TOWARDS CONSTRUCTIVE CHANGE IN ABORIGINAL COMMUNITIES

# Towards Constructive Change in Aboriginal Communities

## A Social Psychology Perspective

DONALD M. TAYLOR AND
ROXANE DE LA SABLONNIÈRE

McGill-Queen's University Press
Montreal & Kingston · London · Ithaca

© McGill-Queen's University Press 2014

ISBN 978-0-7735-4430-7 (cloth)
ISBN 978-0-7735-4431-4 (paper)
ISBN 978-0-7735-9657-3 (ePDF)
ISBN 978-0-7735-9658-0 (ePUB)

Legal deposit third quarter 2014
Bibliothèque nationale du Québec

Printed in Canada on acid-free paper that is 100% ancient forest free
(100% post-consumer recycled), processed chlorine free.

McGill-Queen's University Press acknowledges the support of the
Canada Council for the Arts for our publishing program. We also
acknowledge the financial support of the Government of Canada
through the Canada Book Fund for our publishing activities.

Library and Archives Canada Cataloguing in Publication

Taylor, Donald M., author
   Towards constructive change in Aboriginal communities :
a social psychology perspective / Donald M. Taylor and Roxane de la
Sablonnière.

Includes bibliographical references and index.
Issued in print and electronic formats.
ISBN 978-0-7735-4430-7 (bound). – ISBN 978-0-7735-4431-4 (pbk.). –
ISBN 978-0-7735-9657-3 (ePDF). – ISBN 978-0-7735-9658-0 (ePUB)

   1. Native peoples – Canada – Psychology. 2. Native peoples –
Canada – Social conditions. I. La Sablonnière, Roxane de, 1975–,
author II. Title.

E78.C2T298 2014          305.897'071          C2014-904220-5
                                              C2014-904221-3

This book was typeset by True to Type in 10.5/13 Sabon

*This book is dedicated to all those who are, and who feel, like family.
Your inspiration and patience with our time-consuming and
sometimes reckless missions never goes unnoticed.*

# Contents

# Figures

# Acknowledgments

This is a book about ideas and empirical research formulated and conducted over many years. The result is that the number of people who have contributed directly and indirectly is enormous. To begin with, we have learned so much from Aboriginal and non-Aboriginal friends and colleagues from remote communities across the country. We learned as much from you at informal gatherings in your homes, in small airports, and on the land as we did from formal sessions focused on pedagogical and policy issues. Your voices echo throughout this volume. We hope we listened well.

Our academic social psychology colleagues, post-doctoral, doctoral, and master's students at McGill and the University of Montreal shared their feedback privately and in formal seminars with us, encouraging us to be clear and to the point. Undergraduate students who had to process earlier drafts of chapters were invaluable in terms of pointing to where more (or less) elaboration and clarity were needed.

Financial support for the laboratory- and community-based research that informed the present project over the years includes grants from SSHRC (Social Sciences and Humanities Research Council) and the FQRSC (Fonds québécois de la recherche sur la société et la culture). Additional financial and "in kind" support was provided by partners across the country, including the Kativik School Board and the governments of the Northwest Territories, Nunavut, and Nunatsiavut.

Finally, we thank Jonathan Crago, Ryan Van Huijstee, and Joanne Richardson from MQUP for their guidance, and Meghan Watson for editorial help with indexing and formatting.

TOWARDS CONSTRUCTIVE CHANGE IN ABORIGINAL COMMUNITIES

# 1

## Aboriginal People and the Canadian Psyche

Canada is defined by two unique environments: its vast and varied physical environment and its equally varied human environment. The physical environment serves as a constant backdrop to Canada's human environment, which revolves around bilingualism, biculturalism, multiculturalism, and Aboriginal peoples – First Nations, Inuit, and Métis. The politics of biculturalism and multiculturalism are ever-present, ebbing and flowing, oscillating between pride and tension. Aboriginal peoples constitute only a fraction of the Canadian population, many living on remote reserves and in isolated communities, and yet they have, are, and will be essential to the definition of Canada. Moreover, the impact of Aboriginal peoples is felt at the emotional core of every single Canadian from coast to coast to coast.

Why is it that this small, widely dispersed group of people has such a broad and profound impact on the national psyche? The answer lies in a unique configuration of realities that conspires to place Aboriginal peoples front and centre in the ongoing national agenda. The realities are these: Aboriginal communities have been, and are, suffering social dysfunctions ranging from economic depression and academic underachievement to substance misuse, family violence, and alarming rates of suicide among their youth. Non-Aboriginal Canadians maintain a negative stereotype of Aboriginal peoples that highlights these realities. Given this negative image, it would be easy for non-Aboriginal Canadians to dismiss Aboriginal peoples as a small underclass that is not worthy of much attention. But another critical fact is that Aboriginal peoples were the "first" peoples, the "indigenous" peoples of Canada. They are the peoples who first occupied and became integrated into Canada's vast and varied landscape. They did this long before the ancestors of today's Canadian non-Aboriginal population arrived and, through internal colonization, displaced and banished Aboriginal peoples to remote corners of this vast nation. This "being-here-first" reality has important psychological implications. It is precisely the special status accorded to being first, or having the most seniority, that generates the angst felt, in one form or another, by every single Canadian. Formal attitudinal surveys, informal conversations, and political structures, institutions, and rhetoric all point to this Canadian angst. On the one hand, Canadians hold negative stereotypes of Aboriginal people; on the other hand, they accord them special, revered status as the original settlers of Canadian territory. Add to this the recognition that it was European colonizers, the ancestors of today's non-Aboriginal Canadians, who were and are wholly, or at least largely, responsible for the current plight of Aboriginal peoples. Juxtaposing these realities, we arrive at a nation of people in which each and every person struggles with a fundamental attitudinal and psychological conflict. The psychological challenge for every Canadian is how to come to terms with the fact that Aboriginal peoples are extremely disadvantaged that we have a negative image of them, that they were here first, and that we caused their disadvantage.

It may seem presumptuous to suggest that every Canadian struggles with this psychological angst, but we believe it to be true. You might be saying to yourself: "Some people might constantly wrestle with this angst, but it is not an every-day issue for me." This may be true, but it does not mean that such angst does not define our national identity. Psychologically, none of us enjoys psychological angst, and so we develop psychological mechanisms to deal with it. We may deny the possibility that we will become ill, fully believe our relationship will last forever (despite the consistently high divorce rates), or, if terror management theory (Greenberg, Pyszczynski, and Solomon 1986) has any credibility, socially construct cultures and religions to cope with the existential reality of our own death. Closer to the issue here, the ability to point to a government that has an entire department focused on the welfare of a small number of Aboriginal peoples helps us deal with our basic angst. If we can find reasons to blame Aboriginal peoples for their disadvantage, our angst is minimized. Media attention to Aboriginal issues, the public funding of Aboriginal programs, and even the occasional political acknowledgment of concern (or, even rarer, a partial apology) all allow us to move forward on a day-to-day basis without being saddled with the internal psychological conflict that defines our nation. But the angst is there, and it is at the core of Canadian identity.

What continues to be a relentless and inescapable psychological struggle for every Canadian is the focus of this book. From colonization and assimilation to empowerment and decolonization, every mean-spirited, benign, or enlightened intervention or program designed to address the problems in Aboriginal communities has failed. From the brutal legacy of residential schools to the optimistic revitalization of traditional Aboriginal cultural solutions to community problems, the outcomes have been astonishing in their ineffectiveness. The rising frustration among all Canadians and policy makers in all jurisdictions and regions, be they non-Aboriginal or Aboriginal, has led to what can only be described as a crisis of conscience and a crisis of action. No one knows what to do.

In this book we outline a new way of thinking about and framing the challenge of addressing the social dysfunction and disadvantage that plagues Aboriginal communities. We challenge the current approach, shared by Aboriginal groups and non-Aboriginal Canadians alike, which takes the following form: Aboriginal communities are suffering because of a legacy associated with colonialism. Canada has, in the past, been colonialist in its programs and interventions. Thus, governments imposed non-Aboriginal cultural solutions on communities whose culture was and is very different from that of the mainstream. Canadians now see that these programs must be designed so as to respect and accommodate the differences between non-Aboriginal culture and Aboriginal culture. With this enlightened view, and working in concert with Aboriginal groups, the issues can be successfully addressed. In short, traditionally, the problem was thought to be a matter of "cultural mismatch," and the solution was thought to be more respect for Aboriginal culture.

In this book, we challenge this perspective. Colonialism may be the culprit, but cultural mismatch is not the problem. The problem, we argue, is that colonialism represents, first and foremost, a direct and pervasive attack on Aboriginal cultural identity that, in domino fashion, leads to a perfect storm with regard to community dysfunction. An assault on Aboriginal identity means that every Aboriginal person is socialized without the benefit of a shared set of clearly defined values and accompanying long-term goals. No long-term goals means that no one is motivated to exercise self-control. Why pass up immediate gratification when there is no long-term goal to be compromised?

You might as well party, spend, gamble, engage in risky sexual behaviour, enjoy junk food, and live in the here and now since there is no reason not to. It is not that Aboriginal culture is different from mainstream culture; rather, the root cause of dysfunction and disadvantage is the lack of a clearly defined Aboriginal cultural identity. Our analysis forces us to describe the nearly impossible social psychological hurdles that we face in order to overcome this attack on Aboriginal identity. However, it also points to what we believe can be a different, meaningful, and successful Aboriginally owned and driven national strategy to address the issues confronting Aboriginal communities.

Our mission, analysis, and proposed solutions are far-reaching, and they challenge current thinking. They are rooted in years of teaching and conducting research in Aboriginal communities, which has afforded us the privilege of learning from our Aboriginal friends, colleagues, and elders. This work is the result, and our efforts will be entirely worthwhile if we have heard, and understood, their voices.

## THE POLITICAL CLIMATE

Now that Canada has offered an official public apology to Aboriginal peoples; now that non-Aboriginal governments are genuinely trying to design constructive community programs and cooperative interventions; now that conditions in many Aboriginal communities have reached crisis proportions; now that Aboriginal communities are talking openly about the social, economic, and academic challenges they confront; now that there is a window of opportunity to propose new directions; now that there may be a readiness to consider serious alternative proposals for constructive community change; now, understandable trust issues notwithstanding, we believe that the time is ripe for genuine dialogue and the consideration of strategies for change. It is in this optimistic spirit that we offer this book.

### Current Zeitgeist

There are no shortage of programs and interventions in Aboriginal communities across the country. Moreover, the interventions range widely from economic, academic, and judicial to health, social, and psychological. Sadly, the vast majority of these initiatives have yielded disappointing results, to say the least.

The widespread failure of these many and varied interventions requires a broadly based explanation – one that applies to First

Nations, Inuit, and Métis from every corner of the country. The convenient explanation that has evolved proposes that there is a "cultural mismatch" between Aboriginal culture and non-Aboriginal culture. Basically, the idea is that any non-Aboriginal intervention imposed on an Aboriginal community is doomed because Aboriginal cultures are fundamentally different from non-Aboriginal cultures.

Cultural mismatch theory is appealing for three reasons. First, it is appealing because there are so many obvious examples of non-Aboriginal solutions being imposed on Aboriginal communities. Non-Aboriginal cultural institutions and processes (such as schooling, health care, elderly care, social services, and non-Aboriginal judicial and political systems) have been superimposed upon Aboriginal communities. The colonialist mentality behind such a practice aside, the cultural mismatch is blatant.

Second, cultural mismatch theory is appealing because it is broad enough to cover the failure of all current interventions in Aboriginal groups. What do all these Aboriginal groups have in common? They have all been affected by the same European colonizer, and, whatever the cultural differences among Aboriginal groups, they are all, collectively, very different from the groups that comprise non-Aboriginal culture.

Third, cultural mismatch theory is appealing because there is evidence that its zeitgeist is manifested in current adjustments to interventions in Aboriginal communities. For example, there is a widespread movement across all communities and all institutions to incorporate more and more elements of Aboriginal culture. In schools, this might mean teaching via an Aboriginal language and including classes on Aboriginal culture in the curriculum. Social services are incorporating traditional ceremonies, and the judicial system is consulting with elders in matters of sentencing. Clearly, these are all designed to reduce the cultural mismatch.

For all these reasons, a cultural mismatch theory that accounts for failed interventions in troubled Aboriginal communities is compelling. More broadly, the cultural mismatch idea is wholly consistent with present-day initiatives shared by both Aboriginal peoples and non-Aboriginal governments. Popular labels such as "empowerment" and "decolonization" are evoked to rationalize land claims initiatives, self-government movements, and the demands of Aboriginal groups for more control over their institutions. For example, Aboriginal groups want not only their own schools but also their own colleges and universities, and they want their own social services and legal procedures.

These demands by Aboriginal groups have at least two interesting features that are related to cultural mismatch theory. First, they all involve a push for further autonomy and control, made necessary by a colonialist legacy that has robbed Aboriginal people of collective self-control over their own destiny. Second, this push towards autonomy is entirely directed towards making all of the institutions that touch individual life more culturally consistent with Aboriginal culture.

Again, the theme of cultural mismatch is front and centre, and this is precisely why Aboriginal aspirations for collective autonomy are shared by non-Aboriginal governments. Both have adopted cultural mismatch as the explanatory mechanism for the challenges confronting Aboriginal communities. Of course, negotiating autonomy will be a difficult process since non-Aboriginal governments and people have much to lose. But the process is being engaged in because of a shared vision that non-Aboriginal processes and institutions are incompatible with Aboriginal culture: hence, the failure, to date, of all interventions to improve the quality of life in Aboriginal communities.

## CULTURAL IDENTITY CLARITY: THE REAL ISSUE

Our own analysis begins with a challenge to the cultural mismatch explanation for the failure to adequately address problems relating to Aboriginal communities. The idea of a cultural mismatch assumes that (1) there is a clearly defined Aboriginal culture, (2) there is a clearly defined non-Aboriginal culture, and (3) these two cultures are incompatible.

Our theory begins with the proposition that a person's well-being depends upon a healthy self-concept. A healthy self-concept, we argue, is one that is clearly defined and positive. The process of developing a healthy self-concept begins with *a clearly defined cultural identity* (Taylor 2002).[1]

---

1 Small portions of this book were reproduced and adapted from two sources that have been published elsewhere. First, some ideas and text on cultural identity clarity mentioned in chapter 5 are from Taylor (2002). Second, some of the ideas and text in chapter 4 regarding collective self-control, from chapter 6 regarding the normative structure of a community, and from chapter 9 regarding survey research has been adapted from Taylor and de la Sablonnière (2013).

It is at this point that we take issue with the cultural mismatch model. We attempt to show that what plagues Aboriginal communities is not a mismatch of cultural identities but, rather, a complete rupture of Aboriginal cultural identity. Put simply, the most devastating effect of colonialism is that it has left present-day Aboriginal peoples with an *unclear cultural identity*. The result is that individuals in Aboriginal communities are not in a position to engage the vital psychological processes that are needed to articulate a healthy self-concept and, by extension, personal well-being.

The challenges confronting people in Aboriginal communities are wholly consistent with the idea of a compromised cultural identity. The challenges seem varied, ranging from academic underachievement and underemployment to substance misuse, unhealthy sexual behaviour, and domestic violence, but all have the same root cause: issues related to self-control. That is, they all involve the need to pass up the temptation of immediate gratification in order to achieve more important long-term goals. In order to have the motivation to wrestle with self-control issues, one must have very powerful, well-defined long-term goals. Who is going to pass up immediate gratification for no reason? The long-term goals that lie at the heart of the ability to exercise self-control may be found in a clearly defined, consensually endorsed cultural identity. If one is to appreciate the importance of academic success, the need to be well rested and on time for one's job, and the need to overcome immediate frustration for the sake of a lasting loving relationship, then one needs to believe that academic success, job performance, and good interpersonal relationships are worthwhile long-term goals that are central to a clearly defined cultural identity.

In non-Aboriginal society, where the benefits of a clearly defined cultural identity are fully operable, most people are able to exercise self-control. Those individuals who cannot tend to stand out, thus requiring some form of constructive intervention. In the case of Aboriginal communities, which lack the benefit of a clearly defined cultural identity, every Aboriginal person is robbed of important long-term goals. This being the case, every Aboriginal person struggles with self-control issues. Thus, we do not refer to self-control challenges but, rather, to *collective* self-control challenges.

Our conclusion about the importance of a clearly defined cultural identity, and the lack of clarity in the case of Aboriginal communities, arises from our proposed psychological theory of self-concept – a theory that we have begun to test empirically. We need to describe our self-concept theory in full in order to demonstrate its importance for understanding the crisis in Aboriginal communities, in general, and for countering the current cultural mismatch theory, in particular.

Are we suggesting that there is no such thing as an Aboriginal identity? Absolutely not! What we are suggesting is that, for any given Aboriginal group, what was once a clearly defined cultural identity was obliterated by colonialism. When family structures are torn apart, when a group's language and cultural ceremonies are made illegal, and when an entire way of life is fundamentally altered, all semblance of an intact, clearly defined cultural identity is lost.

Aboriginal communities cannot simply reach back to some point in the distant past, import what was once a clear cultural identity, and then apply it to present-day reality. The task of crafting an up-to-date, functional, clearly and consensually arrived at cultural identity is a daunting one. And each Aboriginal group needs to engage in the task of defining its own cultural identity. This is the necessary first step towards building healthy, motivated communities. A clearly defined cultural identity will articulate not only Aboriginal values but also the collective long-term goals that reflect those values and that help to address widespread collective self-control issues.

The content, the values, the long-term goals, and the detailed scripts that a newly formed cultural identity must provide rest solely with Aboriginal groups. However, the shared colonialist history of all Aboriginal groups, coupled with present-day reality, provides at least a starting point for this crucial exercise. There is little doubt that any newly defined cultural identity will not involve the salient and dysfunctional collective self-control elements of current community life. We say this not only because such behaviours are non-normative from a non-Aboriginal cultural perspective but also because they are just as non-normative from an Aboriginal cultural perspective: Aboriginal people are voicing the need to decrease the prevalence of these collective self-control behaviours in their communities. There is little doubt that any newly defined Aboriginal cultural identity will include elements of traditional Aboriginal cultural identity as well as elements of modern non-Aboriginal cultural identity. What proportions of each, how they are integrated, and, indeed, what they are is the responsibility and right of every Aboriginal group. As long as the result of the process is a clearly defined collective identity, then the normal processes of attaining a healthy identity will be available to each and every group member.

*Clarifying Cultural Identity Is No Easy Matter*

All of us operate on the assumption that once we have correctly identified the source of a problem we are half way to finding its solution. For example, it was once received wisdom that disadvantaged children perform poorly in school because of low self-esteem. The solution was obvious: design programs to boost self-esteem. Similarly, the current focus on cultural mismatches leads to solutions designed to alter the cultural balance in Aboriginal communities (Brady 1995).

We are proposing that neither cultural mismatch nor low self-esteem is the major issue; rather, it is the lack of a clearly defined cultural identity. The problem is that it is not at all obvious who is going to initiate the process of defining a clear cultural identity. Are we to imagine that, all of a sudden, some form of spontaneous community combustion will have Aboriginal people collectively and simultaneously waking up with the realization that it is time to engage in the process of carving a new, clear, consensually defined Aboriginal identity? Not likely.

So, who is going to take up this daunting challenge? Let's review the possibilities. Non-Aboriginal governments, teachers, researchers, organizations, and caring non-Aboriginal people cannot and should not be at the helm. Indirectly, non-Aboriginal institutions have certainly tried: pouring money and human resources into selected Aboriginal programs is a de facto attempt to influence the direction and structure of Aboriginal identity. But the legacy of colonialism rules out any non-Aboriginal intervention. Trust issues aside, what do non-Aboriginal people know about what Aboriginal peoples want? This does not mean that the former cannot be useful. If a relationship can be established such that the power structure places Aboriginal communities in the driver's seat, then Aboriginal people might, at their discretion and on their terms, solicit input and specific expertise from non-Aboriginal organizations and individuals. The bottom line is that non-Aboriginal Canadian institutions, leaders, and organizations cannot and should not be the major contributors to the content and structure of Aboriginal identity.

Another candidate for initiating the generation of a made-for-today's-reality Aboriginal cultural identity is Aboriginal leaders. Indeed, Aboriginal leaders might seem like the obvious choice: Who better to instigate change than Aboriginals who have proven their leadership to the point that they have the support of other Aboriginals and are positioned and, indeed, expected, to promote constructive change?

Strange as it may seem, most Aboriginal leaders are not likely to instigate change designed to generate a clear cultural Aboriginal identity. Interestingly, it is due to their own personal success that Aboriginal leaders are unable to appreciate this particular issue. Their inability to grasp the cultural identity crisis is a product of their journey to a position of leadership. They have battled the odds and risen above the dysfunctions challenging Aboriginal communities. Out of the cultural vacuum resulting from colonialism, Aboriginal leaders have somehow crafted a blueprint for living that provides them with long-term values, goals, and dreams. Some are even relatively unscathed by the ravages of residential schooling and have returned to their communities on a mission. It is their exceptional success that makes Aboriginal leaders so special; however, paradoxically, it is also what makes them blind to the cultural identity issue confronting the vast majority of Aboriginal people. Moreover, Aboriginal leaders, like all leaders, are not predisposed to relinquish power. They attained their lofty position in the context of the current cultural climate and, therefore, are not motivated to initiate serious changes to it. They have nothing to gain and a lot to lose.

So, who is going to initiate and regulate the process of cultural renewal? Aboriginal peoples themselves.

### Appreciating the Challenge of Carving a Clear Aboriginal Identity

Obviously, creating a grassroots movement whose purpose is to clearly define a cultural identity is a daunting task. This is surely the juncture at which any insights that might make the task more manageable need to be offered. Unfortunately, the task is even more difficult than we might imagine. Indeed, attempting to craft a new, clearly defined Aboriginal identity is very much like attempting to make a river flow backwards up a mountain.

To appreciate this challenge, we need to analyze how groups develop a normative structure through which they actualize their group identity. Only by knowing this can we develop a strategy for changing the norms so as to arrive at a clearly defined cultural identity.

Groups – ranging from family and friends to companies, institutions, classrooms, hospitals, entire communities, and even nations – all have collective identities that involve values and goals that require complex normative structures to satisfy the group's identity. For any societal group to be successful, each group member must contribute to the group's goals. These goals, and how to achieve them, must be clearly defined. The group's goal may be successfully raising children, earning a profit for shareholders, treating the ill, keeping neighbour-hoods safe, educating young people, or crafting a healthy and suc-cessful community. Whatever the group's goals, 100 percent effort on the part of each group member is what maximizes the chances for success.

Of course no group is fortunate enough to be able to count on 100 percent of its members all pulling in the same direction. There are always a few lazy, trouble-making, high maintenance group members who do not contribute to, and may even sabotage, the group's identi-ty and goals. We capture this reality by evoking what we call the 80–20 percent rule (Taylor and de la Sablonnière 2013). The percentages are not meant to be exact and are chosen purely for illustrative purposes. In fact, we fixed upon 80–20 because, as adapted from the Pareto prin-ciple (e.g., Juran 1954), these numbers have been applied to a whole host of normative contexts.

Our point is that most successful groups, while aiming for 100 per-cent normative participation, will actually function quite well if 80 percent of their members are behaving normatively and making a constructive contribution to the group's goals. There will always be a minority of 20 percent who are not contributing, but this percentage is not large enough to derail or destroy the group's functioning. Applied to the context of Aboriginal communities, a successful, healthy community would be one in which 80 percent of communi-ty members are doing their part to contribute to the health of the community, with only 20 percent failing to do so. A healthy commu-nity, then, might be one in which 80 percent of young people are exer-cising self-control and pursuing formal education or training while only 20 percent are in a non-normative state.

All groups are preoccupied with maintaining this 80–20 structure of normative functioning. For example, in most communities in Canada, 80 percent of teenagers are functioning effectively, but our attention is constantly drawn to the trouble-making, underachieving juvenile delinquents who constitute the 20 percent. It is these young people who attract media attention, and it is they who are the focus of police officers, social workers, the courts, teachers, and distraught parents.

Two points are critical here. First, there is an important reason that the 20 percent are the focus of so much attention and resources. The community does not want that 20 percent to grow to 25 percent, 30 percent, or even higher. If the percentage does grow the group might cease to function effectively and could well collapse. The company might go bankrupt, the school might fail to prepare young people for the future, and the community might cease to be a healthy and safe place for everyone. So, it is the 20 percent who are juvenile delinquents that receive all the attention, and this attention has a purpose: it is designed to bring the 20 percent back into line – to convert them into the 80 percent. If successful, the new normative structure might be 90-10 or 95-5. It will never reach the idealized 100 percent, but anything better than 80–20 will ensure that the community functions very effectively.

The second critical point in the 80–20 normative structure for effective group functioning is the forgotten role of the 80 percent. We have noted how the 80 percent quietly go about their business and thereby contribute to effective group functioning. We have also noted that it is the 20 percent, the minority, who receive the lion's share of attention. We tend to forget that the 80 percent are crucial to group success. For example, the 80 percent of functioning teenagers do more than contribute to group success: they define what is normal and, thereby, serve as ongoing role models for how to function. Clearly, the more role models the better, and the more pressure they can put on those who are not functioning in the best interests of the community. So, when the 80 percent drops to 75 percent, 70 percent, or even lower, there are even fewer role models and less pressure on the non-normative 20 percent, who are also growing proportionally.

Now let's turn our attention to the normative structure of Aboriginal communities. By their own admission these communities are experiencing levels of dysfunction that extend way beyond 20 percent. The precise ratio would be difficult to determine, but, for the sake of illustration, imagine it is not 80–20 but 20–80. This would mean that 80 percent of community members are not working towards the overall health of the community and that only 20 percent are serving as role models. Of these 20 percent, only a few would be positioned to try to pressure the 80 percent to join them.

Crafting a clearly defined Aboriginal identity is the necessary condition for constructive social change in Aboriginal communities: the magnitude of that task now confronts us squarely. We now have some appreciation of why the myriad number of interventions that have targeted Aboriginal communities with overwhelming human and financial resources have produced disappointing results. Non-Aboriginal interventions are designed to address 20 percent of the population, with 80 percent serving as role models. These interventions, which involve 20 percent attempting to change community norms endorsed by 80 percent, will not suffice.

Our 80–20 analysis of the normative structure of successful groups also explains why the current rush to apply traditional Aboriginal interventions will be equally disappointing. Prior to European colonization, Aboriginal groups functioned effectively, benefiting from their own clear cultural identity and their own 80–20 normative structure. The innovative and effective interventions Aboriginal groups developed to deal with their challenges in terms of justice, illness, relationships, and learning all involved an 80–20 group structure. But these traditional Aboriginal interventions, like their non-Aboriginal counterparts, were designed for an 80–20 normative structure; neither Aboriginal nor non-Aboriginal interventions were designed to deal with the reversed 20–80 normative structure. That non-Aboriginal interventions are doomed is disappointing enough, but the failure of Aboriginal interventions not only leaves community problems unresolved but also unfairly reflects badly on Aboriginal culture.

Our analysis, thus far, has proceeded from one overwhelming challenge to the next, without any apparent room for optimism. However, our focusing on seemingly insurmountable problems is not motivated by a desire to lower expectations, excuse failure, or blame the victim. Quite the opposite. We firmly believe that an understanding of the processes governing community reality is the only foundation for designing workable solutions. This is what motivates us to think differently about the link between cultural identity and collective self-control issues and, thereby, to challenge cultural mismatch theory. It is also the reason for our 80–20 analysis of the type of normative structure needed for effective community functioning. At first glance, it might seem that the more our quest for understanding proceeds, the more overwhelming the challenge to imagine any reasonable solution.

Well, nobody said it would be easy. Indeed, the social issues in Aboriginal communities have been notoriously resistant to virtually every intervention to date. If defining the issue is the first step towards a constructive solution, then the onus is on us to take the second step. And this is what we now intend to do.

## MOBILIZING CONSTRUCTIVE COMMUNITY CHANGE

Confronted with community dysfunction in the form of widespread collective self-control issues, the main task is to mobilize that community to carve a new, clearly defined cultural identity. Accomplishing this while faced with a 20–80 normative structure is the task at hand.

But wait. Some might argue that one person's 20–80 is another person's 80–20. That is, if groups in non-Aboriginal society follow an 80–20 normative structure, then clearly the 80 percent represent the norms valued by that society. Defining Aboriginal communities in terms of 20–80 surely means that these communities have a different set of cultural values than do non-Aboriginal communities – indeed, it is the inverse of what is found in the latter. This would be true if Aboriginal people endorsed the 80 percent norms in their 20–80 structure. But they do not (Taylor and de la Sablonnière 2013). Aboriginal people in communities across Canada have courageously spoken out about the collective self-control problems that, in their view, are rampant. They are adamant in their collective rejection of the values and behaviour patterns that characterize their communities. They want to reverse the 20–80 normative structure and craft a new Aboriginally defined and controlled 80–20 normative structure.

## TURNING THE CORNER: FROM DAUNTING CHALLENGES TO CONSTRUCTIVE SOLUTIONS

In rejecting cultural mismatch theory as an adequate tool for assessing the challenges confronting Aboriginal communities we discuss a number of linked concepts, including colonialism, cultural identity, collective self-control, and a 20–80 normative community structure. These are presented in Figure 1.1, which illustrates the links among them and their implications.

Each new concept we introduce makes the challenges seem greater and the prospects more bleak, leaving us in an apparent state of hopelessness. But this is not our purpose. The concepts are linked, and they lead us to conclusions about the root cause of social dysfunction, which, in turn, leads us in a new direction. Our admittedly depressing analysis offers the basis for embarking on a potentially constructive game plan.

We now turn our attention to addressing community problems by reversing the current 20–80 normative structure in order to craft a

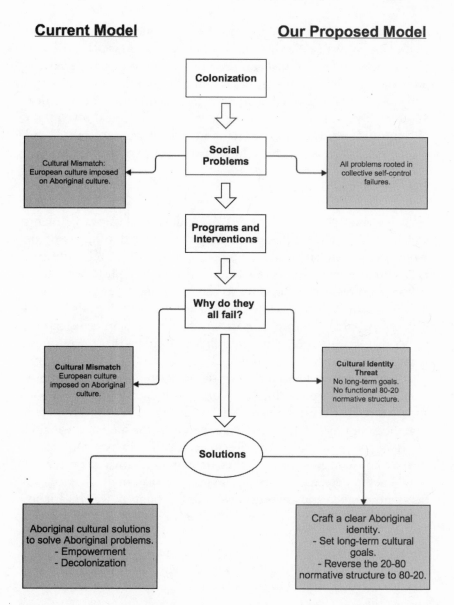

**Current Model**                    **Our Proposed Model**

Colonization

Social Problems

Cultural Mismatch: European culture imposed on Aboriginal culture.

All problems rooted in collective self-control failures.

Programs and Interventions

Why do they all fail?

Cultural Mismatch European culture imposed on Aboriginal culture.

Cultural Identity Threat No long-term goals. No functional 80-20 normative structure.

Solutions

Aboriginal cultural solutions to solve Aboriginal problems.
- Empowerment
- Decolonization

Craft a clear Aboriginal identity.
- Set long-term cultural goals.
- Reverse the 20-80 normative structure to 80-20.

Figure 1.1   Diagram contrasting current cultural mismatch theory with our proposed threat to cultural identity model

clearly defined Aboriginal identity and its concomitant long-term goals. This, in turn, will enable us to adequately address collective self-control issues in Aboriginal communities. We offer three interrelated processes that these communities might call upon to reverse the current 20–80 reality and set in motion the attempt to achieve a new 80–20 reality. These three processes involve: (1) the social psychology of "minority influence," (2) a careful analysis of "zero tolerance," and (3) survey research as a vehicle for constructive community change.

### Minority Influence

Social psychology has a rich history of conducting classic experiments and offering much theorizing regarding the powerful influence of the group on individual group members (see Cialdini and Goldstein 2004; Bond and Smith 1996). Parents desperately plead with their teenagers to resist peer pressure to use drugs and to engage in risky sexual behaviours. They say things such as: "If all your friends jumped off a cliff, would you jump too?" Parents hope that their teenagers will respond: "Of course not!" But research demonstrates that the response is more likely to be: "Sure. I might close my eyes, but I would jump." This dramatically underscores how the majority influences the individual. Indeed, so powerful is majority influence that observers of society often use expressions such as "we are a nation of sheep" to capture the extent to which the individual is under the spell of the majority. It is precisely this normative majority, this 80 percent, that is invoked to change the behaviour of the non-normative 20 percent.

Whenever we teach classes on the topic of majority influence, students are stunned and are provoked to reflect on its power. Invariably, a few will ask: "If majority influence is so powerful, how do you explain people like John F. Kennedy, Martin Luther King, Stalin, Hitler, Mandela, Gandhi, and Jesus Christ – individuals who changed the majority?" In essence, they are asking: "How can a minority change the majority?" Or, in our terms: "How can the 20 percent change the 80 percent?"

Social psychologists have studied the topic of minority influence, and there is much to be learned about reversing the 20–80 normative structure of Aboriginal communities. Majority influence overwhelms the minority and has the benefit of numbers. This is not the case with minority influence. Thus, in order to be persuasive, the minority must be doggedly vocal, self-assured, and consistent in its arguments. Faced with such a determined minority, the majority, while not under numerical pressure to comply, may begin to engage in what theorists call a validation process. This validation process involves members of the majority 80 percent beginning to question and perhaps even doubt their own views. It may be difficult for the 20 percent to provoke the validation process, but, when it succeeds, it can stimulate genuine social change.

Minority influence, then, may be a good place to start. It offers the 20 percent in any community a game plan consisting of a clearly defined and simple set of norms that they must pursue with a vengeance. Clearly, it is a difficult task for the minority 20 percent to turn around the majority 80 percent. Thus, at this point, we turn to a potential tool.

### Zero Tolerance: A Response to 20–80 Normative Imbalances

"Zero tolerance" is a slogan, or buzz word, that can be heard everywhere. School, community centre, and public building walls are decorated with signs announcing zero tolerance for every conceivable inappropriate behaviour, from smoking, drugs, and carrying weapons to bullying, littering, and driving while drunk. Unfortunately, the initial introduction of a socially significant policy – zero tolerance – for addressing problematic behaviour has been watered down to the point at which it has come to function as a mere suggestion. In the face of rising non-normative behaviour, anything short of following zero tolerance to the letter is doomed.

A genuine zero tolerance policy is employed when there is a normative crisis. For example, when drugs and violence overrun a school to the point that students and teachers are petrified daily, a zero tolerance policy may be necessary to re-establish constructive school norms. A zero tolerance rule for violence would be simple, extreme, and unyielding, and the consequence for any violation would be immediate and irrevocable expulsion. In terms of violence, this would mean if one student as much as gave another student a slight shove, the student would be removed from the school for good.

What makes a zero tolerance policy especially noteworthy is that, on the surface, it violates societal norms of equity, fairness, and justice. Both in our formal justice system and in the everyday regulation of behaviour, the punishment is supposed to fit the crime: the more serious the offence, the harsher the punishment. Zero tolerance violates this norm of fairness by pronouncing that the same severe consequence will follow the smallest as well as the most extreme offence in a particular domain. The student who attacks another with a weapon and the student who merely administers a small shove will both receive the same harsh punishment. Thus, the implementation of a genuine zero tolerance rule is a serious undertaking, and it is always hoped that its imposition can be lifted once a more normative state is restored.

A genuine zero tolerance policy might well be useful in turning the 20–80 normative structure of Aboriginal communities in the direction of a new, more constructive, 80–20 structure. The challenge would be to select one behaviour at a time, and then, through minority influence, develop sufficient support from authorities to ensure that that behaviour is not tolerated. One failure to follow through on a zero tolerance policy renders it totally ineffective. Applied with rigour, however, it can be an effective strategy for inculcating a rapid change in normative structure.

*Survey Research as a Vehicle for Constructive Community Change*

A third potentially effective strategy for inducing social change, and one that may have long-term implications, is the application of community-based survey research. Currently, in many Aboriginal communities, scientific research is neither valued nor practised. Why? Simply put, because, for Aboriginal communities, scientific research symbolizes the worst features of colonialism.

Research conducted in Aboriginal communities was, and too often continues to be, conducted by non-Aboriginal researchers who have little or no relationship with the people in the community and little sensitivity to their preoccupations. Typically, this so-called "helicopter" research is designed by a non-Aboriginal scientist who descends on a community, collects data of interest only to her or himself, and then retreats to the laboratory in order to analyze this data and write obscure academic articles. This research benefits the researcher's career, but it was not instigated by the community and its results do not benefit the community. To make matters worse, the research often betrays and disrespects the community because the researcher is oblivious to, or simply does not care about, its culture. Thus, the researcher often asks the wrong questions, imports culturally inappropriate measures, and misinterprets the results of her/his research. These results are reported to a naïve non-Aboriginal audience and tend to highlight and promote negative stereotypes of Aboriginal communities. As Goyce Kakegamic, a respected elder of the Nishnawbe Aski nation, so eloquently puts it: "Our history with researchers is one of 'give and take,' we gave and they took. We gave views, information, teachings and wisdom, and researchers used this information for their own purposes, not ours, and in most cases we were neither credited nor provided access to the completed research" (quoted in Garrick 2008, para. 3).

These colonial research practices are being slowly, with an emphasis on "slowly," replaced with genuine community-based research. Indeed, Inuit regions now have licensing procedures in place to monitor research in communities and to ensure that it is designed to meet their needs. Many First Nations and Métis communities have similar formal procedures for controlling research, and these are implemented in a rigorous and highly selective manner.

Given this legacy, along with the current reality of research in Aboriginal communities, what possible role could research play in reversing a 20–80 normative structure? The answer may be found in our own experience with how different the research process is in Aboriginal communities compared to non-Aboriginal environments. How is it different? In Aboriginal communities, when a survey is conducted there is 100 percent participation, and, rather than wanting to remain anonymous, community participants want their name front and centre. In order to appreciate these differences, and their potential link to community change, we need to examine non-Aboriginal practices with regard to survey research.

In non-Aboriginal society, countless scientific surveys are conducted daily on every conceivable issue. There are so many surveys that most non-Aboriginal people try to avoid them, either because the issue is not important to them or because there are simply too many survey requests. Faced with this reluctance, and a large population, the survey methodologist is forced to focus on a *sample* of community members rather than attempt to survey everybody. So the researcher might be happy to survey a mere 10 percent of a population and never even approach the remaining 90 percent. This means that the researcher must use the results of a small 10 percent sample to extrapolate to the entire population. Of course, the survey methodologist is careful to select a representative 10 percent sample, making sure that there are sufficient respondents, including, for example, women and men, young and old, and rich and poor. Survey sampling methods are sophisticated, complex and precise, and, when conducted carefully, they can provide a community with very useful information.

In addition to the sampling issue, surveys conducted in a southern non-Aboriginal context are careful to ensure that respondents have their anonymity respected. The assumption is that people will be more honest when responding, especially to sensitive issues, if their names are not made public.

However, survey research in an Aboriginal community is a very different experience in terms of sampling and anonymity. When an Aboriginal community is controlling the research, it is only when an issue of vital concern to the entire community arises that a survey will be conducted. For example, several communities in Nunavik (Arctic Quebec) were concerned about the survival of their language, Inuktitut, and the role the school should play in promoting it. When we conducted a survey on language ability and language use, *every member of the community over the age of fifteen completed it.* This full participation never occurs in a southern, non-Aboriginal context. The fact that virtually everyone in an Aboriginal community responds to a survey means that everyone has a voice and that all voices are equal.

Next, many Aboriginal community members were surprised at our insistence that their survey responses remain anonymous. We reinforced this anonymity because survey research in southern, non-Aboriginal communities has found that, unless anonymity can be guaranteed, respondents may be unwilling to complete the survey (and even if they do, their answers may not be truthful). Our Aboriginal respondents, however, cared about the issue of language and very much wanted their names on the survey instrument; after all, it was their language and their opinion, and they were proud of both. This full participation and pride in their opinion makes surveys conducted in Aboriginal communities very different from surveys conducted in non-Aboriginal communities. The two issues of sampling and anonymity demonstrate that scientifically based research surveys in Aboriginal communities are genuinely participatory exercises – exercises that can be used to instigate a change in normative structure.

There is no better mechanism than a survey for reaching everyone in a community. Call for a community meeting, and only those who are not threatened by the issue or who already act in line with it show up. FM radio reaches everyone, but it is received only passively. A survey, on the other hand, reaches everyone, and it requires the active engagement of each person. Involving everyone in the community is vital when the issue concerns changing norms. Norms, after all, involve a consensual agreement about what behaviour is appropriate.

Now that communities are beginning to discuss openly the collective self-control challenges they confront, they may be poised to begin addressing them. Survey research may be the appropriate vehicle for reversing a 20–80 normative structure and resulting in a clearly defined cultural identity. What might this process involve? It would need to begin with the community choosing the issue upon which it wants to focus. Now the numerous issues confronting Aboriginal communities are all interconnected in that they all involve issues of self-control. But any community would be overwhelmed by attempting to address all of them simultaneously. Moreover, some issues are more threatening than others, and it is likely that communities will want to begin by choosing an issue that is very important but not one that is especially threatening. This way, the community can gain confidence in the process before moving on to the more threatening issues.

Imagine that a community decides to address the issue of academic underachievement, including poor school attendance and high dropout rates. A community survey could be designed to gauge the attitudes and experience of every adult in the community as every adult is involved with socializing young people in an Aboriginal community. Following the usual demographic questions, the community, in concert with a survey specialist, might design an array of questions to determine the actual experiences of community members with formal schooling, how useful they believe it to be, how they feel when they enter the school, and how they feel regarding the importance of formal education to future success and its potential role in promoting Aboriginal culture and language. The responses to these questions, according to some standard answering format, would provide invaluable information. They would provide an attitudinal profile for the community and point to the barriers that need to be addressed in order to build a stronger community commitment to the formal education of the community's young people.

Up to this point, the survey in question would be like any other survey that has been rigorously designed, conducted, and analyzed so as to provide important information about the community's attitudes regarding formal education. In order to expand the role of the survey so that it can be instrumental in reversing the 20–80 normative structure of Aboriginal communities, we need to add new, specially designed, questions. Specifically, we need to add questions that have two characteristics: (1) they need to focus on the new norms that the community wishes to establish, and (2) they must not be designed to address a norm with which respondents are not yet willing to engage. In other words, questions must be designed to elicit strong support from respondents. "Would you be willing to help your child get to school on time?" might be one such a question; a more action-oriented question might be: "Would you be willing to wear a T-shirt on special days that says 'I support my child's education'?" Clearly, the community has to know just what adults in the community would be willing to endorse. If too much is asked, there may be less than full endorsement.

It goes without saying that the survey must include a few minimalist, certain-to-be-endorsed demands on school personnel to contribute to a new norm of fuller student participation (e.g., asking the school to provide students with something to drink at recess, or teachers to write a brief note for each student to take home). This would ensure balanced participation on the part of both the school and the community with regard to taking the initial steps to change the normative structure.

The actual norm reversal process is launched at the point at which the community is provided with feedback about the survey results. The feedback process is crucial to all genuine community-based research. It is the community that owns and controls research data; thus, feedback must first go to the community, and it is the community that must decide who has access to the data and how to act upon them.

The mechanisms for community feedback typically involve community meetings, pamphlets, and brief written reports (to be distributed to everyone) as well as announcements and discussions on the local FM radio station. Feedback usually occurs over several days, after which the information is used by policy makers, politicians, and specialized groups. The community-based groups come up with their own recommendations and implementation strategies.

The feedback process for changing community norms needs to do more. Feedback should begin through the usual mechanisms but with a special focus on normative items. That is, the community would be confronted with those items that resulted in a close to 100 percent consensus, an almost unheard-of level of agreement on surveys. The community would be challenged to follow through on the item immediately, and with the assurance that every other adult in the community fully endorsed it. Anyone not complying with her or his stated intention would not only be behaving counter to her/his individually expressed intention but also to the normative intentions of the whole community. Under these circumstances, and following the feedback on the normative items, established community leaders would be asked to monitor and promote adherence to these norms. This is how the "push back" would begin. The normative survey items may be modest to begin with, but the survey process can be a useful vehicle for getting the process started.

## STRUCTURE OF THE BOOK

In the chapters that follow, we take the broad strokes outlined in the introduction and explore them in depth. We begin our journey in Chapter 2, with a direct statement about where we stand on Aboriginal issues. Specifically, we discuss who we are as authors, the cultural diversity of Aboriginal groups, and Aboriginal resilience. In Chapter 3, we describe the constellation of issues that is challenging virtually every Aboriginal community. In the process, we underscore what amounts to 150 years of less than fruitful interventions. In Chapter 4, we introduce our concept of collective self-control. In Chapters 5 and 6, we outline two theories that we propose are at the root of collective self-control issues. First, in Chapter 5, we introduce our theory of self-concept. We present this idea elsewhere (Taylor 1997, 2002), but since the importance of collective cultural identity is the foundation of our analysis of the challenge confronting Aboriginal communities, we need to review it in some detail. Second, in Chapter 6, we present a new normative analysis of the 20–80 normative structure of Aboriginal communities – an analysis that explains the root cause of collective self-control issues (Taylor and de la Sablonnière 2013). The result of this analysis is discouraging; however, it serves to focus attention on how we might reverse the legacy of failed interventions. In Chapters 7, 8, and 9 we shift our attention from the challenges confronting Aboriginal peoples to the three interrelated strategies for constructive social change. We begin in Chapter 7 by applying social psychological theory regarding minority influence, and we follow this in Chapter 8 with our view on zero tolerance. In Chapter 9, we introduce a novel role for survey research as a potential vehicle for constructive social change. Finally, in Chapter 10, we integrate the various strands and offer a blueprint for constructive community action.

Throughout our analysis we have much to say about Aboriginal identity and the normative structure of Aboriginal communities. There is, however, one important distinction that we need to make. Our focus is never on *what* the content of Aboriginal identity or the content of a new normative structure should be – that is the sole prerogative of Aboriginal peoples. Rather, our focus is on the *process* of how identity and norms interrelate.

WHY US?

We are a curious pair to be writing this book: an English-Canadian male senior academic and a mid-career Québécoise female academic, neither of whom is of Aboriginal heritage. However, both of us share whatever biases are associated with non-Aboriginal experimental social psychology and its emphasis on theory-driven research and the rigours of the laboratory. We have also spent years conducting field research in various countries, from the United States, Southeast Asia, and the Middle East to Russia, Kyrgyzstan, and Mongolia.

That said, our biggest commitment to genuine community-based research has been, and continues to be, First Nations and Inuit communities across Canada. It is in this context that the worlds of community research and theory-driven laboratory research confront one another. And this might explain the style of this book. We lay out a series of ideas, some of which reflect the collective findings of a discipline, some of which reflect our own theorizing, and, more important, some of which reflect our absorption of the wisdom of Aboriginal friends, colleagues, and elders. The absorption process goes way beyond what we have learned from formal exchanges with Aboriginal colleagues at community meetings; rather, it involves the osmosis that arises from sharing flights in small planes to community after community, from sharing hours and hours waiting for weather to clear, being out on the land, co-teaching in remote communities, testing hundreds of young students, and participating in lengthy community meetings at which research results are shared and discussed. This is where trust develops, ideas are shared, and the stereotype of Aboriginal people as quiet, unobtrusive, and low-key is put to rest. It is in these contexts that our ideas have been shaped. Here, although we present these ideas in a non-Aboriginal manner, much of what we have gleaned has come from what Aboriginal friends, colleagues, and elders have taught us. During the entire ongoing process neither they nor we realized that mutual teaching and learning was such an important and ongoing "bi"-product.

Both our academic and community based-realities are reflected in the style of this book. At times we attempt to support our theorizing with research from the social sciences. Equally often we illustrate our arguments with anecdotes regarding our personal experiences in Aboriginal communities. The combination, we believe, accurately reflects our vision.

# 2

# Aboriginal Voices, Cultural Diversity, and Aboriginal Resilience

In this chapter we address three fundamental issues that are ever-present but rarely openly discussed when Aboriginals and non-Aboriginals sit together and focus on important topics. The first concerns the balance of Aboriginal and non-Aboriginal voices in discussions of any substance. In this day and age, it would seem that there are few undertakings more presumptuous than two non-Aboriginal Canadians contributing to the legacy of colonialism by writing a book on Aboriginal peoples in Canada. So why do it?

The second issue concerns categorizing all Aboriginal people under the umbrella term "Aboriginal." Why not distinguish and respect cultural differences by referring to specific Aboriginal groups, each of which makes a unique contribution to the fabric of Canadian society?

The third issue concerns the concept of Aboriginal resilience. Our analysis leads us to conclude that there is a genuine crisis in Aboriginal communities. Readers, indeed we ourselves, have concerns about the negative impact and stereotypes that might be unintentionally promoted by our book. Implicitly, Aboriginal resilience is at the heart of this volume: Amidst the challenges and issues at hand, is there hope for the future of Aboriginal people? We can camouflage this question with platitudes in order to appear to emphasize the positive. We choose, instead, to speak honestly.

## WHERE IS THE ABORIGINAL VOICE?

The challenges we face as non-Aboriginal authors are exacerbated by the stance that we take regarding the present circumstances in Aboriginal communities. We argue that over one hundred years of failed interventions demands a new course of action as the hardships facing Canada's Aboriginal peoples today are greater than the published statistics and public testimony portray.

We conclude our introductory chapter with the question: "Why us?" And here we must offer a nuanced rationale. The question is not really "Why us?" but, more accurately, "Why is there no Aboriginal author?"

This is a fundamental question and one with which non-Aboriginals like ourselves wrestle with every day when we teach, give workshops, conduct research, consult on Aboriginal policy issues, and, indeed, author a book within an Aboriginal context. Between us, we have been wrestling with this authorship issue for forty years. Do we have a definitive answer to the question? No. Nobody does. To suggest that the absence of an Aboriginal author is "perpetuating a legacy of colonialism" is superficially satisfying to some, but it neglects the depth of the complexity that is involved. Before elaborating on the issue of authorship, let us simply say: To not write a book may very well be the ultimate act of exclusion of, and disrespect for, Aboriginal peoples.

Here is the reality: if Aboriginal communities across the country had detected a hint of a colonial or exclusory attitude, then we would never have been able to conduct our teaching, research, and policy work for so long and in so many communities. We take some pride in being among the first to talk with residential school survivors in our Aboriginal classes in remote communities and to develop university-level courses for which we insist upon having Aboriginal co-teachers who ultimately take responsibility for each course. We take pride in the fact that, at regional, national, and international education meetings, it is almost exclusively our research group that features Aboriginal presenters who usually present in their Aboriginal language. So between us we have partnered with, lived with, hunted with, travelled with, and socialized with Aboriginal friends and colleagues for forty years.

Does this mean that we are immune from contributing to Canada's legacy of colonialism? Absolutely not. It may well be that unconsciously and inadvertently we are prolonging a colonialist mentality while deluding ourselves that our intentions and the style and structure of our community engagements are contributing positively to the decolonization process. This is precisely why we continue to wrestle with this issue at every step.

So why not have Aboriginal authors? To answer this question, we present two main arguments. First, the academic expertise we offer complements the efforts of our Aboriginal colleagues who devote their time to teaching and implementing policies within their communities. Our Aboriginal friends and colleagues have important, demanding jobs in education and community service. They partner with us by choice and how they find the time is a miracle. Anyone with community experience across the country knows that skilled and respected Aboriginal people are stretched to the limit. For example, to become a certified Aboriginal teacher is a great accomplishment. Their reward is to bring their ability and cultural richness to the classroom. But in addition they are the ones asked to develop cultural materials, translate and head up community committees, and attend meetings across the country, all the while pursuing their professional certification and actually teaching, or heading up departments, full time.

Our Aboriginal colleagues encouraged us to write this book as they share with us the strong belief that Aboriginal policy has been, and continues to be, misguided. Our academic background in social psychology complements the expertise of our Aboriginal colleagues who teach and implement policies at the community, regional, and national levels. Our rationale is rooted in social psychological theory and research. No Aboriginal friend or colleague would have the time, training, or inclination to participate in writing an academic book. When working with Aboriginal colleagues and friends on cultural issues, we observe and learn, but we would never pretend to be Aboriginal culture experts. For example, even if our research program showed that learning in Inuktitut (versus French or English) from kindergarten to Grade 3 had great advantages for children, we would not interfere by implementing policy or by developing a curriculum for the children focused on Aboriginal culture. Thus we, as non-Aboriginals, have had the privilege of sitting on Aboriginal committees designed to monitor and offer advice to non-Aboriginal organizations. Being asked to sit on the committee as one of the few non-Aboriginals was a great privilege, but we would never expect to be – nor should we have, nor were we – considered for the position of rotating chairperson of the committee.

Similarly, our Aboriginal colleagues would not be comfortable writing an academic treatise. As one elder expressed it to us, "Go out and put a voice to our pain." Simply put, it would be unfair to our Aboriginal partners for us to speak for them, or to include their names as authors, as any negative repercussions that emerge need to remain ours and not theirs. For example, if an initially defensive reaction to our book emerged among Aboriginal and/or non-Aboriginal readers, our Aboriginal authors might unknowingly be caught in the crossfire without being fully versed in the theories of social psychology and so being unable to defend their arguments. They might be asked to explain the scientific background of the theories that have been used or to speak about details of the experimental conditions that led to the results reported in this book.

Aboriginal leaders who are working tirelessly for their communities walk a fine line between instigating change (and the threats and pushback that change brings) and trying to maintain the respectful ear of community members whom they hope to influence. Any inadvertent or unexpected connection with ideas that might distance them from their constituents could be catastrophic. Co-authoring a book with Aboriginal authors might work fine for 90 percent of the content, but there could be some abstract theoretical dimension that, even though it might constitute only 10 percent of the argument, would be enough to derail the entire mission of the dedicated Aboriginal author.

Our Aboriginal colleagues are, however, the natural experts to whom we must turn with regard to the community initiatives we propose. This will become clear in the later chapters, where we attempt to outline a series of concrete, constructive community-based programs. The enormous contributions our Aboriginal team members have made to these community initiatives is evident. What we as authors attempt to do is document the social psychological underpinnings of their design. We also document the many presentations and workshops our Aboriginal team members have developed for Aboriginal leaders in different regions in order to come up with policies to improve school attendance by expanding the ideas offered in this book. These presentations were prepared by Aboriginal team members because they are the individuals with the expertise in these domains.

The second argument we present in response to the question "why not have Aboriginal authors?" refers to the broader issues of authorship legitimacy. Can a female writer realistically have a male protagonist as a central character in a novel? Can a non-user of performance-enhancing drugs analyze professional sports culture? Can a non-Aboriginal author make a constructive contribution to Aboriginal life or an Aboriginal author offer insights into the challenges confronting modern cities?

These are complex social and moral questions with no easy answers. Perhaps the most appropriate form of answer rests in the realization and recognition of the contextual specificity of each situation. In other words, the only decisive answer we can offer is the rather lame: "It depends!"

A few Aboriginal examples might illuminate the complexity of the question of author legitimacy. On more than one occasion a university has proudly announced that it will be offering courses for credit designed to teach an Aboriginal language. In one specific example, one whose details are familiar to us, the non-Aboriginal academic community applauded itself for being so inclusive and for showing such respect for the Aboriginal language and the people who speak it. An uncomprehending shockwave ran through the university community when the Aboriginal chiefs of the language group in question demanded that their language *not* be taught. The chiefs argued that their group had lost so much that virtually all that remained was the integrity of their unique language. Having linguists and anthropologists teach non-Aboriginal students the essence and subtlety of the Aboriginal language would rob the Aboriginal group of its last culturally distinctive identity. Clearly, this is an example of a mismatch in cultural power that renders the proposed exercise both inappropriate and threatening. If members of the Aboriginal group were to teach the language to young members of their own group, there would be no problem: it depends.

So what if non-Aboriginal teachers or writers were to communicate their ideas to an Aboriginal audience and non-Aboriginal policy makers in the domain of Aboriginal issues, assuming those ideas did not represent a threat to Aboriginal autonomy, distinctiveness, or identity? What if non-Aboriginal consultants helped design hospitals, hockey arenas, and social services? The input cannot be guaranteed to be constructive – so again, it depends.

Taking the argument one step further, some contend that there are advantages to having members of one group share their perceptions of another group. Maybe there are benefits to having a Western movie director produce a movie focused on India (e.g., *Slumdog Millionaire*), or a British cook write a book on Italian cuisine, or a therapist treat a client who is from a different cultural group. In all three examples the argument is the same: sometimes an outsider sees things that someone living the experience fails to recognize because he or she is so immersed in the group's way of life. How life unfolds for group members is so normal that it would never occur to any member to question the group's norms. An outsider may well be struck by what she or he sees because it is novel to her/him, and sometimes raising basic normative questions can be constructive. But, of course, sometimes outside perceptions are naïve and biased. Again, it depends.

In sum, our answer to the question "Why is there no Aboriginal author?" ultimately sidesteps all the many thorny issues and rests on a simple premise: the responsibility for the ideas expressed in this book is genuinely that of the authors and no one else. The enormous contributions to our thinking that have come from Aboriginal and non-Aboriginal colleagues and friends is a given, but to burden those who have so freely shared their insights with us purely for appearance's sake would be disingenuous. We chose to author this work in order to protect our Aboriginal colleagues, from whom we have learned so much, from any unpredictable and potentially costly negative repercussions.

## THE DIVERSITY OF ABORIGINAL CULTURES

Throughout the book, we constantly refer to the challenges faced by Aboriginal people in Canada, the misguided efforts to address these challenges, and the need for a different approach. It may seem as though we believe that it is legitimate to refer to Aboriginal peoples as a single cultural group, with no appreciation for the array and magnitude of the cultural differences that make up the overarching label "Aboriginal peoples." It was Washburn (1975) who asserted "there was and is no single Indian culture" (15-16), a sentiment that has been echoed by recent authors (e.g., Waldram 2004). However, we believe it is legitimate to focus on "Aboriginal peoples" when the processes concern all Aboriginal groups. The issue is one of functional social categorization. Specifically, we argue that, when the focus of attention is one single factor common to all Aboriginal peoples, it is legitimate to refer to them as a cohort. Thus, it is the issue or context that determines the appropriate level of cultural categorization. Indeed, the label "Aboriginal peoples" is frequently used, including by Aboriginal leaders themselves, when discussing pan-Aboriginal issues (Royal Commission on Aboriginal People 1996). Likewise, we happen to be addressing an issue that is indeed shared by all Aboriginal groups, bands, and communities: internal colonization.

We might begin by asking: Why is there such sensitivity surrounding cultural labels for Aboriginal peoples? "Native peoples," "Indigenous peoples," "Aboriginal peoples," and "First peoples" are all labels referring to the culturally and linguistically diverse inhabitants of North America prior to European colonization. The labels have changed, evolved, and have been used differently in Canada and the United States as a response to changing political and social realities. What all these labels emphasize is a category of people who predated Europeans and thereby position themselves as the first inhabitants of the land. And when a people, any people, feel disrespected, group labels take on a special significance. Residents of Quebec are certainly vigilant and sensitive about group labels. Labels such as "French-Canadian," "Québécois," and "francophone" each has its own social and political sensitivity (Henderson 1999; Kircher 2009; Lambert et al. 1960). Equally, labels such as "Canadians," "mainstream Canadians," "dominant Canadians," and "non-Aboriginal Canadians" all refer to the culturally and linguistically more numerous and powerful inhabitants of Canada. Each has subtle political and social connotations, ranging from the allusion to power associated with "dominant Canadians" to the emphasis on cultural distinctions among groups associated with "non-Aboriginal." The broader point is that there are situations in which negotiation, tension, and conflict can be traced to fundamental differences between the pre- and postcolonial inhabitants of this land.

There are, of course, circumstances in which the functional relations between groups require a different level of cultural focus. Early on in the Canadian context a distinction was made between "Indian" and "Eskimo," or, more appropriately, between "First Nations" and "Inuit." Labels such as "Indian" and "Eskimo" have been judged to be derogatory and are raised here to illustrate that, with broad category labels, as with all cultural labels, their meaning is emotionally charged. More important, "Aboriginal peoples" as an overarching label frequently becomes further categorized into "First Nations" and "Inuit." Why? Because cultural differences between First Nations and Inuit were not only pronounced but also especially important in terms of policy. Inuit, for example, were far less numerous than First Nations and were not subject to a "reserve" system but instead concentrated in remote communities. As such, they felt that policies negotiated with First Nations groups were not relevant to the Inuit experience. Insisting on a category distinction between First Nations and Inuit, it was hoped, would maximize the chances for distinct policies to meet distinct cultural differences. Only recently have Métis people earned an official designation as a culturally distinct Aboriginal people. We have thus arrived at the current state of respect for cultural differences, with official designations of Aboriginal people referring to three culturally distinct groups: First Nations, Inuit, and Métis.

Beyond the official classifications of First Nations, Inuit, and Métis lie a myriad of subtle and not so subtle cultural differences, and, depending upon the context, those cultural differences may be crucial. We have experienced these differences first-hand across the country. For example, in the early 1990s we were involved in discussions when IBM wanted to create an Inuktitut keyboard for Inuit computer users. In Nunavik alone, however, there are three distinct dialects that need to be respected. This meant that, if one dialect group was chosen over the others, that group would have been validated to the detriment of the other two dialect groups. Given that so many Aboriginal tongues have been lost forever, it is easy to appreciate the tenacity with which a particular Inuit group insists upon its specific culture and dialect being recognized and respected. Add to this the Inuit groups. who write with syllabics as opposed to Roman orthography. Every region and community is different. The variability is real and needs to be respected, depending upon the issue.

Now we turn to the crux of the matter. Some would say that because we, in this volume, most frequently use the overarching label "Aboriginal peoples," we are thereby unaware of, or ignoring, or indeed disrespecting, important cultural differences. Our response to this is that the category of, label for, and specificity of the cultural group chosen depends on the issue and the context. In this volume the seminal trigger for the processes and solutions upon which we focus is internal colonization, a process that affected every Aboriginal person – First Nations, Inuit, or Métis. We argue that the issues are pan-Aboriginal and, thus, that "Aboriginal peoples" is the level of categorization that is appropriate. It is also why our solutions need to be pan-Aboriginal and inclusive of all groups.

These cultural differences issues arise constantly. In Canada we often, in official and informal circles, hear the label "Asian." Of course, those of Korean, Japanese, Taiwanese, or Chinese descent may well feel that their particular cultures are not being respected by such an all-inclusive category. Our point would be, using the label "Asian" would only be appropriate when the issue under examination is one that is shared by all Asian groups. If it is not a pan-Asian issue, it would be disrespectful, or perhaps even reflect genuine ignorance, not to focus on the level of cultural differences appropriate to that issue. And this may require being attentive to cultural subgroups within a national group, again depending upon the issue.

"Canada" as an overarching label is fraught with the same issues. Who represents Canada? We are a culturally diverse nation, comprised of provinces and territories that jealously guard their distinctiveness. So don't tell us that Quebec, Ontario, or British Columbia speaks for the whole nation. If I live in Manitoba or Nova Scotia, how do I respond to those who divide Canada into five regions: Atlantic provinces, Quebec, Ontario, the Prairies, and British Columbia?

Our point is that the appropriate level of cultural categorization must be chosen in accordance with the common factors that are shared among groups, while at the same time acknowledging the differences and diversity of cultural entities therein. To choose the wrong level of cultural analysis, either too broad or too narrow, may have destructive consequences. If the focus is on creating meaningful educational materials for students, then the local community culture will need to be the focus. The whole reason for pursuing a relevant curriculum for students is a consequence of the colonialist practice of imposing non-Aboriginal curricula on Aboriginal students with the result that the educational content with which they are presented neither offers nor respects their lived reality. To supplant this with a very broad "Aboriginal" content might be preferable, but it would still impose upon students material that is alien to any specific community. Ceremonies from a forest-dwelling First Nations group would have little relevance for an Inuit community from the Eastern Arctic.

Conversely, if it is a question of regrouping subgroups of Aboriginal peoples, then local cultural norms and dialects may have to give way to the similarities that cut across these different subgroups. For example, if First Nations peoples across the country wish to regroup into a larger political body in order to share strategies and have a larger impact on the Canadian landscape, then each band may have to sacrifice aspects of its cultural distinctiveness and emphasize the common elements.

Local culture or broader culture? It depends on the issue. For the present volume the focus is on the challenges facing Aboriginal peoples – all Aboriginal peoples. It is indeed shocking to find that, despite the wide variety of cultural and historical differences among Aboriginal communities when it comes to the pressing problems, you find an identical array of social challenges from coast to coast to coast. And it doesn't end there: Indigenous peoples in the United States, Mexico, Central America, South America, the Caribbean, and the entire circum-polar region all suffer the same array of collective challenges. How is it possible? The one common factor? Internal colonialism (see Ponting 1986).

This volume addresses the impact of colonialism. This is a pan-Aboriginal issue, and, thus, we focus on the shared experiences of all Aboriginal peoples. This is not to neglect or disrespect cultural differences among Aboriginal groups and subgroups; rather it is to make a conscious decision to focus on an issue that crosses Aboriginal cultural differences – internal colonialism.

ABORIGINAL RESILIENCE

In the chapters to follow we launch into an analysis of the challenges confronting Aboriginal communities, and the theme of widespread dysfunction is ever present. Spending so much time in Aboriginal communities makes this a difficult undertaking for us. For many years we have not voiced the problems of Aboriginal communities outside of these communities. The public stereotype of Aboriginal peoples was, and still is, negative enough without its being exacerbated by non-Aboriginal perceptions. Recently, however, there has been a dramatic change: Aboriginal leaders and community members have begun to openly and courageously talk about the problems in their communities.

In fact, public discourse in Aboriginal communities about social dysfunction has become so pervasive and intense that a new theme has emerged: "Why are we always emphasizing the negative? Let's focus more on the positive." When you spend considerable time in communities and at community meetings, you quickly appreciate this sentiment. As well, the emergence of this new sentiment is a testament to the extent to which public Aboriginal discourse has emerged from silence to meeting the issues head on. We, of course, echo the need for addressing the issues squarely, and, as noted earlier, we argue that conditions are actually, and unfortunately, worse than the public. discourse concludes.

All the more reason, then, to pause and reflect on the positives, to make sure that, before proceeding to focus on the challenges, we underscore the unique positive qualities that are the bedrock of Aboriginal communities. Our sentiments should be obvious since the amount of time we have, do, and will spend in Aboriginal communities is a concrete indicator of the positivity of the experience. And as much as the land has its attractions, weather and mosquitoes notwithstanding, it is ultimately the people that draw us back time and time again.

But this is not the place to toss out empty platitudes about how wonderful Aboriginal people are. As with any group of people, you encounter "the good, the bad, and the ugly." There is a family in a remote community whose home we would stay at any time we were in the community. It was a mixed family – anglophone man, Inuit woman, and their three children. These were treasured visits, but there was always a tinge of "white guilt" that the family balance was upset by the frequent onslaught of two more southern whites to the family dynamic. On one visit a phone call to the home led to the announcement that an Inuit friend would be coming to join the family for a week. We openly expressed delight at the news, saying to our Inuit host: "For once you will have some cultural balance to offset our frequent invasions of your home." Her response was spontaneous and dug far deeper than cultural stereotypes. She simply said: "When you are sharing your home where people are in your face all the time, all you really care about is the person, not the group – I can't stand her." Talk about putting white guilt in its place and underscoring individual variation within groups! Of course, it did lead to a great gossip session as our host described what would drive her, and all of us, crazy for the next week.

So what are the genuine positives that strike any visitor to an Aboriginal community? The answer is simple, pervasive, and impressive: the resilience of Aboriginal people. Resilience refers to a general individual ability to "maintain a state of equilibrium" in face of adversity or trauma (Bonanno 2004, 20). For Aboriginal people, resilience is conceived at the community level (Kirmayer et al. 2011; Kirmayer et al. 2009); thus, resilience observed in Aboriginal communities refers to "a process linking a set of networked adaptive capacities to a positive trajectory of functioning and adaptation in constituent populations after a disturbance" (Norris et al. 2008, 131). In other words, resilience for Aboriginal people is seen as an ability to redress their trajectory in light of profound trauma that has often touched entire generations.

To place Aboriginal resilience in perspective we need only remind ourselves of the legacy of colonialism. There is a vast literature detailing the destructive history of the colonization of Aboriginal peoples, but, for our purposes, Thomas King's (2012) brilliant *The Inconvenient Indian* offers a number of telling quotes that capture why Aboriginal resilience is an awesome testament to the Aboriginal spirit. Here are a few King's offerings from pages 60 and 61 of his book:

In a few years, perhaps, they will have entirely disappeared from the face of the earth. (Heckewelder 1876, 40)

Little can be hoped for them as a distinct people. The sun of their day is fast sinking in the western sky. It will soon go down in a night of oblivion that shall know no morning. (John Benjamin Sanborn 1869, quoted in Willson and Sanborn 1887, 673)

The Indians are children. Their arts, wars, treaties, alliances, habitations, crafts, properties, commerce, comforts, all belong to the very lowest and rudest of human existence. (Horace Greeley 1860, 151)

To quote Thomas King (2012, 61) himself: "Problem was, Live Indians didn't die out. They were supposed to, but they didn't." Instead, "live Indians were forgotten, safely stored away on reservations and reserves or scattered in the rural backwaters and cityscapes of Canada and the United States. Out of sight, out of mind. Out of mind, out of sight" (ibid.).

These short passages speak eloquently to the collective resilience of Aboriginal peoples. They are still here, and that alone is profound. But when we speak of the positives in Aboriginal communities in the form of resilience, we are not focusing on collective resilience per se but, rather, on how, for Aboriginal peoples, such resilience is demonstrated in everyday life at the individual level. The collective experience of colonialism has left in its wake a legacy of individual and collective hardships that would challenge any human being to the core.

Every time we give a course or workshop in a community, individual challenges and resilience are on wrenching display. We have never given a course among a group of fifteen adult students when at least ten or eleven of them were not in the process of being rocked with tragic news. This news ranged from a sudden serious health issue, a death or accident in the family, a child in a desperate legal situation, or a loved one lost on the land. Each of these events would be enough to challenge a person's physical, emotional, and spiritual health should they occur once or twice in her/his adult life. The reality is that Aboriginal people face these individual dramatic events consistently, and they touch all community members at the same time. For example, if a suicide occurs in a community, it is not only a disaster for the close family members but also for the community as a whole since everyone knows everyone else. As such, Aboriginal people constantly cope with adversity, yet they survive, support each other and share, retaining their sense of humour. In the end they are able to concentrate on moving forward, albeit only to get knocked down again.

Visit any family and ask "how's it going?" and you will receive the standard answer: "Same old, same old," or "it's going," or "OK." Fifteen minutes into a conversation you will learn of the myriad life stressors with which individual, family, and extended family members have been hit. Each one would bring a family to its knees, but Aboriginal resilience conquers, and you feel humbled by the depth of their ability to cope.

Our search for positives begins and ends with resilience. It is an Aboriginal characteristic that is real, and it benefits all who encounter it. It is also the unspoken theme of this book. Our contention is that conditions in Aboriginal communities are worse than formal statistics and public portrayals present, that these conditions affect all Aboriginal communities, and that so far interventions have been misguided. We advocate a new direction based on the assumption that collective challenges require collective solutions. Our entire rationale is predicated on a celebration of Aboriginal resilience.

# 3

# Colonialism's Legacy:
# A Litany of Community Challenges

Our goal for this chapter, which is to describe the breadth and depth of the challenges confronting Aboriginal communities, might seem straightforward, but its achievement is fraught with complexity. This necessitates a lengthy preamble before we touch upon any actual statistics. We must go beyond these statistics to show how even they, bleak as they are, consistently underestimate the Aboriginal reality. And we must document the long list of failed interventions.

The more difficult part of the journey involves balancing the need to document the challenges facing Aboriginal communities without playing into and exacerbating the already negative stereotype that non-Aboriginal Canadians have of the quality of life in these communities. Our analysis, therefore, focuses less on the easily retrievable statistics and more on the challenges that Aboriginal communities are, often for the first time, speaking about openly.

The presentation of comparative numbers is delicate because Aboriginal people have very conflicting views about statistics and, indeed, about the entire research process. Recognizing this dilemma, we present objective data to underscore the challenges confronting Aboriginal communities. We are guided, however, by the priorities that Aboriginal communities themselves have chosen to highlight. Specifically, we tend towards those statistics that validate what Aboriginal leaders and community members are speaking about openly and publicly.

Our lengthy introductory comments on a chapter designed to present the "hard data" regarding the challenges confronting Aboriginal communities might lead readers to conclude that we are less than comfortable with "quantitative" research. Let us put that conclusion to rest. We are both products of a discipline – experimental social psychology – that has a rich tradition of experimentation. Like all social psychologists we have conducted, and continue to conduct, laboratory experiments related to basic social psychological processes. In addition, however, we are committed to field research, where we aim to bring the rigours of experimental social psychology to the real world. The process of conducting community-based field research requires knowing communities well and feeling comfortable with their rhythms and preoccupations. The result is that we have become involved in a variety of activities beyond those that are strictly research defined. The first of these is a direct offshoot of our research and involves teaching statistics, research methodology, and social psychology in an array of contexts. These range from teaching traditional university classes with non-Aboriginal Canadian and American students to teaching at universities in emerging nations and, finally, to teaching in remote Aboriginal communities in Canada. Our community-based research has also meant participating in community contexts on policy issues, dealing with social and personal concerns, as well as accompanying hunters, fixing generators, baking, playing volleyball, and painting. Thus, while our commitment to rigorous research is unwavering, we are very much affected by the realities of community-based research and the very personal relationships they involve.

BEYOND COLD STATISTICS

The most salient image that non-Aboriginal Canadians have of Aboriginal communities involves an array of social problems, including academic underachievement, under-employment, substandard housing, substance abuse, physical and sexual violence, reckless sexual behaviour, and suicide. There are others, but here we focus on those that Aboriginal communities themselves are voicing.

Two important points must be underscored before we present our statistical portrait. The first point is that, when reporting statistics, or especially when reading about them, there is a tendency to dehumanize the individuals depicted (Bernard, Ottenberg, and Redl 2003). Any time members of a group are dehumanized, it legitimizes treating them as less than human. Labelling the enemy in an armed conflict as "dogs" or "goats" implies that they are less than human and, therefore, not worthy of full human treatment. Subtler forms of dehumanization involve implying that a group does not experience the full range of emotions, as do other human groups. According to Harrell-Bond (1986, 206), some Western aid workers tend to believe that the people they are dealing with don't react like Westerners and, therefore, ultimately conclude that they "are used to death and suffering and therefore no longer feel these things." This suggests that other people don't experience the emotional depths that "we" experience. It dehumanizes them and, in so doing, legitimizes our being less concerned for their welfare. Cold statistics can have the same impact, and their dehumanizing effect has been eloquently captured by such observations as: "Statistics are human beings with the tears wiped off" (Brodeur 1985, 355). Or the more sobering: "A single death is a tragedy, a million deaths is a statistic" (Joseph Stalin quoted in Knowles 2004). As Arthur Koestler (1944, 88) famously wrote in order to shock his American readers during the Second World War: "Statistics don't bleed; it is the detail which counts. We are unable to embrace the total process with our awareness; we can only focus on little lumps of reality."

To underscore the dehumanizing potential of statistics, consider those rare occasions when someone we know personally commits suicide. We feel the impact and, regardless of the circumstances, there is a profound sense of loss, to the point that, for a period of time, we feel personally vulnerable. We feel a wide range of emotions, which might include anger, sadness, and disarray. In contrast, when a tragic event is reported in the form of a percentage rate or a statistic, it is but a simple number and is often personally meaningless, even when, as in the case of Aboriginal people, it is shocking. When we read a statistic, we may link it to a personal experience or to a story we have heard firsthand, but rarely do we feel the full range of emotions that are experienced by the actual individuals who comprise the statistic. To truly digest the impact of a statistic, the best we can do is to reflect on what it would be like if each individual it depicts were a loved one. When emotions are linked to statistics we may have a greater appreciation for their impact and, hence, for the resilience portrayed by Aboriginal people on a daily basis.

The second point to consider when analyzing any statistical profile of Aboriginal peoples is their unique demographic distribution. The Aboriginal population is very much younger than the non-Aboriginal Canadian population, and this reality affects the implications of any comparative statistics. When demographics point to a preponderance of young people, the smaller adult population is challenged to secure the future for its community – a challenge that is exacerbated by the fact that an entire emerging generation will lack the support of an older generation in its formative years. When there are more younger people than older people in a community, and when the former are facing serious challenges, there are fewer adults to socialize them and to provide them with guidance and a normative framework within which to function effectively.

In terms of specifics, Canada's Aboriginal communities are growing significantly faster than the mainstream population. From 1996 to 2006, the Aboriginal population grew by 45 percent, compared to 8 percent for the non-Aboriginal Canadian population (Statistics Canada 2006c). Children and youth under twenty-four years of age constitute almost half (48 percent) of the Aboriginal population, whereas they form less than one-third (31 percent) of non-Aboriginal Canadians (ibid.). Proportionally, children nine years old or younger are nearly twice as numerous in the Aboriginal population (19 percent) than they are in the Canadian population (11 percent).

The point we wish to emphasize is that, when analyzing statistics for Aboriginal communities, we need to appreciate that the challenges they indicate are exacerbated by the age distribution, which is skewed towards the very young. For example, if the unemployment rate is higher in Aboriginal communities than it is in the non-Aboriginal population, it means that an inordinate number of the unemployed are relatively young. It also means that unemployed youth will be relatively numerous, with few mature adults to spearhead economic activity. Young people are the voice of the future and the vitality of their communities depends on them; however, for Aboriginal communities, an entire generation of young people will not have the guidance of a mature generation to help them through to adulthood.

## CHALLENGES CONFRONTING ABORIGINAL COMMUNITIES

### Academic Underachievement

#### ABORIGINAL LEADERS SPEAK OUT

Many Aboriginal leaders describe academic underachievement as a shocking problem that needs to be solved immediately. Community leaders are vocal in acknowledging that the school dropout rate has reached crisis proportions. The recently retired national chief of the Assembly of First Nations, Phil Fontaine, has been especially outspoken about this challenge, stating: "More than half our people are under the age of 25. We must invest in education and training for First Nations so that Canada can remain a productive and competitive country. We literally cannot afford to lose this generation" (Assembly of First Nations 2009, para. 7). Similarly, Patrick Brazeau, national chief of the Congress of Aboriginal Peoples, concludes: "Better education and training are the means to overcome dependency. They are the gateway to economic opportunity and the best means of staking your claim on prosperity" (Congress of Aboriginal Peoples 2009, 4).

STATISTICAL REALITY

The raw statistics on school attendance alone underscore how desperate the situation is. Simply put, the school dropout rate has reached crisis proportions. In 2001, in the over fifteen-year-old Aboriginal population, 48 percent did not have a high school certificate and only 4 percent had a university degree, compared to 31 percent and 15 percent, respectively, for non-Aboriginal Canadians (Mendelson 2006). The situation is even worse for Aboriginal people living on reserves: as many as 59 percent over the age of fifteen did not have a high school diploma, whereas only 2 percent had a university degree (ibid.). In Nunavut, the rate of Inuit youth aged between fifteen and thirty-four years old who don't have a high school diploma reached 70 percent (Statistics Canada 2003). Perhaps the most disturbing statistic is the dropout rate of Aboriginal youth living on reserves: by the age of twenty, only 36 percent have obtained their high school diploma (64 percent dropout-rate) compared to 84.6 percent of non-Aboriginal youth (Health Canada 2009).

The difference between Aboriginal and non-Aboriginal rates is frightening, especially considering that, when dropout rates reach levels higher than 25 to 30 percent in a non-Aboriginal region, panic sets in: politicians and educators are mobilized to address the problem and every available measure is taken to encourage youth to pursue their education. For example, Quebec's minister of education has recently instigated an ambitious mission to lower the dropout rate from 31 percent to 20 percent before 2020 (Quebec 2009).

Given that a dropout rate of 31 percent is considered a crisis, how can we even begin to comprehend a 64 percent dropout rate in an Aboriginal community? The dropout rate is more than twice as high as that in the non-Aboriginal population, and there are even three times more twenty-five to thirty-four-year-old Inuit than non-Aboriginal Canadians who have not obtained their high school diploma (Inuit Tapiriit Kanatami 2005). A dropout rate of this magnitude means that students drop out of school at a young age and that doing so has become normative. In the context of conducting longitudinal research in schools in Aboriginal communities, we have, unfortunately, witnessed this phenomenon first hand. One of our longitudinal research projects requires that students be tested every year, beginning in kindergarten. What we are struck by each year is the number of students who have dropped out of our testing as early as Grades 3, 4, and 5. When we reach our last year of testing in Grade 6, only a handful of students attend school regularly. Thus, dropping out of school at a young age is more common than we might imagine; it has become routine and, indeed, normative for many Aboriginal communities.

The 64 percent dropout rate among Aboriginal students living on reserves portrays a disappointing reality, a reality that is even bleaker when we look beyond the statistics. To put it bluntly, the 64 percent dropout figure is an underestimation. The statistics do not consider the fact that, although some students do not officially drop out of school, they nevertheless only attend sporadically. For example, when we conduct our longitudinal research, we have difficulty testing all the children on the class list. Sometimes we begin to test a child, but, because it is lunch time or the end of the school day, we send the child home with a plan to continue the testing after lunch or on the next school day. Frequently, the child does not return to school that afternoon, the next day, or for several days. It has become so normal for children to attend school on a "drop-in" basis that no one is surprised by this practice. The result is that, at the end of the school year, these students pass to the next grade, even when clearly not all the skills required by the curriculum have been mastered. The reality is that it is such a challenge for teachers to keep students in their class that, even if they attend sporadically and are far behind in the curriculum, they are considered to be "going to school." Can a teacher fail most of her/his students because they attend school sporadically when most, if not all, of them do so?

This raises a more philosophical question with respect to educational standards in Aboriginal communities. If the educational standards demanded for students in Aboriginal communities were the same as those required for non-Aboriginal Canadian students, the dropout rate would dramatically increase. In fact, even students who do succeed in graduating from secondary school are at a disadvantage compared to students in non-Aboriginal schools who have achieved the same level of education. In other words, the statistics on school dropout rates are higher than the numbers portray, especially when one takes into account the fact that this 64 percent reflects the statistics obtained from schools that have lower educational standards. Hence, students in Aboriginal communities do not reach the same level of knowledge as do their non-Aboriginal counterparts. For half of all Canadians literacy is "below the acceptable range, and the reality is that Canada's Aboriginal peoples have even lower literacy rates. One indicator of this is that the proportion of Registered Indians with less than a Grade 9 education in 1996 was approximately double that of other Canadians" (Movement for Canadian Literacy 2004, 3).

Clearly, the reported dropout rate of 64 percent would be even higher if non-Aboriginal standards were rigorously enforced. Many observers have railed against the practice of lowering standards, arguing that it is necessary to apply non-Aboriginal standards to Aboriginal students in order to challenge them and to enrich the quality of their academic achievement (Dingle 2009; Richards and Vining 2004). This is, however, an unrealistic solution since applying stricter standards in Aboriginal communities is likely to have negative repercussions. Changing the curriculum to more rigid and challenging standards might further discourage Aboriginal children from attending school and, in turn, lead to even more school dropouts. What schools and educators have chosen to do is lower their standards and revise their objectives in the hope that students do not become discouraged. The hope is that young people will enjoy the school experience and that, in time, standards will gradually be increased until they ultimately match those in the non-Aboriginal population. Adjusting the educational standards was thus deemed necessary in order to encourage children to attend school. However, this reality underscores the fact that a dropout rate of 64 percent on average, – a rate that climbs as high as 70 percent in some communities – would be even higher if these communities had to meet the same standards as do their non-Aboriginal counterparts.

## FAILED INTERVENTIONS

Over the course of Canadian and Aboriginal history, there have been numerous interventions designed to address the dramatic underachievement of Aboriginal students. Only a few of these have been successful and none has been successful enough to positively affect the gap between Aboriginal and non-Aboriginal Canadians. Indeed, "a shocking number of Aboriginal young adults are not completing high school," and many fewer continue on to postsecondary education (Mendelson 2006, 35).

Prior to the arrival of European settlers, Aboriginal groups had complete responsibility for providing their children with the knowledge and skills they needed to become constructive group members. Upon their arrival, European colonizers introduced formal schooling designed explicitly to assimilate Aboriginal young people. Nomadic Aboriginal groups were forced to settle in designated reserves or communities and send their children to school. In some communities a school was built, but in most communities Aboriginal children were moved, far from their families, for months at a time, into non-Aboriginal communities. All were designed to replace Aboriginal culture and language with what was deemed a "superior" (i.e., European) culture and language.

It was in this context that the now infamous residential schools came into being, their explicit mission being to assimilate Aboriginal students into mainstream Canadian society (Anglican Church of Canada 2009). Draconian steps were taken to remove all traces of Aboriginal culture and language: children were removed from their Aboriginal communities and placed in European-Canadian schools, and their parents were most often legally compelled to turn over custody of their children to residential school authorities (Royal Commission on Aboriginal Peoples 1996). A national survey among Aboriginal people in Canada reported the well-being and health of half of those who survived the residential school ordeal were negatively affected by this experience (First Nations Centre 2005). As adults, "graduates" of these schools struggle daily with their identity and with low self-esteem after having been raised in an environment of fear, loneliness, and hatred. Now, as parents, they lack the requisite skills to raise their own children, instead turning to violence and neglect. In this way the residential school experience disrupted the transfer of parenting skills from one generation to the next (Royal Commission on Aboriginal Peoples 1996). Years ago we had a personal encounter with this reality when teaching Inuit adults, many of whom had been forced, as young students, to stand outside the school, naked, in -47 degree weather, for uttering a sentence in their own language. Little did we appreciate how widespread such inhuman practices were.

As if a policy of assimilation were not misguided enough, its legacy of widespread violence and sexual abuse represents a sad chapter in Canada's history. Over time, residential schools have closed one by one, but the damage has been immeasurable and the impact is still felt today in terms of attitudes towards formal education on the part of First Nations, Inuit, and Métis peoples. Recognition of the failed mission of assimilation culminated in the public arena on 11 June 2008, when Prime Minister Stephen Harper offered a formal apology on behalf of the Canadian government to former students of residential schools, acknowledging the rampant physical, psychological, and sexual abuse of Aboriginal children and the institutionalized cultural genocide (Prime Minister of Canada 2008). This discourse continues with the establishment of the Aboriginal Healing Foundation and the Truth and Reconciliation Commission. Clearly, the assimilation experiment has failed.

The failed assimilationist policy gave way to a more "enlightened" vision that involved developing a formal school system that was still modelled after Western European pedagogy but more inclusive of Aboriginal culture. In some Aboriginal communities, this meant that schools were built within the community itself. In others, often those closer to mainstream Canadian cities, Aboriginal children were, and still are, sent to mainstream schools. Clearly, this poses a major challenge in terms of including an Aboriginal cultural component in the curriculum.

Currently, the operative philosophy builds on the popular concepts of "empowerment" and "decolonization." This involves placing more control for formal education in the hands of Aboriginal groups and communities. The emphasis has shifted towards reducing the cultural mismatch or discontinuity between the culture of the community and the culture of the school "to foster bicultural competence" (Royal Commission on Aboriginal Peoples 1996, 5:13). The result is a core "mainstream" curriculum supplemented by culture classes and Aboriginal language classes and that, in some cases, uses an Aboriginal language as the language of instruction (either for some courses or for entire grades).

Given the discouraging statistics we have presented, it would be tempting to conclude that moving towards a more culturally relevant curriculum has failed to produce the desired results. No and yes. "No" because it is too early to draw a fair conclusion; moreover, cultural relevance requires trained Aboriginal teachers, culturally appropriate materials, and time to develop first-rate lesson plans. "Yes" because the major hurdle seems to be actually attracting students to attend school on a regular and committed basis, and this has not yet happened. No curriculum, however culturally appropriate, will succeed without having students attending school regularly, physically and psychologically healthy, and eager to learn. Until school is valued, and its relevance to the quality of life for Aboriginal people concretely demonstrated, school attendance will be a major issue. No curriculum, no matter how culturally relevant, can succeed when school attendance is sporadic at best.

So, even though Aboriginal groups are more involved with the education of their children, and despite the millions of dollars that have been invested in developing a culturally relevant curriculum, the dropout rate remains at crisis levels.

## Unemployment

### ABORIGINAL LEADERS SPEAK OUT

Unemployment and economic development are two sides of the same coin, and Aboriginal leaders are extremely vocal about both. The economy, Aboriginal leaders argue, lies at the heart of personal development, self-actualization, and well-being. For its part, at the collective level, economic development is viewed as central to Aboriginal aspirations for increased self-control, autonomy, and the resolution of outstanding land claims. Phil Fontaine, the former national chief of the Assembly of First Nations, stepped down in 2009, and five candidates vied for his title. All of them proposed focusing on stimulating the economy, and this, they argued, was especially pivotal, given today's global economic crisis. For example, Shawn Atleo (2009, para. 1), the victorious candidate, declared: "This is our time to empower our fast growing youth population in ways that will ensure a future of opportunity, success and prosperity." Perry Bellegarde (2009, 1), another candidate, argued: "One of the hallmarks of a people's ability to be truly self-governing is economic self-sufficiency. We must continue to move toward economic self-sufficiency by taking strides to: 1) Facilitate strategic partnerships with the private and public sectors, 2) Create opportunities for resource revenue sharing, and 3) Facilitate sustainable economic development projects." In the speech launching his campaign, candidate John Beaucage (Adams 2009, 17) declared: "Together, through Nation Building, we will work towards eliminating poverty, building economies, empowering our citizens and our youth through unity with pride."

## STATISTICAL REALITY

A recurring theme in terms of the consequences of unemployment is captured in a song from the famous Quebec poet and composer Felix Leclerc (1972): "the best way to kill a man is to pay him to do nothing." Widespread unemployment gives rise to these figurative "killing" conditions, and this is precisely the statistical portrait that arises when comparing unemployment rates between Aboriginal and non-Aboriginal communities. A report from Statistics Canada indicates that, in 2006, the unemployment rate was 23.1 percent for First Nations people between twenty-five and fifty-four years old living on reserve, and 12.3 percent for those living off reserve (Gionet 2009a). For the same-age population in the same year, the unemployment rate was 8.4 percent for Métis (Gionet 2009b) and 19.0 percent for Inuit (Gionet 2008). That year, the unemployment rate among non-Aboriginal Canadians was 5.2 percent (Gionet 2009a). And, indeed, the highest unemployment rate ever recorded for all Canadians was 12 percent in 1983 (Statistics Canada 2008).

These numbers are worrisome when one considers that an unemployment rate of 8 percent in the mainstream population signals a societal problem: the priorities of the Prime Minister of Canada following the economic crisis were all oriented towards addressing unemployment (Prime Minister of Canada 2009). Only to support families and communities that were hit by the economic crisis, the government of Canada invested $15.5 billion in order to fund programs protecting jobs, to provide employment insurance and training, and to freeze employment insurance rates (ibid.). The Canadian federal government plunged into deficit for the first time since 1996, and predictions indicate that this deficit will rise to $85 billion before the budget returns to the black (*Economist* 2009). The unemployment figures are much higher in Aboriginal communities, but for some reason this does not provoke the extreme measures that are taken when unemployment rises in non-Aboriginal communities.

Government funding for Aboriginal issues is more concentrated on employment insurance and welfare payments rather than on sustainable economic development. Indeed, welfare has been called the "single most destructive force" in Aboriginal communities because of the high dependence rates and the anti-productivity environment it creates (Royal Commission on Aboriginal Peoples 1996 3:170). For example, one focus of these government programs is the issue of housing. Insufficient housing leading to overcrowded living conditions is a crisis in Aboriginal communities across the country. Despite this crisis, housing is heavily subsidized, taking financial pressure off most community members. It thus becomes difficult to motivate many of them to pursue job opportunities. We have seen situations in which an airline cannot find anyone to clean airplanes that land in the community. The mind-boggling solution is for the airline to fly non-Aboriginal staff up to the remote community to clean the airplane and then fly back again on the same plane.

This "pay-people-to-do-nothing" theme is, however, not entirely captured by unemployment statistics. We have witnessed first-hand a series of bizarre, but not uncommon, situations. For example, non-Aboriginal contractors in Aboriginal communities are often required to hire a certain percentage (e.g., 10 percent) of Aboriginal employees – a well-meaning policy. The unfortunate reality is that very often contractors will hire Aboriginal workers but pay them to stay away from the job.

FAILED INTERVENTIONS

The domain of employment is probably the one on which the government and Aboriginal communities work together most closely in order to improve the situation. In the last thirty years, the Canadian labour movement has taken steps to address the "barriers to Aboriginal employment and recommend solutions to facilitate the development of a workforce representative of Aboriginal people in this country" (Canadian Labour Congress 2005, sec. 5, p. 3). For example, in 1998, a partnership agreement between the Canadian Labour Congress and the Congress of Aboriginal People was developed to support Aboriginal people in their quest for full equality and justice. Also, to further integrate Aboriginal people into the workforce, the federal government has introduced a number of initiatives aimed at helping them find job opportunities and, it is hoped, lower social assistance dependency. Examples of these are the $85 million Aboriginal Skills and Employment Partnership Program and the $1.6 billion Aboriginal Human Resources Development Strategy (Human Resources and Skills Development Canada 2009).

Although such initiatives are to be applauded, the outcome in terms of economic improvement is not convincing and certainly calls into question the appropriateness of the myriad number of interventions already in place. What is most worrisome is the gap, in terms of participation in the labour force, that continues to increase between Aboriginal people (51 percent) and non-Aboriginal Canadians (81 percent), and it is even wider for young Aboriginal women and men between the ages of fifteen and twenty-four (Canadian Labour Congress 2005). Indeed, high unemployment still represents a chronic feature of Aboriginal communities: unemployment rates reach as high as 85 percent in some communities. Not only are there large numbers of people out of work in Aboriginal communities but many more cannot find employment that matches their skills (ibid.). Specifically, there is a structural feature to employment in Aboriginal communities that militates against a healthy work profile. There are very few professionally educated and trained Aboriginal people in fields such as education, law, medicine, and business. That is problematic enough as it means that the few professionally trained personnel are dramatically overworked, while the vast majority of community members lack any employment possibilities.

In sum, it seems that current initiatives designed to stimulate Aboriginal communities in terms of economic development offer "too little to be more than band-aid measures" (Canadian Labour Congress 2005, sec. 3, p. 21). These programs are often temporary and are not sustained beyond a one- or two-year period. One factor that makes it difficult to motivate communities to invest in education and training, with a focus on improved job possibilities, is the belief that, in Aboriginal communities, education is not related to employment opportunities. For example, it is often the case that a water truck driver or a custodian with minimal formal education will receive the same pay as a teacher. Similarly, employees may be doing the same job and receive the same pay yet have widely differing education levels. With situations such as these being the rule rather than the exception, it is hard to make a case for the importance of education when it comes to obtaining a decent job in Aboriginal communities. While there may be some truth to this, it is nevertheless true that education is critical for desirable employment. For example, there is a difference of more than $11,000 between the average income of Aboriginal women who have a university degree ($22,572) and the vast majority who do not ($11,326) (Canadian Labour Congress 2005).

*Crime, Violence, and Sexual Abuse*

ABORIGINAL LEADERS SPEAK OUT

Crime, violence, and sexual abuse are three related problem areas that have commanded attention in Aboriginal communities across the country. Among Aboriginal people, it is well known that these problems are not localized to specific individuals or nuclear families but, rather, directly or indirectly affect most, if not all, members of every community across the country. Indeed, in one of its reports, the Canadian Council on Social Development (2009, para. 1) concludes: "Aboriginal people in Canada are at greater risk both for being victimized by violent and personal crimes, and for being negatively involved in the criminal justice system." The First Nations Child and Family Caring Society of Canada (2002) dramatically notes that a First Nations young person is more likely to be incarcerated than to graduate from secondary school. Indeed, statistically, "incarceration rates of Aboriginal people are five to six times higher than the national average" (Canadian Council on Social Development 2009, para. 3).

The scope of the problem can be summarized by the Pauktuutit Inuit Women of Canada (2006, 6), who report that "most Inuit have been victims of sexual, physical or emotional abuse or have witnessed a close family member being abused, assaulted or killed." If we carefully examine this claim, the magnitude of the problem is illuminated. The word "most" stands out since it implies that the majority, at minimum more than 50 percent, have been victims. This overwhelming claim is echoed by what teachers, nurses, police officers, social workers, and community members tell us when we meet with them informally. Indeed it is rare, when we are in a community, that we don't work closely with community leaders and professionals on ongoing issues of violence in one form or another. Throughout our work in Aboriginal communities, we have been privileged to be trusted with people's concerns and worries about their communities. They also admit that almost all of the children in their communities have been victims of some form of violence at some point in their lives and that this continues. The word "most" is a frightening one, and it points to a challenge that few non-Aboriginal Canadians can fathom.

STATISTICAL REALITY

According to findings arising from the 1999 General Social Survey (Statistics Canada 2006b), Aboriginal community members were three times more likely to be victims of violent crimes (specifically sexual assault, robbery, and physical assault) than were members of the non-Aboriginal Canadian population. Although Aboriginal people have inordinately high rates of crime, violence, and sexual abuse, they are also victims of personal acts of violence. According to Statistics Canada (ibid.), between 1999 and 2004, 21 percent of Aboriginal people, including 24 percent of women and 18 percent of men, reported having been a victim of violence at the hands of a current or previous spouse or common-law partner. This 21 percent rate compares with 6 percent for non-Aboriginal people, which illustrates, once again, the severity of the situation. In Aboriginal communities, 21 percent of spouses are victims of a crime as opposed to 7 percent of spouses in the non-Aboriginal population (Statistics Canada 2006a). Twenty-five percent of Aboriginal children have witnessed their fathers being abused and 40 percent have witnessed their mothers being abused (ibid.). In non-Aboriginal cities and communities, even with numbers that do not come close to 21 percent, there is constant pressure for more women's centres, preventive programs, transitional homes for men and women, and more governmental assistance generally. This only serves to magnify the gravity of the situation for Aboriginal communities.

This sad reality is also reflected in the high violent crime rate in Nunavut, which is the highest in Canada (Statistics Canada 2007). In 2004, the rate of spousal violence was three times higher for Aboriginal women (24 percent) than for non-Aboriginal women (8 percent), and Aboriginal women were more likely to report the most severe forms of spousal violence, such as having been beaten up or worse (Statistics Canada 2006a). In terms of spousal homicide, the rate was eight times higher for the murder of Aboriginal women (4.6 percent) than for the murder of non-Aboriginal women (0.6 percent) and thirty-eight times higher for Aboriginal men (3.8 percent) than for non-Aboriginal men (0.1 percent) (Statistics Canada 2006a). Finally, the rates for sexual offences in the territories were between two and fourteen times higher than in the rest of Canada (ibid.). An in-depth study (Rojas and Gretton 2007, 257) concludes: "Aboriginal youths were more likely than their non-Aboriginal counterparts to recidivate sexually, violently, and non-violently during a 10-year follow-up period. Furthermore, the time between discharge and commission of all types of re-offences was significantly shorter for Aboriginal youths than for non-Aboriginal youths."

We need to reflect on the numerous statistics that show a discrepancy between Aboriginal and non-Aboriginal Canadians. When examining these numbers, we have to bear in mind that, as with the statistics for academic underachievement and unemployment, the statistics on all forms of violence are underrepresented in Aboriginal communities across Canada. Just as in all non-Aboriginal societies, it is well known that crimes, be they of a violent or of a sexual nature, are underreported. Thus, the crime rate reported by police authorities is widely believed to be an underestimation of actual violence rates. A Statistics Canada (2008) report indicates that most victims of violence tend to turn to their families, neighbours, or friends for support instead of to authorities.

Unfortunately, the gap between reported and actual crimes is more pronounced in Aboriginal communities than it is in non-Aboriginal communities. This can be explained by the fact that what is defined as a crime largely depends on what each society or community considers to be normative. For example, if violence and crime exist in large proportions, as in Aboriginal communities, then when crimes do occur they will be taken less seriously and, therefore, will be less likely to be reported.

Another factor that might explain why crime could be more frequent than what the statistics portray concerns the lack of resources, especially police officers. Too often, an officer on duty is over-worked and can't take the time to deal with "minor infractions" – a categorization that, given their frequency, often applies to domestic assaults. In the case of spousal abuse, unless it is extremely severe, we can presume that it would be very difficult for officers to deal with all abusive spouses as there are simply too many of them.

Finally, a report from Statistics Canada (2006b) indicates that crime rates in Aboriginal communities are probably underestimated in the data collected during general surveys and in the federal census. The reason is simply that it is very difficult to reach Aboriginal communities and that those community members who are reachable are not likely to be those who are facing the most serious problems.

FAILED INTERVENTIONS

The fact that violence and crime are normative and are underreported may be explained by a basic psychological process: social comparison. Social comparison may also explain why past and current interventions have failed to improve conditions in Aboriginal communities. Social comparisons are the mechanism that people use to evaluate their own situation (Festinger 1954). Thus, individuals will compare their own behaviour, thoughts, and feelings with those of others in order to determine whether they are normal, what they should do, and whether they are good people. Imagine a teenage girl in an Aboriginal community who gets beaten by her boyfriend and suffers a broken nose. If she evaluates her personal situation by comparing herself to her girlfriends who also have abusive boyfriends, or to her parents whom she has witnessed engaging in abusive behaviour, it is unlikely that she will report her own abuse. Instead, she might very well feel "lucky" to only have a broken nose. Thus, if a person lives in a community in which there is frequent violence and sexual abuse, and she herself is victimized, it is unlikely that the social comparison process will lead her to be proactive. Conversely, in communities in which violence and sexual abuse are clearly non-normative, the same person might, through a process of social comparison, be quick to report the incident to the authorities. Clearly, there is a pressing need to change the social norms as these are the necessary foundation for helping individuals in difficulty.

For decades, there have been interventions designed to help reduce crime, violence, and sexual abuse in Aboriginal communities. For example, the Institute for the Prevention of Crime, based at the University of Ottawa, recommends increased investment in programs such as *Safe Streets* and *Women's Safety* in order to make non-Aboriginal communities safer environments (Monchalin 2009). But such interventions might not be as effective in Aboriginal communities as in non-Aboriginal communities because of the differences in their respective normative structures. For these interventions to be effective, key differences – not in culture but in normative structure – between Aboriginal and non-Aboriginal communities need to be appreciated. This entails creating a normative structure in which the vast majority of community members are not involved with, and do not sanction, violence and abuse. It is also worth considering that policing small communities, wherever they may be, is a major challenge. And the problems associated with this challenge are exacerbated when communities are comprised of two or three large extended families. A local police officer will be constantly in conflict with family members, and outside police officers will never be integrated. Quite a dilemma. Perhaps these structural and normative realities explain why, to date, no effective intervention has been found.

## Suicide

ABORIGINAL LEADERS SPEAK OUT

The disturbingly high suicide rate in Aboriginal communities speaks to the depth of the psychological distress in these communities across the country. To many Aboriginal leaders, suicide is one of the most devastating issues because of its association with other health and social problems. The tendency for suicides to occur in clusters is particularly problematic. Given the small, tight-knit nature of Aboriginal communities, this causes a devastating "ripple effect" whereby the suicide of one is likely to negatively affect the entire community and potentially contribute to the suicidal and self-destructive tendencies of others (Health Canada 2003a). Leaders emphasize the urgency of the situation: "Over several years, in 172 days of public hearings in 92 communities across Canada, the Commissioners heard that suicide was one of the most urgent problems facing Aboriginal communities" (Chénier 1995, 1). Researchers are aware "that the Canadian Aboriginal population is experiencing an alarmingly high rate of suicide, especially in young Aboriginal males" (White and Jodoin 2003, 11).

STATISTICAL REALITY

Recent statistics support people's deep concerns about suicide rates in Aboriginal communities. It is striking that the general suicide rate among Aboriginal peoples across Canada is more than two times higher than that for the general Canadian population (Kirmayer 1994). The suicide rate is 11.8 per 100,000 inhabitants in the non-Aboriginal population, but for First Nations communities the rate is a striking 24.1 per 100,000 inhabitants (Health Canada 2004).

In Inuit communities, these proportions are even more devastating. Their suicide rate is a full eleven times higher than the rate in the rest of the country (Health Canada 2006). And in 1999, in Nunavut, more than one death out of four (27 percent) was a suicide (Khan 2008). Sadly, incidents of children and youth committing suicide are not all that rare. If we examine these numbers in greater detail we see that they are among the highest in the world. According to the international suicide rate (World Health Organization 2009), the First Nations suicide rate ranks eighth among countries worldwide, just below the rates for countries from the former Soviet Union – Hungary (26.0), Kazakhstan (26.9), Lithuania (30.4), and Russia (30.1) –

and just above Japan (24.4). The Inuit suicide rate (135.0) is not only the highest worldwide but it is also far ahead of the next country, Belarus (35.1).

These numbers are disturbing, especially considering that the suicide rate in Aboriginal communities is on the rise (Boothroyd et al. 2001; Khan 2008) while suicide rates in non-Aboriginal communities are decreasing (Kirmayer et al. 2007). Suicide used to be rare among Aboriginal people in Canada; tragically, however, suicide has increased dramatically in the last few decades (White and Jodoin 2003). In fact, for First Nations, suicide rates between 1979 and 1994 have increased by approximately 10 percent over the past few years, while the rate for the general Canadian population has been relatively stable over the same period (Kirmayer 1994; White and Jodoin 2003).

Adolescents and young adults are at the highest risk for committing suicide. Aboriginal teenagers between the ages of fifteen and twenty-four are five to seven times more likely to commit suicide than their non-Aboriginal peers (Kirmayer 1994). This means that young Aboriginal women are 7.5 times more likely to commit suicide than the average Canadian adolescent female, while young Aboriginal men are five times more likely to commit suicide than the average Canadian adolescent male. According to Health Canada (2009), the leading causes of death for First Nations up to the age of forty-four are suicide and self-inflicted injuries.

These statistics are dramatic, to say the least. But, like underachievement, unemployment, and criminality, they are underestimated. First, the numbers reported here represent only the suicide rates among Aboriginal peoples who have treaty status (or are "registered") and of Inuit living in remote communities. Excluded are "unregistered" non-status Aboriginal peoples, Métis, and Inuit living outside traditional Nunavut territories (White and Jodoin 2003). This inevitably leads to an underestimation of the actual numbers, thereby underestimating the problem of suicide among Aboriginal peoples.

Moreover, the number of accidental deaths is four to five times higher in Aboriginal communities than it is in the rest of the Canadian population (White and Jodoin 2003). It has been estimated that a number of these accidental deaths are actually suicides; more precisely, up to 25 percent of unknown deaths are not accurately recorded and, therefore, include unreported suicides.

FAILED INTERVENTIONS .

The suicide rate makes it clear that current interventions are ineffective or, at best, insufficient. Importing mainstream programs does not seem to work, and there may well be a need to refocus. Suicide is an extreme act, and, despite the alarming statistics, is only engaged in by a small minority. For example, in a community of five hundred people in which the suicide rate is relatively high, one person a year might commit suicide. In other words, only a few will choose suicide as an option. Clearly, suicide is not the normative option for most of those who are coping with inordinate stress. The point is that those few who reach the point of suicide would, at an earlier phase, have struggled with a variety of less extreme but nevertheless debilitating psychological pathologies. Moreover, for every person who commits suicide there are bound to be many, many more who, while never reaching the extreme of suicide, suffer psychologically. Perhaps there needs to be an enhanced focus on psychological problems, such as widespread anxiety and depression, which are closer to the "suicide" end of the continuum than the "well-being and happiness" end.

Thus, we might consider the suicide rate as a poignant indicator of widespread distress in Aboriginal communities. In tackling the high suicide rates, Aboriginal leaders have noted that the losses they have endured in terms of land and cultural identity "have contributed to anger that has no harmless outlet, grief that does not ease, damaged self-esteem, and a profound sense of hopelessness about the future" (Royal Commission on Aboriginal Peoples 1996 3:141). Indeed, this sense of identity loss is "a major risk factor for suicidal behaviour among young Aboriginal people" (Royal Commission on Aboriginal Peoples 1996 4:145). For every suicide there are many more who silently suffer from depression, anxiety, or despair. For instance, the World Health Organization (2009) estimates that, if 1 million people committed suicide in the year 2000, about ten to twenty times more attempted suicide. Furthermore, 19 percent of Aboriginal women and 13 percent of Aboriginal men have attempted suicide, as opposed to 4 percent of non-Aboriginal women and 2 percent of non-Aboriginal men (First Nations Centre 2005). Finally, during the course of their lives, 15 percent of Aboriginal adults have tried to kill themselves, and 31 percent have thought about doing so (ibid.).

While statistics indicate that Aboriginal communities have higher rates of major depression and dysthymia than do non-Aboriginal communities (First Nations Centre 2005), we have to remind ourselves that there may be crucial elements, aside from depression, that contribute to suicidal behaviour (Kirmayer et al. 2007). Aboriginal people suffering from depression or other psychiatric disorders may be more vulnerable to the demoralizing effects of social problems; however, insufficient data on the prevalence of psychiatric disorders in Canadian Aboriginal communities makes it difficult to determine what proportion of suicides are linked to such disorders (ibid.). According to the First Nations Centre (2005), 18 percent of Aboriginal adults suffer from major depression and 30 percent report having felt sad, blue, or depressed during two consecutive weeks in the past year. Furthermore, in 2001, the Canadian Community Health Survey indicated that, in comparison to 7 percent in the Canadian non-Aboriginal population, 12 percent of First Nations people who resided off-reserve have had an episode of major depression and that the rate among those who live on-reserve could be even higher (Canada 2006). Among Inuit in Nunavik, almost a quarter of suicides (23.5 percent) were related to depression, personality disorder, or conduct disorder, while almost half (47.1 percent) were associated with a past psychiatric history (Boothroyd et al. 2001). Given the hardships Aboriginal peoples have faced and continue to face, it is not difficult to conclude that interventions should target a wide range of psychiatric symptoms and mental health issues before they escalate into suicide ideation and attempts. Both Aboriginal leaders and the Canadian government have acknowledged the need for broader mental health initiatives. Researchers also stress that "focusing attention exclusively on the problem without attending to its larger social context can do more harm than good" (Kirmayer et al. 1993, 71).

To better understand the scope of the problem and to appreciate why all interventions to date have failed, let us return to our community of five hundred people. In such a context, it should be relatively easy to raise youth awareness on the subject of suicide. You would think that the millions of dollars that have been invested in suicide prevention would be very effective in the context of small communities, where everyone knows everyone else. But, as we have seen, the number of suicides is on the rise, and this is for two reasons. First, most interventions only attract those who are comfortable navigating non-Aboriginal workshops or community meetings, where it is assumed that a simple community arrangement will be sufficient to bring people to any given meeting. Second, current intervention programs for suicide prevention assume that most people in a community are psychologically healthy and thus able to provide support and resources to those few community members who are struggling. Indeed, in a mainstream context, it has been well established that social support from friends and family is indispensable for helping someone who is not psychologically well (Cohen 2004). Even though 60 percent of Aboriginal people turn to friends for help, and approximately the same number seek help from their immediate family (First Nations Centre 2005), we have to remember that, in Aboriginal communities, friends and family are often struggling themselves and so are not well positioned to provide the social support that is so vital. No wonder the usual counselling and intervention programs are less than successful.

## Substance Abuse

### ABORIGINAL LEADERS SPEAK OUT

Substance misuse, relating to alcohol, drugs, and solvents, has to be the most salient non-Aboriginal stereotype of Aboriginal people, and it is one that is often targeted as the root of all other social problems. Recently, Aboriginal leaders have begun to acknowledge and address this widespread problem. The chief of Splats' First Nation, Wayne Christian, illustrates this new openness: "Many young people in our communities are addicted, suffering in isolation and still grappling with the legacy of physical and sexual trauma that has been passed down from one generation to the next" (Christian and Spittal 2008, 1132). Today, this vicious cycle continues, with the use of illicit drugs being linked to problems such as high rates of alcohol-related violence, accidents, unemployment, family problems, and risky sexual behaviour (Health Canada 1998).

The substance abuse problem has reached such proportions that alcohol-related deaths are six times higher and drug-induced deaths are three times higher for Aboriginal people than for non-Aboriginal Canadians (First Nations Centre 2005). Angrily, Chief Lawrence Joseph, head of the Federation of Saskatchewan Indian Nations, urges his province to start paying attention to the problem and to take action: "Saskatchewan municipalities should stop worrying about potholes and start focusing on the 'rampant' crisis of substance abuse in the Aboriginal community" (cited in Graham 2008, para. 1). But what seems to worry Aboriginal leaders even more is the fact that substance abuse seems to be on the rise. In support of this worry, Health

Canada (1998) reports that the use of prescription and illicit drugs is increasing, even though drug consumption has historically been secondary to alcohol consumption.

Recently, more in-depth reports have documented epidemiological information about substance abuse. For instance, the Aboriginal Peoples Survey indicates that, in Manitoba, 73 percent of all Aboriginal people feel that alcohol abuse is a problem in their community (Health Canada 1998). Even more worrisome, 63.9 percent of Aboriginal people believe that no progress is being made regarding substance and alcohol abuse problems; only 6.6 percent believe that some progress is being made (First Nations Centre 2005).

STATISTICAL REALITY

What Aboriginal leaders and community members report concerning substance abuse is corroborated by statistics. For example, 26.7 percent of First Nations adults consumed marijuana in the past year compared to 14,1 percent of adults in the Canadian population (Assembly of First Nations 2007). According to a national survey among Aboriginal people, 27 percent admitted to suffering from problems with alcohol (First Nations Centre 2005). Also, one out of five Aboriginal youths living in Manitoba has reported using solvents, and a full half of these users were under the age of thirteen (Health Canada 1998).

Such frightening numbers are difficult to ignore. Eleven-year-olds, even fourteen-year-olds, are surely too young to be struggling with substance dependencies. Early adolescence is a crucial developmental stage, associated with many physical, psychological, emotional, and social changes. Given that Aboriginal demographics lean heavily towards young people, the early onset of substance dependence will negatively affect the future for entire communities.

The challenge of addressing the problems underscored by the statistics on substance misuse is magnified by their association with numerous other social problems within the communities. With the elevated statistics on substance abuse among young people, it is not surprising that going to school every day and graduating from high school is an anomaly rather than a routine expectation. The lack of structures to support those who have dropped out of school also contributes to this grim reality. The absence of support for children in need leads to more problems. Many of the children who have dropped out of school find themselves wandering around the communities at all times of the day and night. For example, when working in Aboriginal communities, we were initially surprised to see children as young as eight or nine years of age playing in the streets until long past midnight. As a large proportion of children and teenagers learn though modelling their parents and other close family members, it is quite possible that seeing them consume alcohol and drugs leads them to believe that this is what people normally do.

An important theme related to alcohol consumption in Aboriginal communities concerns the pattern of concentrated, heavy drinking. Aboriginal people actually drink less than non-Aboriginal Canadians on a daily basis (2 percent versus 3 percent) as well as on a weekly basis (35 percent versus 46 percent), and abstinence is much more common among Aboriginal people than among the mainstream population (15 percent versus 8 percent) (Health Canada 1998). However, 16 percent of Aboriginal people drink heavily every week compared to 8 percent of non-Aboriginal people (Health Canada 2009). This pattern of consumption, which naturally leads to intoxication, corresponds to what is often labelled as "binge drinking" (Brady 2000; Shkilnyk 1985), which includes high levels of alcohol consumption over a short period of time. Unfortunately, this behaviour is directly linked with major health problems, trauma, and social or behavioural disorders (Chansonneuve 2007).

Having 82.9 percent of young adults report that they drank alcohol in the past year is especially problematic (Assembly of First Nations 2007). Aboriginal people are more than twice as likely to binge drink than are members of the general drinking population (Anderson 2007). At a more specific level, the habit of binge drinking was reported by 37.7 percent of the Saskatchewan Aboriginal adult population, which is similar to the statistics for the Aboriginal population of the Northwest Territories, where one-third reported drinking heavily (Health Canada 1998). These numbers can be compared to those of the non-Aboriginal Northwest Territories population, 16.7 percent of whom engaged in binge drinking (ibid.). Epidemiological studies of Aboriginal people find that greater amounts of alcohol are consumed during an episode of binge drinking than during any other time. These statistics demonstrate not only that more Aboriginal people binge drink but also that they drink greater amounts while doing so. Given the negative array of outcomes associated with this pattern of drinking, these numbers are doubly concerning.

Alcoholism and binge drinking have debilitating consequences beyond those experienced by the person with whom they are directly associated. Many problems in the community are related to alcoholism. For instance, almost half (48 percent) of Aboriginal spousal abuse victims have revealed that their partner drank prior to the incident, whereas this proportion drops to a third for non-Aboriginal victims (Brzozowski, Taylor-Butts, and Johnson 2006). Also, alcohol is a major risk factor for suicide (Kirmayer et al. 2007), and, in a study covering suicides in Manitoba, the mean alcohol blood level was more than twice as high for Aboriginal people who took their own lives as it was for non-Aboriginal Canadians (Malchy et al. 1997).

Aboriginal males tend to binge drink weekly in a higher proportion than do Aboriginal females (20.9 percent versus 10.2 percent) (First Nations Centre 2005). However, not only do a higher proportion of First Nations women binge drink weekly than non-Aboriginal women (3.3 percent), they also binge drink in a higher proportion than do non-Aboriginal men (9.2 percent) (Adlaf, Begin, and Sawka 2005). This not only affects a variety of related social problems but also increases the chances that a newborn will suffer from fetal alcohol syndrome (FAS) (Health Canada 1996). In fact, even though no study has provided reliable statistics for the prevalence of FAS among Aboriginal peoples, it is widely accepted that it is very high (Health Canada 1998). The situation is even more worrisome since the proportion of women drinking is increasing (ibid.).

As we can see, alcohol misuse, and binge drinking in particular, has a number of negative spin-offs. Binge drinking alone has been implicated in a variety of health problems, including psychiatric disorders (Robin et al. 1998). The National Native Addiction Partnership Foundation Inc. reports that the rate of injury and poisoning for First Nations people is four times higher than that for the non-Aboriginal population. It also reports that high rates of hospitalization and death due to injury, poisoning, and suicide are related to substance and alcohol abuse (Health Canada 1998). In summary, binge drinking in Aboriginal communities is a significant public health concern for the community at large.

The statistics on alcohol misuse, and binge drinking in particular, grossly underestimate the reality. The numbers point to binge drinking rates that are twice as high among Aboriginal communities as they are among the non-Aboriginal Canadian population (Health Canada 1998). Beyond the numbers, it is interesting that information on substance abuse in Aboriginal communities is extremely difficult to find and that what little exists is often contradictory. Indeed, even though substance abuse is one of the more serious problems confronting Aboriginal communities, we found this section most difficult to write because we were often unable to obtain reliable or consistent information. Perhaps this can be explained by the fact that there is a negative stereotype linking Aboriginal people to substance abuse – so much so that Aboriginal people themselves feel uncomfortable speaking about it outside of their own community. Hence, it is difficult to gather data on the topic. In some cases, the response rates to surveys that asked questions about substance abuse were poor (First Nations Centre 2005; Health Canada 1998). This leads us to believe that, since alcohol is prohibited on several reserves and communities, people that do have a drinking problem will tend to under-report their consumption rates. This corroborates what we have observed in some of the "dry" communities (i.e., those that vote to severely limit alcohol in their environs), where, nevertheless, mountains of empty bottles could be found piled up a discrete distance from the community.

Binge drinking also has spinoff effects with regard to everyday community functioning. For example, for several days following their bout with alcohol, binge drinkers will not be functional members of their communities. In the years we have been working in Aboriginal communities, we have seen countless examples of the long-term impact of binge drinking and its disruptive effect on community life. To take a concrete example, given the importance of knowledge transfer, we are frequently asked to train Aboriginal students for a variety of pedagogical and research roles. Trainees typically show great enthusiasm for the project and demonstrate great potential. Training involves cumulative knowledge and, thus, interruptions are most disruptive, as are absences from work once the trainee has important leadership responsibilities. Binge drinking would often, disruptively and unpredictably, take very promising trainees and employees away for days at a time. Since many trainees supervised young people, these interruptions were especially problematic. When 33 percent of the population engages in binge drinking (Health Canada 1998), the repercussions are serious.

There is, of course, a predictable relationship between binge drinking and money. When people have money, they have access to alcohol and drugs. This association can be seen quite clearly in Aboriginal communities. The few days following the issue of paycheques or welfare cheques are particularly conducive to binge drinking. Everyone in the community knows that the schools, places of work, and government offices will not be functioning as usual because of the high number of those who will use their money to engage in binge drinking. In a small community, this means that everything virtually shuts down. Moreover, there are increases in crime, violence, and accidents. Not a pretty picture.

## FAILED INTERVENTIONS

Knowing that levels of substance abuse have risen and that non-Aboriginal governments and Aboriginal institutions at all levels are investing millions of dollars to improve the situation, we can only conclude that all the interventions aimed at reducing this problem in Aboriginal communities have failed. What explains this failure, we argue, is the fact that these intervention programs are designed to be implemented in communities that are structurally and normatively different from those of Aboriginal communities. For example, Alcoholics Anonymous is a popular rehabilitation program that has had some success with many non-Aboriginal Canadians. For such programs to succeed, individuals who have a dependency must come to realize, either by themselves or with the help of social feedback, that they have a significant problem with substance abuse and that this problem is negatively affecting their entire lives. By using social comparisons, an individual would quickly become aware that s/he represents a small minority and that most people consume alcohol in a moderate fashion. When the individual is ready, s/he might then join a program to address the dependency. If the program is successful, the person will be encouraged to develop new, more appropriate social networks and avoid the previous circle of friends with whom s/he shared a lifestyle centred on drinking. Thus, pivotal to the success of these intervention programs are two conditions: first, it is essential that the person comes searching for help by him- or herself once s/he recognizes that s/he is different from the norm – and different in a destructive manner; second, it is important that the person change her or his circle of friends in order to avoid the influence of previous forces, implicit and explicit, that could lead to a relapse.

In Aboriginal communities it is virtually impossible to meet these two necessary conditions. First, since substance abuse is so normative, and because the social comparison process leads individuals to compare themselves with those who also have alcohol-related problems, Aboriginal people are unlikely to become aware of their own consumption problem. They might realize that they do drink considerably but think that this is not problematic since others in the community are worse than they are, and that the impact of the problem (e.g., not going to work) is common in the community. Second, it would be very difficult for people seeking help in a program to avoid contact with those people who are a "bad influence" on them. The communities are small, often isolated, housing is overcrowded, and everybody literally knows everybody else.

CONCLUSION

In our classes in urban Canadian universities, we carefully report statistics in order to illustrate the array of problems confronting Aboriginal communities. How do our non-Aboriginal students digest this information? Our sense is that the statistics are incomprehensible. We say this because, when we return to the communities after a semester of teaching, although we are excited and happy to be with our Aboriginal colleagues and friends, we are also dismayed by the magnitude of the challenges, even though we have continuously been reminded of it by the statistics upon which we focused during our recent teaching. Clearly, first-hand sustained experience in the communities is needed to understand the depth and breadth of the challenges. If this is true for us, then our students are surely not positioned to grasp the enormity of the issues. And what of our policy makers and elected officials?

In this chapter we underscore an array of challenges about which Aboriginal leaders are speaking publicly. The problems upon which we focus have a wide range of consequences for the quality of life of all Aboriginal peoples. The mortality rate among Aboriginal adults is higher than it is among the non-Aboriginal population, with an increased risk of death for both men and women from alcohol abuse (including from cirrhosis of the liver), homicide, suicide, and pneumonia) (MacMillan et al. 1996). These figures have remained relatively unchanged over time.

This implies that other health-related issues have and will emerge. These include obesity, diabetes, fetal alcohol syndrome, and depression, to name a few. Diabetes, in particular, is more prominent in Aboriginal communities: one First Nations adult out of five is diabetic, and this rate is probably an underestimation (First Nations Centre 2005). Depending on the age group, the prevalence of diabetes among Aboriginal people is two to six times higher than it is in the general Canadian population (ibid.).

Simply put, Aboriginal people who live off-reserve experience poorer general health than do non-Aboriginal Canadians (Tjepkema 2002). In a review of the Aboriginal health literature, MacMillan and colleagues (1996) conclude that Aboriginal people are generally more at risk for physical diseases. For example, infant mortality rates are about twice as high (13.8-16.3/1000) as they are for non-Aboriginal Canadians (7.3/1000) (ibid.). This high rate is mostly due to "postneonatal causes of death, including infectious diseases, respiratory illness, sudden infant death syndrome (SIDS) and injuries" (ibid.,1573; see also Waldram, Herring, and Kue Young 1995). Fetal alcohol spectrum syndrome is another major health issue confronting Aboriginal communities with serious implications for the future. While exact rates have been difficult to determine, its prevalence in Aboriginal communities has been consistently higher than it has in non-Aboriginal ones (Canadian Paediatric Society 2002). Another contributor to the diseases that are so prevalent in Aboriginal communities is inadequate housing: overcrowding is exacerbated by the fact that the water supply is inadequate, either in quantity or quality, in one housing unit out of four (Health Canada 2009).

To make matters worse, it seems that every new threat to the quality of life for Canadians as a whole hits Aboriginal communities even harder. From environmental contaminants and climate change to AIDS and the HINI influenza, Aboriginal communities get hammered. Is the answer more financial and human resources? Certainly that would help. For example, the Pauktuuit Inuit Women of Canada (2005, 6) argue: "Those who work in abuse prevention and community services – shelter workers, crisis counsellors, Inuit healers, and police – are also discouraged. As people on the front lines say, 'it's all talk and no action.' A considerable sustained effort, with adequate resources, is urgently required. We need to do more, now."

Money and the political will may well be part of the solution, but we believe that our entire understanding of the myriad challenges facing Aboriginal communities needs to be reformulated. This reformulation will point to a "C" shift in strategy in terms of addressing the array of challenging issues. As a first step, in the next chapter we attempt to pin-point the fundamental factor that lies at the heart of all the problems we have described in this chapter: collective self-control.

# 4

# Collective Self-Control:
# Towards an Understanding of Community
# Challenges

Our review, in Chapter 3, of the challenges that Aboriginal leaders and community members are voicing can't help but provoke a number of feelings, ranging from sadness and sympathy to guilt, anger, and helplessness. One inescapable reaction is to simply feel "overwhelmed" – overwhelmed by the sheer number of challenges and by the magnitude of each issue. Feeling overwhelmed brings with it a sense of paralysis, and, if we are to move forward in a constructive manner, we need to begin by bringing some order to the litany of challenges identified.

So, how are we to organize our thinking about the array of challenges that are confronting First Nations, Métis, and Inuit communities? Each challenge is, of course, a major issue in and of itself. We could treat each issue as a discrete challenge, and, indeed, there have been numerous and serious programs and interventions designed to address each and every one of the issues we have highlighted. The sheer number of the intervention silos created by such an approach is both incomprehensible and doomed from the outset. Treating each issue separately ignores the common cause associated with all of them.

Not surprisingly, then, beyond treating each issue as a distinct challenge, there have been serious attempts to consider possible relations among these issues. The aim is to find any common denominator that might offer a focus. Addressing this common denominator should have a constructive impact on all the issues associated with it. The most popular form of conceptualizing a common denominator is to pin-point which of the long list of issues might be the one that gives rise to all the others. Indeed, it would be cause for hope if one of the issues could be deemed the primary cause that, if addressed, could, in domino fashion, have a constructive impact on all the others.

For example, some argue that the long-standing economic depression in Aboriginal communities is the main issue and that all the other problems are the result of people trying to cope with unemployment, underemployment, and a reliance on government programs (e.g., Kendall 2001; Tookenay 1996). Poverty, it is argued, is the common denominator, the root of all the challenges confronting Aboriginal communities. The possibility of reducing the vast array of community challenges to a single source is compelling. It suggests that solving the issue of poverty should be the major focus of human and financial resource allocation and that its reduction will, with time, alleviate all the other problems. Unfortunately, the "poverty" argument has not proven to be the simple fix. This is not to suggest that poverty is not a major issue or that attempts to raise Aboriginal communities out of poverty have been sufficiently addressed. However, the fact is that years of direct financial aid have failed to alleviate poverty levels in Aboriginal communities.

Others point to alcohol misuse as the prime mover (e.g., Saggers 1998). It is alcohol that leads to social dysfunction and a lack of motivation to achieve any form of success. Alcohol seems to be clearly related to crime, violence, and a number of health issues. Solve the alcohol problem and the other issues will fall away in due course. Again, there is no doubt that alcohol abuse is indeed related to other issues, but it has proven to be a stubborn issue to address. Moreover, it would seem that, even if alcohol issues were brought under control, there would still remain an array of community issues with which to deal. So again, we applaud the attempt to pin-point the primary issue, and there is no doubt that alcohol is a reasonable candidate, but it is not the most primary.

Still others point to education, or a lack thereof, as the primary cause of the problems in Aboriginal communities (e.g., Richards 2006; Preston 2008). The argument is that formal education builds literacy and the problem-solving skills that are necessary for making constructive life decisions. Information is power, and, thus, every human decision, from informed political voting to employment possibilities and healthy eating, requires education. We have no doubt that education is important, and no doubt that formal education can have constructive implications for any number of life domains. But education is not be the single, underlying factor that drives all the challenges these communities are facing.

In summary, we support efforts to infuse order into the overwhelming list of community challenges. Any constructive approach to addressing such a vast number of serious issues requires organization. However, the type of organization chosen cannot be superficial or misguided because once a primary cause is articulated, resources will be focused on it. If the search for this primary cause is misguided, or falls short, then those resources will, at least to some extent, be wasted.

We have witnessed this phenomenon first-hand in a completely different domain. A large telecommunications company in a major metropolis was concerned about the never-ending complaints from its cadre of middle managers. The company had wrestled one by one with each of these complaints, which ranged from vacation schedules to overtime to working conditions to office size and structure, to no avail. The company was well intentioned and genuinely responsive to these complaints but its responses were directed at each separately. Like the government with regard to the challenges in Aboriginal communities, the company had not put an adequate effort into discovering the root cause of the managers' complaints. Finally, a careful analysis revealed that their root cause was one that the managers themselves couldn't put their finger on and that this was why they were voicing a series of concrete, easily visible complaints. A deeper analysis revealed that the real issue was that they felt threatened by their lack of autonomy. Their opportunities for using their talents in such a way that they would have some impact on their departments were minimal. Unbeknownst to them or to their superiors, this was the real issue. The point is that all the company's efforts to deal with the managers' complaints (e.g., vacation schedules and office structure) did not address the underlying problem: their lack of agency and autonomy in guiding their departments.

Obviously, the situation involving Aboriginal people is much more complex and profound than that facing the company. It requires us to go beyond the list of presenting problems and to search for the underlying issue. The hope is that, if we are able to do this, then, instead of addressing each issue separately and in an uncoordinated fashion, we can offer a genuine focus and direction for constructive change.

## SELF-CONTROL (WILLPOWER)

For our part, rather than focus on one particular issue as being most important, or as the causal agent for some, or all, of the other issues, we seek to find a common underlying cause. That is, we attempt to pin-point the basic psychological process at the heart of each and every community issue. It is our contention that the common psychological process is self-control.

Self-control, often understood more broadly as self-regulation, or more colloquially as *willpower,* is a complex and sophisticated process that requires individuals not to give in to an immediate impulse but, instead, to engage those challenging behaviours that maximize the chances for longer-term success (Baumeister and Tierney 2011). Formally, Baumeister, Vohs, and Tice (2007, 351) define self-control as "the capacity for altering one's own responses, especially to bring them into line with standards such as ideals, morals, and social expectations, and to support the pursuit of long-term goals." The ability to refrain from taking a drink, overindulging in junk food, playing instead of studying, and engaging in unprotected sexual behaviour are all classic examples of behaviours that require the effective exercise of self-control. It has been postulated that this ability not to give in to immediate gratification lies at the heart of human success and well-being. In terms of scientific research, inadequate self-control has been linked with behaviours that range from overeating, alcohol and drug abuse, crime and violence to overspending, sexually impulsive behaviour, and smoking, all the way to academic underachievement, failures at task performance, emotional problems, and difficulties with interpersonal relationships.

Many of the examples in this list are recurrent themes and issues that Aboriginal communities have voiced. Let's begin with a simple every-day example to help us appreciate the extent to which self-control mechanisms are pervasive and crucial for effective human functioning: the world of work. If we begin with having and holding a job, what could be more basic than showing up to work on time and ready to earn that paycheque? This might seem like a simple matter of setting the alarm clock for 7:00 AM, knowing that it will take an hour to get ready, gobble down some breakfast, and get to work. To do all this in one hour is realistic in Aboriginal communities, where the commute time is not a factor. Now, the intention to wake up at 7:00 AM, and the setting of the alarm clock at suppertime the night before, is not a huge issue. Self-control issues begin to emerge when an offer for a night out at the bar to shoot some pool arises. Self-control would say: "I better pass on this or else I'll be a basket-case in the morning and it will affect my work performance, which, after all, is my livelihood." Our worker is exercising self-control because the immediate fun of a night out must be sacrificed for the longer-term reward that comes with good, consistent work habits. However, our worker might think: "Well, it will be hard to wake up on time if I go out, but as long as I'm prepared to force myself out of bed and really apply myself despite sleep deprivation, why not head out tonight?" True enough, but self-control becomes front and centre the minute the alarm goes off at 7:00 AM. Now, the desired immediate response would be to pull the plug on the alarm clock and go back to sleep, not worrying about vague, long-term goals such as consistently good work performance. The worker who doesn't go out the night before, or who does but toughs it out the minute the alarm goes off, is exercising the essence of self-control: overriding something positive right now for a greater gain later on. The worker who gives in to the immediate reward is displaying no self-control and the result of this strategy will be undesirable outcomes for the long-term goals that are presumably far more important than some minor immediate gratification.

Of course, our worker has confronted these same self-control issues while pursuing whatever education and training was necessary to obtain the job. Do I study or party tonight? Do I skip classes and get caught up on my sleep or struggle to be sure I maximize my chances for long-term success? If I do go out tonight, do I pass on the alcohol to make sure I can at least get up in the morning or do I enjoy the taste and feeling I get from just one drink? Of course, the same self-control dilemma arises for the next drink and the next drink. Eventually, alcohol or not, our worker might from time to time feel frustrated and, despite knowing that abusive behaviour toward anyone close to him would be certain to destroy the relationship, the opportunity to vent frustration on a weaker and proximal person right now raises self-control issues.

We have put our worker through the full gamut of everyday self-control, or willpower, dilemmas in order to illustrate that the array of apparently very different challenges confronting Aboriginal communities share the same psychological root: self-control. What are the common elements to each and every challenge that we have highlighted? In each case, successful human behaviour requires an ability to refrain from giving in to an immediate, small reward so that a longer-term, far larger reward can be obtained. By longer-term reward we mean success at school and work, healthy interpersonal relationships with loved ones, and behaviour choices that do not include violence, substance misuse, and unhealthy eating habits. Short-term pain for long-term gain: that is the essence of self-control, or willpower.

Definition:

## COLLECTIVE SELF-CONTROL

The research evidence relating to the importance of self-control for human success and well-being is impressive. Indeed, self-control and raw intelligence appear to be the two human characteristics that compete for importance in terms of success and well-being. Importantly, intelligence is viewed, for the most part, as a characteristic that is genetically based or hardwired; therefore, each of us is more or less stuck with the hand we've been dealt. But self-control, a characteristic that is equally important for human well-being, can be taught (Baumeister and Tierney 2011).

Ego depletion

This is not to suggest that learning to exercise self-control is easy. Current theorizing (e.g., Muraven and Baumeister 2000) suggests that exercising self-control is analogous to exercising a muscle. Passing up a slice of chocolate cake when on a diet requires energy (ego depletion), as does a muscle when you lift heavy weights. At some point the muscle tires and you are unable to lift any weight. In a similar fashion, a person who has to exercise self-control will frequently run out of psychological energy, and, in this state of ego depletion, s/he will likely give in to temptation rather easily. Given the large number of self-control issues that Aboriginal people face, they may well be in a constant state of ego depletion. For example, all teenagers face a litany of self-control challenges. They must wake up early and get ready to go to school, complete whatever homework they are assigned, resist the temptations of peer pressure, take care of daily family chores, and so on. For Aboriginal teenagers, generally speaking, each of these self-control challenges is more difficult than it is for non-Aboriginal teenagers. She must wake up early to go to school, for which she will most likely face ridicule from fellow students for being so dutiful. She must complete her homework, likely without parental support, and she must do so knowing that most of her peers are dropping out of school. Not surprisingly, then, our Aboriginal student is already ego depleted. So when the opportunity to eat unhealthy food, or skip a training session, or take a nap arises, she, despite the best of intentions, lacks the willpower to resist. And thus some of our student's long-term goals are compromised.

A compelling experiment illustrates nicely how exercising willpower takes a toll on the individual in terms of ego-depletion (Baumeister et al. 1998). Two groups of university students, neither of which had eaten for at least three hours, were brought to a laboratory where an appealing bowl of cookies and a less than attractive bowl of radishes were placed on a table in front of them. The groups were then divided into two experimental conditions: the "cookie" condition and the "radish" condition. In the cookie condition, participants were told that they should eat two or three of the delicious cookies; in the radish condition, participants were asked to eat a few radishes and leave the cookies alone. The experimenter then exited the room, leaving the poor participants in the radish condition to exercise self-control and not give in to eating any of the cookies.

Experiment:
on self-
control &
ego depletion

The experimenter then returned and asked participants in the cookie and the radish conditions to perform a number of frustrating and difficult cognitive tasks. The participants who were required to resist the urge to eat the tempting cookies performed very poorly on subsequent tasks that also required self-control – evidently having already fatigued their willpower reserves. By comparison, the cookie-eaters, who were permitted to eat their desired treat without having to exert their willpower, performed extremely well.

Another compelling experiment demonstrates how often we are required to exercise self-control and the toll it takes on our willpower muscle. It focuses on women dieters who were brought to a laboratory and asked to view a scene from a classic movie – a real tear-jerker. Half the women were required to exercise self-control by suppressing their emotions while watching the movie ("don't show your emotions"); the other half were encouraged to express their emotions freely ("let your feelings and tears flow naturally").

The dieters were then escorted to a lounge where, normally, they would have been required to exercise their willpower because they were offered ice-cream to snack on. You guessed it: the women who had been required to exercise self-control over their emotions during the movie gave in and ate more ice-cream than did the other women (Vohs and Heatherton 2000). So, controlling emotions takes psychological energy, and, as we have seen, exercising self-control in one domain weakens our control in other domains. Imagine the challenge for people who must constantly exercise self-control in a number of different domains.

Results such as these suggest that our reserves, even as adults, are finite, and the allocation of willpower resources affects future performance on similarly challenging events. However, the good news is that, when, over and over again, a muscle is used to the point of fatigue, it grows stronger. So, too, when a person confronts self-control issues again and again, her/his psychological muscle grows stronger.

In summary, our emphasis on self-control as the psychological root of the diverse challenges facing Aboriginal communities is fundamentally optimistic. It suggests that, while a less than desirable environment may foster a lack of self-control, a change, albeit a dramatic one, in one's environment can give rise to adaptive behaviours when self-control is exercised.

So what is the environment that might have given rise to entire communities displaying a variety of maladaptive behaviours, communities in which lack of self-control is central and pervasive? The key here is that theorists who study self-control focus on why individuals differ from each other when it comes to exercising this behaviour. The student in the class who acts out impulsively, the alcoholic and the gambling addict, the smoker and the junk food lover, and, indeed – the new self-control problem – the young person addicted to internet games: these individuals, along with whatever biological or environmental factors make them different from their peers, are our focus.

If there were only one or two individuals in a community who were plagued with self-control issues, we would focus on what unique circumstances functioned to make them different from everyone else. In the case of Aboriginal communities, however, we are confronting a genuine social issue – an issue that challenges a significant subset of the entire community. Thus, our approach has to be different. The traditional self-control question is: "What are the factors that make this individual impulsive and incapable of exercising self-control? Is it family upbringing, genetic predisposition, a cognitive deficit, or lack of meaningful long-term goals?" Our question is: "What are the factors that might be affecting the entire group? What common experiences has the group as a whole been exposed to that might explain such widespread self-control challenges?"

## GOAL-DIRECTED BEHAVIOUR IS IMPOSSIBLE WITHOUT A GOAL

When it comes to analyzing where to begin our search for the collective cause for the state of Aboriginal communities, there is no need to look very deeply. In order to ask people to pass up short-term pleasure there must be a powerful long-term reward on the horizon. First and foremost, then, self-control requires well-defined, highly rewarding long-term goals (Baumeister, Schmeichel, and Vohs 2007). You better be committed to the goal of successfully completing secondary school if you are going to pass up an outing with your buddies to study for an exam the next day. You better proceed slowly on this first date if you really want to establish a long-term, meaningful relationship. And you certainly better pass on the booze and junk food if you really want to be a professional ice-hockey player.

If you could care less about education, having a meaningful relationship, or achieving athletic superstardom, then there is no need to exercise self-control. Thus, long before we explore deeper complex causal factors, our first stop needs to be on the extent to which people in Aboriginal communities have an array of long-term goals to which everyone subscribes. We believe that herein lies the problem. It is important to reiterate that we are not focusing on any specific individual's long-term goals; rather, we are searching for the collective long-term goals of entire Aboriginal communities.

## SELF-CONTROL, LONG-TERM GOALS, AND TIME

The capacity to reflect on the self is uniquely human. One consequence of this is the complex role that time plays in human functioning. We all live in the present, but we have the capacity to think about, contemplate, and place ourselves in the future, and that future may range from very soon to very distant (Zimbardo and Boyd 2008). As a young person we can imagine ourselves many years in the future having an important job and living in a big fancy house. Or we can imagine ourselves two weeks into the future lounging by the pool at the all-inclusive vacation spot in Cuba that our parents have arranged for a winter getaway. Equally, we can contemplate the past, usually focusing on selected memories that may involve either the immediate or the distant past. We might be on a coffee break at work on a Monday morning thinking about the amazing young woman/man we met at a party last Saturday night. Or we might remember how frightened we felt when, as a child, we got separated from our parents for a few hours in a crowded shopping centre. Interestingly, while we actually experience the present, moment by moment, our past and future are not experienced but, rather, psychologically constructed (ibid.). So there we have it: we live in the present but with a unique ability to focus on the past, present, or future.

This simple reality, it turns out, has profound implications for successful human functioning and well-being. People use this ability differently in terms of the emphasis they place on the past, present, and future (Zimbardo and Boyd 1999, 2008). We all know people who dwell a little too much on one of these three time perspectives. The one we hear about most often is the person who is living in and driven by the future and so is encouraged to "stop and smell the roses" or "enjoy the moment"; in other words, to "focus a bit more on the present." Others focus more on the past, to the point that their entire view of the present and future is filtered through some past experience, usually a dramatic or traumatic one. It might be a woman who now interacts with every man she meets as though he will be just like her first love of ten years ago who was an abusive deadbeat. Or it might be a refugee who escapes from a repressive government and now has difficulty trusting civil authorities. And then, finally, we have those who are focused only on the present, embracing reward and eschewing punishment, with little homage to the past or concern for the future. It is these predominantly present-oriented people who are the focus of this chapter, for it is they who are the ones who are prone to seek instant gratification and to have difficulties with self-control (Zimbardo and Boyd 1999, 2008).

These individual differences in time perspective are not trivial. It turns out that those who tend to be future-oriented are the ones who are highly successful, achievement-oriented, socially adjusted, and experience higher levels of well-being (Zimbardo and Boyd 1999). Any appreciation for the importance of exercising self-control by delaying gratification and becoming future-oriented must begin with a remarkable experiment conducted by Mischel and his colleagues: the famous "marshmallow experiment" (Mischel and Ebbesen 1970; Mischel, Ebbesen, and Zeiss 1972). Young children, at about the age of four, were brought one by one to a comfortable laboratory. Here they were asked to select which they would rather eat: a marshmallow or a pretzel. Upon selection, the experimenter explained that he had to leave the laboratory room but that, when he returned, the desired food could be eaten. Crucially, the children were also told that they could summon the experimenter's return at any time but that this would be at the expense of getting to eat the food they preferred. Once the experimenter left the child alone in the room, the challenge presented itself: could the child exercise willpower and wait for her/his preferred treat?

Ten (Mischel, Shoda, and Peake 1988) and fourteen years (Shoda, Mischel, and Peake 1990) later, Mischel returned to assess the same children and observed a number of striking differences between them. Those who at the age of four had opted for their preferred treat by patiently waiting for the return of the experimenter now scored much higher on standardized college entrance exams, were less moody, more confident, worked better under pressure, were more independent and cooperative, and less prone to jealous rages. Forty years later (Casey et al. 2011), the same preschoolers who were assessed in the original marshmallow experiment were again visited. This time the analysis was on their capacity to focus their attention. The results showed that, as adults, individuals who were less able to wait for their preferred treat as young children had a lower capacity for sustained attention.

The long-term benefits for those with the capacity to delay gratification and to exercise self-control was established in stunning fashion. Indeed, these studies have been replicated many times, and self-control has been the subject of numerous scientific publications over the years (Metcalfe and Mischel 1999). The famous marshmallow studies stimulated much research, and soon a valid and reliable measure of self-control was developed. Consistently, students who score high on self-control obtain better grades. Managers in the workplace who score high in self-control are rated more favourably by their subordinates and their peers. More generally, people who exercise self-control form more satisfying relationships with other people, and they tend to be more empathetic, more emotionally stable, and less prone to anxiety and depression (Baumeister, Heatherton, and Tice 1994).

Finally, a long-term study conducted in New Zealand tracked one thousand children from birth to the age of thirty. The children with high self-control were, in adulthood, found to be physically healthier, less obese, and to have fewer sexually transmitted diseases. Those low in self-control as children tended to grow into adults with lower-paying jobs and little money in the bank or put aside for retirement. They also tended to be single parents more often than did the children with high self-control (Moffitt et al. 2011). Clearly, self-control is a funda-mental skill.

The ability to exercise self-control and delay gratification has pro-found implications. We had an opportunity to test the importance of "delay of gratification" among a group of Aboriginal children. We administered to young students a forty-five-minute battery of cogni-tive/language tests in a one-on-one testing situation. The young stu-dents, aged eleven to fourteen, enjoyed the experience but did have to concentrate for a long period of time. Before beginning the test we made the same offer to each student: "You can have one treat now before we begin the tests *or* you can wait until after the testing is com-pleted and have two treats." The treats in question were cookies, which at the time were a community favourite. Our Aboriginal stu-dents behaved just like those in the classic experiments. The students who decided to wait until the testing was completed to receive two treats scored higher on our battery of tests than did those who opted for one treat at the beginning. Clearly, for our Aboriginal students, the ability to delay gratification was associated with a better academ-ic outcome.

It would seem that those who focus on the future, on long-term goals, and are willing to forego present short-term rewards are headed for success. It would also seem that those who are rooted in the pre-sent are doomed. These are the ones who will drink now because it feels good, with no consideration of long-term consequences. These are the ones who will gamble, pursue risky sexual behaviour, party, avoid work and study, and act out violently, with little concern for where this may lead (Zimbardo and Boyd 1999).

What is equally clear is that the past, present, and future play im-portant roles in every decision a person makes. It is a question of bal-ance. The person who is always focused on the future, never on the past or present, may be successful but will be unresponsive to present realities. This is the person who is encouraged to "live in the moment" because life – the present – is passing her/him by. The person who is rooted in the past is often encouraged to "get over it" since s/he is not dealing well with the present and has no future-oriented goals towards which to strive. Finally, as we have highlighted, the person focused exclusively on the present fails to learn from the past and to enact future-oriented, goal-directed behaviour to guide her/him towards more successful outcomes.

## COLLECTIVE SELF-CONTROL (WILLPOWER)
## IN ABORIGINAL COMMUNITIES

If we put the pieces together, we arrive at a potential insight into the daunting list of challenges that confront many Aboriginal communities. Poverty, alcohol misuse, and lack of formal education are certainly fundamental problems that might be related to the numerous issues associated with the challenges confronting Aboriginal communities. As such, paying particular attention to these "big three" in the hope that they will also positively affect the many other problems may well pay dividends.

We have attempted to delve deep into the issues facing Aboriginal communities, and our analysis leads us to conclude that, even more fundamental than the "big three," is the issue of self-control (or lack of willpower). We argue that self-control issues lie at the heart of every issue (currently being separately treated) that seems to plague Aboriginal communities. Thus, we also argue for a concentrated focus on, and an allocation of human and financial resources devoted to, managing and teaching self-control in every domain of life that Aboriginal people deem important. Crucially, this is not an impossible mission. Self-control is not hardwired: it can be learned and it can be taught.

While self-control is crucial to basic psychological health, it has always been viewed and treated as an individual problem. Here we introduce the concept of "collective self-control" in order to signal that self-control can be a shared community issue, a collective issue. Individual self-control issues require an investigation into the individual circumstances and experiences that might lead a particular person to have difficulties exercising self-control or willpower. Similarly, collective self-control issues require an investigation into the shared circumstances that might lead an entire group to have difficulties exercising self-control or willpower.

When we examine the scope of the self-control challenges confronting Aboriginal peoples, a clear common experience presents itself. First, we need to emphasize that the same constellation of self-control issues seems to be identical for the vast majority of First nations, Inuit, and Métis communities across Canada. Indigenous peoples in the United States and, indeed, around the world are also challenged with these same self-control issues. What do they all have in common? Some would argue that it must be a genetic predisposition. Indeed, this genetic explanation is often alluded to in the context of susceptibility to alcohol. The problem with the genetic argument is that it is not credible to argue that there is a genetic predisposition towards an entire constellation of issues that range from alcohol to drug use to violence and underachievement.

It is not difficult to find the experience universally shared by Indigenous peoples: colonialism. This is what completely changed the lifeways of all Indigenous peoples.

Colonialism, then, is the clear candidate for explaining what we label the collective self-control challenges that confront Aboriginal communities. We have also noted how self-control is teachable, notwithstanding the psychological energy required to learn it. However, the link between colonialism and collective self-control needs to be fully understood if a clearly defined, concrete strategy for addressing the challenges confronting Aboriginal communities is to be developed.

It is not enough to simply point to colonialism as the culprit and then imagine that the problem is solved. Currently there is general agreement that colonialism, in all its manifestations, has been and continues to be the root cause of Aboriginal challenges. It is also generally agreed that the effects of colonialism are decidedly negative. This negativity might be articulated in the form of low self-esteem or internalized negative emotions or psychological trauma. But evoking these broad psychological outcomes is not enough. It doesn't explain the specific effects, why they are passed on from generation to generation, and how they manifest themselves in particular forms. Without delving into the specific *whys* and *hows* of colonialism's impact, there can be no focused coping strategy or effective intervention plan.

If any individual is to be motivated to exercise self-control, she or he must have a long-term goal that is so important, so sustaining and compelling, that s/he is willing to give up immediate reward or gratification in order to achieve that goal. This essential ingredient for the successful exercise of self-control needs to be carefully spelled out, and this is what we do in the following two chapters.

# 5

## Cultural Identity Vacuum: The Real Impact of Colonialism

If colonialism is the shared experience that has given rise to the phenomenon of collective self-control challenges, we need to address a series of fundamental questions. How does colonialism affect Aboriginal people? Why does its impact last for generations? What is the precise link with collective self-control?

The key words in our fundamental questions are "how," "why" and "precise." These are key words because there is a broad consensus among Aboriginal people, scholars, policy makers, and the general public that colonialism was, and is, the root cause of Aboriginal disadvantage. However, beyond appreciating that colonialism is a process with negative consequences, there is little insight into the "hows" and "whys" of the colonialist process, let alone its precise repercussions. Without the "hows" and "whys" and the "precise" repercussions, there can be no effective, targeted solutions.

Thus, the answers to our questions require that we address the links in the chain between colonialism, cultural identity, and the universal collective self-control challenges that are seemingly shared by all contemporary Aboriginal communities. Figure 5.1 depicts the steps we need to take to arrive at our conclusion about the unique form of collective self-control challenges confronted by Aboriginal communities.

In order for people to exercise self-control they must, first and foremost, have a long-term goal. Moreover, this long-term goal must be so important, so salient, so compelling, and so powerful that they are willing to forego immediate gratification in order to maximize their chances of achieving it. Where does a person find such an important long-term goal?

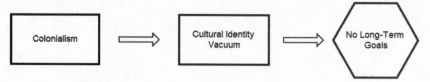

Figure 5.1   Diagram depicting constructs associated with self-concept

*Culture sets up long-term goals*

Our answer is that the culture in which one lives clearly and consensually defines the long-term goals and values that are worthy of pursuit. When an entire culture brings its full weight to bear on the goals it embraces, every member of that culture internalizes, at least to some extent, those long-term goals that are deemed worthy. And pursuing and achieving these culturally defined goals brings status and reward. Now, influenced by the power of cultural values, a person is more likely to align her- or himself with a long-term culturally defined goal that might make it worth passing up an immediate reward. A culture that places a heavy emphasis on formal education, for example, will bring its collective weight to bear on young people so that they will make immediate sacrifices in order to maximize their long-term educational goals. This doesn't guarantee that every young person will dutifully pursue formal education or that all will succeed. But it certainly makes clear to young people what is valued. The fact that school attendance in Canada is a law speaks to the importance Canadian culture places on education as a valued (Heymann 2013), long-term goal and the level of agreement among Canadians about its importance to everyone. Indeed, no Canadian escapes this message, and, as the population has aged, the concept of "lifelong learning" has become increasingly popular. In contrast, there are no laws compelling all young Canadians to be soldiers, play basketball, play a musical instrument, collect stamps, or be able to cook. All of these are desired cultural activities but they do not constitute one of those few culturally defined long-term goals whose pursuit often requires sacrificing immediate gratification. Another culture might collectively encourage its people to retain their heritage culture and language, especially if it is under severe threat; another might demand that its group members become wealthy by any and all means; another might value the acquisition of land; while still others might reify family. Whatever the culture collectively defines as a defining value, or long-term goal, you can be sure that everyone gets the message. You can also be sure that achieving that defined value will require great sacri-fice: there would be no need to trumpet it if everyone could easily achieve it.

We make a straightforward link, then, between collective self-con-trol and a clearly defined cultural identity. This places Aboriginal identity squarely at the heart of collective self-control issues and, by extension, the cluster of daunting challenges that confront Aboriginal communities. In this chapter we elaborate on our theory linking colo-nialism with cultural identity, collective self-control, and, ultimately, psychological health and well-being.

## COLONIALISM DESTROYS CULTURES

Colonialism is not a pretty process. Colonizers are motivated by per-sonal and national gain to the detriment of those being colonized. The result is a long-lasting rupture to the cultural integrity of colo-nialism's victims. The colonialist legacy in Canada is one that has been well documented (Royal Commission on Aboriginal Peoples 1996), and it would be presumptuous of us to pretend that there is much we can contribute to the history of relations between Aborigi-nal and non-Aboriginal peoples in Canada. What we hope to do is to underscore the magnitude of the onslaught on Aboriginal integrity, autonomy, and identity.

What better place to start our broad-brush portrait than the 2008 official apology offered by Prime Minister Stephen Harper on behalf of all Canadians for the assimilation agenda perpetrated upon Abo-riginal Peoples in the form of "residential schools." In King's (2012, 122) judgment, with which we concur: "The Canadian apology, while heartfelt, was, in many ways, a stingy thing, limited only to the abuse that Native people had endured in the residential school system."

The "stinginess" of the apology matters to us in the present context. What we intend to underscore is the fact that the colonialist process "gutted" Aboriginal culture. Colonialism always affects the culture of the colonized. And the British and French together had plenty of experience colonizing a significant portion of the globe. In most instances, be it India, Vietnam, the Middle East, or Africa, entire nations who had long abandoned a hunting-and-gathering lifestyle were the target. The result was that, while resources were stolen and social structures reoriented to a new colonialist reality, much, or at least some, of the culture remained intact.

This was not the case with regard to the impact of colonialism on the hunting-and-gathering cultures that comprised Canada's Aboriginal peoples. In the case of First Nations, Inuit, and Métis peoples, colonialism left nothing of these many and varied cultures intact. The harsh realities paint a devastating picture, one that forces us to recognize that the famed residential school experience was, and still is, but the tip of the iceberg.

Cocker (1998, xiii) pulls no punches: "European consumption of tribal society could be said to represent the greatest, most persistent act of human destructiveness ever recorded." Cocker cites some historians as estimating that as many as 100 million Indigenous peoples perished as a result of colonialism in Canada, the United States, and South America. Indeed, King (2012) suggests that as many as 80 percent of the Indigenous population of the eastern seacoast lost their lives to colonialism. Now these dramatic figures go beyond "military" battles and include factors such as disease and famine. Nevertheless, just the sheer loss of life would decimate a culture, especially when the culture in question is small and is based on a hunting-and-gathering lifestyle. In terms of policy, King argues that colonialism was guided by two impulses: extermination and assimilation. The combination of these has had a devastating impact on the entire social, economic, political, and spiritual life of Aboriginal peoples and their identity.

The destructive impact of a colonialist assault on cultural integrity varies according to the power differential between colonizer and those being colonized as well as according to whether the colonization process is short-lived or perpetual. In the case of Indigenous peoples around the world, the impact was maximally destructive. The power differential between European colonizers and Canada's Aboriginal peoples could not have been wider, and the colonizers came to stay. No short-term disruption of cultural integrity here.

What needs to be appreciated is the extent to which the cultural power differential associated with colonialism dislocates every corner of the colonized group's heritage culture. Simplistic analyses of colonialism allude to the three "M's": military, missionaries, and merchants. In terms of the military, it is clear that the intention was entirely exploitative. Missionaries were often well intentioned, albeit with much political guidance, and merchants were merely trying to "cut the best business deal," a practice they would engage in with any person or group with whom they might trade. But whether the motivation of colonizers is constructive or destructive (something that depends on the eye of the beholder), it is the <u>power differential</u> that ultimately destroys the heritage culture.

Even a cursory examination of the effects of colonization on the culture of Aboriginal peoples illustrates the extent to which their cultural identity has been destroyed. Colonization meant that groups that were largely nomadic, roaming purposely and strategically in small extended family collectives, were now forced to live sedentary lives, either on bounded land-poor reserves in the case of First Nations peoples or in fixed communities in the case of Inuit. Formal schooling and commerce forced families apart. In the case of schooling, children were removed from their family for a good portion of the day or, worse, were sent to schools thousands of miles away, which meant they were separated from their families for months at a time. Meantime, the ravages of new diseases and the mixed blessings associated with new technology radically changed the lifestyle of Aboriginal peoples.

We refrain from a lengthy digression into the inhuman treatment that colonized peoples suffered because our concern is to focus on how the heritage culture of colonized groups was irrefutably damaged. When cultural difference theorists point to severely disadvantaged groups and say the challenge is one of integrating two equal cultures, they are at best misrepresenting the challenge. Given the power differential, what we are looking at is the integration of two cultures, one of which has been severely fractured.

*Power differential*

## COLONIALISM AND ABORIGINAL LANGUAGES

One of the best illustrations of the profound impact of the power associated with colonialism is found in the domain of language and formal schooling. Specifically, in the growing debate over bilingual education, intergroup power is pivotal. The pedagogical challenge, which initially gave rise to bilingual forms of education, was concerned with how to help minority children, whose home language was not English, compete effectively in the school environment. Because the problem was initially framed in purely linguistic terms, the solution was simple: immerse minority-language children in the dominant language, be it English or French, as quickly as possible and for as long as possible. The aim was to maximize the chances that the child would perform well in a school and in a society that functions exclusively in English or in French.

This form of language submersion was so unsuccessful that new solutions were sought. What emerged from the ineffectiveness of submersion, and partly as a response to US legislation proclaiming that insensitivity to the home language of minority children was discriminatory (*Lau v. Nichols* 1974), was a revolutionary concept: bilingual education (Lambert and Tucker 1972). What is so special about bilingual education is that students are not merely taught a language; rather, they are taught through a language. That is, the new language is the language of instruction. Bilingual programs vary widely, but by far the most popular form involves students being taught in their heritage language through the early grades and then transitioning into the dominant language for the remainder of their formal education: hence the label "transitional bilingual program."

How exactly does transitional bilingualism work? Minority students would be taught in their home language for the first two or three years of their formal education, and then they would be transitioned into an all-English (or French) curriculum for the remainder of their schooling. A variant of the same process would involve minority students being given some of their schooling in the home language until such time as their English (or French) skills were sufficient to permit them to function in the regular English (or French) stream. Transitional bilingual programs, therefore, involve using the home language in order to help minority children ultimately participate in a regular mainstream, non-Aboriginal, English (or French) curriculum.

Transitional bilingualism programs have proven to be highly successful for minority students. Their success is based on a simple idea: language transfer. The point is that gains made in the minority language through instruction in the early grades do not compromise development in the dominant language; rather, these gains are transferred quickly to the dominant language. The end result is that a minority child who is taught via her or his minority language for the first few years is eventually more proficient in the dominant language than is a student who is taught exclusively in the dominant language. And this is certainly true for Aboriginal students. For example, Inuit children taught in Inuktitut for the first three years of school are, in Grade 6, as good in English or French as are Inuit students taught exclusively in one or another of those languages (Usborne et al. 2009).

It may seem that transitional bilingualism is an enlightened form of education that is respectful of heritage languages. But let us look a little closer. First, transitional programs are designed to help minority students assimilate to English (or French) rather than to convey any particular respect for the heritage language.

For example, here is how transitional bilingualism works in the United States, where it is widespread. Suppose a child from Portugal with very little fluency in English enrols in a school located in a major American city. The child will be tested in English and, if found lacking, will be stigmatized as an LEP (limited English proficiency) student. The child, so stigmatized, will be pulled from regular classes and given instruction in Portuguese so that he or she will not fall too far behind in terms of course content. At the end of the year, the child will be retested in English and, if minimal standards are met, will be mainstreamed in the all-English regular program. The child, of course, still faces potential failure for, after all, she or he has only reached minimal standards in English. The point here is that, even for immigrants to North America, most bilingual programs are fundamentally disrespectful of heritage languages. Moreover, they are designed to almost guarantee academic failure.

But this pales in comparison to the plight of Aboriginal people. Internal colonization has not been merely disrespectful of heritage languages, it has destroyed them (Dorais 1996). Of fifty-three Aboriginal groups in Canada, only three have a heritage language that has some hope of survival: Cree, Ojibwe, and Inuktitut (Norris 2007). When a child from an immigrant family, be it Portugal, Italy, or Greece, loses his or her heritage language, that is tragic for the child and the family, but no one believes that Portuguese, Italian, and Greek will be lost as world languages. But when one Aboriginal child loses his or her language, it signals the death of an entire heritage language and, by extension, a people.

The implications of internal colonialism for collective identity conflict are clear. The colonizer ultimately expects those who are colonized to assimilate and to participate in society. The expectation, then, is that those who are colonized will divest themselves of their heritage culture and language and, to the fullest extent possible, adopt the dominant culture and language. The conflict in collective identity produced by assimilation is multifaceted. First, it requires giving up a cherished and meaningful set of beliefs, values, and behaviour patterns. Second, it requires embracing a dominant culture and language, which may appear desirable in terms of the power this affords those who do so successfully. But it also involves frustration and loss of esteem when, because of systemic discrimination, those colonized persons who have embraced the dominant culture and language are nevertheless denied the opportunity to participate fully in society.

The impact of colonialism on Aboriginal languages is instructive. The vast majority of Aboriginal languages have been lost forever, and the few that remain are under severe threat (Norris 2007). On the surface, the introduction of transitional bilingualism programs appears to be an enlightened move: there is great enthusiasm for programs that include an Aboriginal language not merely as a course in the curriculum but also as the language of instruction in the early grades. But transitional bilingual programs are essentially assimilationist. There are far more balanced forms of bilingual education, whereby the Aboriginal language would be used not just in the early grades but throughout the entire formal education process. The end result would be fluently bilingual students.

More broadly, what happened to Aboriginal languages illustrates the extent to which Aboriginal cultures were obliterated by the colonialist process. Left facing such a cultural vacuum, you would think that assimilation to European culture would be an inevitable outcome. Why did, and do, assimilationist policies fail? The answer lies in the fact that European colonizers failed, and continue to fail, to fill the cultural void left by the widespread destruction of Aboriginal cultures.

## A CULTURAL IDENTITY VACUUM AND ASSIMILATION

The assimilation theme figures prominently as a coordinated policy with regard to Aboriginal peoples. This raises an important issue: if Aboriginal cultures were destroyed by colonization, then surely, through assimilation, the Aboriginal cultural void was filled by European culture. This being the case, would it not be more accurate to say that colonization destroyed Aboriginal culture but replaced it with European culture? Shouldn't we point to "cultural replacement" rather than to a "cultural vacuum" as the fundamental challenge for Aboriginal groups?

We argue that European colonizers did not do a good or a fair job of exposing Aboriginal people to the essentials of European culture. We suggest that Aboriginal people have been exposed to the superficial trappings of European culture but not to its essential values, goals, and norms. The meritocracy principle, which forms the bedrock of

European culture's social, judicial, political, and economic structure, has never been explicitly shared with Aboriginal peoples.

At the heart of European values is <u>meritocracy</u>, the notion that a person's status is associated with his or her performance based on ability and effort. Aboriginal people were only exposed to superficial bits of European culture and were forced to occupy its lowest positions. <u>They were offered no opportunity</u> to learn or acquire the <u>fundamentals of the European meritocracy</u>. That is, they had no opportunity to learn that they, too, based on their ability and effort, could become merchants and teachers if they so desired.

The fragmented image of European culture that was presented to Aboriginal people is particularly striking in the domain of education. Formal education was a fundamental institution of European culture. It was the mechanism, the vehicle, by which the individual could acquire the systematic body of knowledge necessary to "get ahead" in European culture. Thus, every member of this culture shared the belief that formal education was directly linked to success in the job market. It was clear to everyone that the higher the formal education and the better the performance in school, the higher the status of the job an individual would attain. The correspondence between formal education and job status was certainly not perfect, but the point is that those raised in a European culture believed it existed.

Aboriginal people had European education thrust on them, but they were <u>not provided with a clear understanding</u> of its role and <u>function</u>. There was, and is, no clear link between formal education and job status and, by extension, social status and community influence. Ironically, this apparent lack of a relationship between job status and education operates in two directions.

When formal education was thrust upon Aboriginal people, most of the underlying bases for that education were neither presented nor explained. True, Aboriginal people saw schools being built, teachers being hired, and classes being given. However, nowhere was the fundamental link between education and economic prosperity clearly delineated. At no time were the fundamentals of the principles of merit either explained or modelled.

Examples abound of how the deep structure pertaining to how formal education operates has never been properly explained to Aboriginal people. We have had countless conversations with parents about the sporadic nature of their children's school attendance. What these conversations reveal is that, through no fault of their own, parents have no idea that school curricula are programmatic – that one knowledge element follows from another; rather, they view formal education as the imparting of discrete elements of information, with the learning of one element in no way affecting the learning of another. What has never been explained to parents is that what students learn on Monday needs to be mastered before they can understand the material presented on Tuesday. No wonder the students don't feel compelled to attend school every day, and no wonder they find school incomprehensible.

Let's take a more subtle, but profound, example. Before colonization, traditional education for Aboriginal children was not a game: it was a matter of immediate survival. Young boys and girls learned by observing their parents, and only when they were deemed ready would they be granted the privilege of hunting, fishing, sewing, or cooking regularly with adults. At this stage, there was no more room for error.

Contrast this with European formal education, in which children practise for years on end and face no serious consequences for making an error. European formal education is designed to teach by encouraging students to engage in trial and error and would seem entirely strange from an Aboriginal point of view. Specifically, using a variant of the Socratic method, the teacher poses a question and students compete to provide the answer. If every student could answer the question correctly, the teacher would judge that it was too easy and move on to more difficult material. If the student makes a mistake, the consequences are trivial. Well, to be fair, they may not seem trivial to a student who feels inadequate for having given an incorrect answer, but the teacher will constantly encourage her/him to keep trying, underscoring the fact that there is no shame in failure. The idea is that students are encouraged to acquire information within the safe environment of the school, where mistakes are not costly. The hope is that, through this process, the student will accumulate enough skills to ensure that, when he or she graduates and enters the "real" world, mistakes will be minimized. Traditionally, Aboriginal children are already in the "real world" and so could not enjoy the luxury of constantly making mistakes.

To further complicate matters, in the European tradition the questions the teacher asks of students are not genuine questions. The teacher already knows the answer and the students know this. So the exercise, the heart of formal learning, is disingenuous: it is a game with complex rules that defy common logic. Commonsense would dictate that you ask questions only when you do not know the answer and need the information, but at school you only ask questions when you already know the answer.

And this process begins even before children enter kindergarten. Non-Aboriginal parents spend an inordinate amount of time asking their children questions not for information but in order to encourage and test learning. Children will be asked to name the colours that the parent points to. They will be read the same story dozens of times, with the parent pausing to ask questions about the characters, the setting, and what is going to happen next. Parents will engage in number games, and the "in thing" is for parents to watch carefully selected television programs with their children and then question them about the content. In all these instances, the parents are asking questions to which they already know the answers.

The children are learning a cultural ritual that lies at the heart of formal learning. It is a complex ritual for it requires the child to understand that, in most contexts, one asks questions to obtain information but that, in a formal learning context, questions are asked when the asker already know the answer. Nevertheless, to be successful, the child must either assume or pretend that the adult doesn't know the answer. Only by successfully pretending can the child rationalize answering and thus providing enlightenment to the adult. We suspect that, occasionally, children will intentionally give an incorrect answer in order to check the adult's reaction. This allows her/him to confirm her or his implicit assumption about how the ritual is supposed to unfold. That is, when the child offers an incorrect answer, the parent will quickly remind her/him of the right answer. This confirms for the child that the ritual does indeed require giving answers that are already known by the parent.

This fundamental question-and-answer ritual is essential to a lifetime of formal learning, it begins early in the child's development and becomes implicit cultural knowledge. Even at the university level, in their essays students are asked to explicate theories that they were taught by their professors. Clearly the professor already understands the theories, but the student must pretend he or she does not. Children who are not socialized into this implicit cultural knowledge will experience difficulty in any formal school environment. Such students will appear to be smart enough to the teacher, but they will always manage to not quite deliver the performance that is expected in a formal classroom. Clearly, this puts many students at a disadvantage.

These are but a few illustrations of how, in attempting to assimilate Aboriginal people, colonizers presented them with only the superficial trappings of European culture while neglecting to reveal their deep structure. The result of the process of colonialism is that Aboriginal people have been left with a cultural vacuum on two counts: their own culture was destroyed and they were not presented with a clear alternative. The implications of living in a cultural vacuum need to be spelled out, and so we now direct our attention to understanding the psychology of cultural identity.

## COLONIZATION, THE SELF-CONCEPT, AND THE PRIMACY OF CULTURAL IDENTITY

Colonization, when it involves groups of dramatically different power, and when it involves colonizers who "come to stay," results in a cultural vacuum that will have a profound psychological impact on each and every group member. In the search for a theoretical framework for understanding the psychological impact of colonization, our attention turns to that most "human" of attributes: the ability of individuals to reflect upon themselves. This unique ability allows individuals to form a concept of "self," which is surely the most fundamental, complex, and important psychologically based cognitive process (see Leary and Tangney 2003). It is the process that organizes experience, guides and regulates behaviour, and is the root of psychological meaning and adjustment.

The self is exceedingly complex. It is stable but constantly adjusting to the immediate demands of the environment. It contains elements that are mere fragments of lived realities and yet is experienced as a coherent construct. The individual is exposed to an overwhelming array of social stimuli, but only a select few become internalized as an integral part of the self (see Baumeister 1999).

Despite these mysterious complexities, there is a degree of consensus about certain fundamental dimensions of the self-concept. First, it is clear that one overarching dimension involves the contrast between self-knowledge or cold cognitions (identity), on the one hand, and self-evaluation or hot cognitions (esteem), on the other (see Campbell 1990; Campbell, Assanand, and Di Paula 2003; Campbell and Lavallee 1993). Identity addresses the question "who am I?" whereas esteem addresses the question "am I worthy?"

The emergence of social identity theory (Tajfel and Turner 1979; 1986) has illuminated a second important dimension of the self-concept, one that contrasts personal and collective identity. Traditional theories of the self-concept focus on personal identity, those characteristics that define an individual as unique. For example, when a person describes herself as intelligent, shy, brave, and loyal, she is describing a constellation of attributes that make her unique.

Social identity theory points to the important contribution that the groups to which a person belongs contribute to her or his self-concept. A person's cultural, religious, social class, gender, professional, and, indeed, leisure group may all contribute to her or his self-concept (Ashmore, Deaux, and McLaughlin-Volpe 2004). Our same intelligent and loyal person might also define herself as a young Aboriginal woman. These are aspects of her collective identity in that they refer to attributes that she shares with other members of the categories young, Aboriginal, and woman.

By crossing these two fundamental dimensions of the self-concept (identity versus esteem, and personal versus collective), we arrive at four distinct components to the self-concept: (1) personal identity, which includes personal attributes (I am outgoing and punctual); (2) personal (self-) esteem, which involves a self-evaluation (I am proud to be outgoing and punctual); (3) collective identity, which are the attributes of my group (my group is friendly and non-aggressive); and (4) collective esteem (I am proud that my group is friendly and non-aggressive). Each of these four components of the self-concept has been the focus of psychological attention, with an inordinate concentration on personal (self-) esteem. Indeed, today's pop culture points to low self-esteem as being responsible for all the ills that confront individuals and groups alike.

Our theory argues that all four components of the self are crucial. Extrapolating from all four, we conclude that the psychologically healthy person is someone who has a clearly defined personal identity and a clearly defined collective identity, along with a positively valenced personal identity and a positively valued collective identity.

Theorizing about the self-concept in terms of identity versus evaluation, and personal versus collective, is not novel. Where our theory of the self-concept departs from current theorizing is in terms of the role played by each of its four components. Taylor (1997, 2002) argues that, while each of the four components plays a vital role for

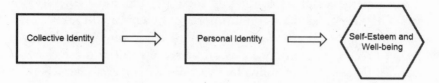

Figure 5.2   Diagram depicting relationship among two key components of the self-concept

a healthy sense of self and well-being, certain components have psychological precedence. Specifically, our argument is that collective identity has psychological priority over the other three components, and personal identity, in turn, has precedence over personal (self-) esteem. The hierarchical arrangement of two key components is presented in Figure 5.2.

The precedence of collective identity arises, we argue, because the attributes that comprise an individual's personal identity are relative. When an individual perceives herself to be intelligent, an element of her personal identity, she is really saying: "I perceive myself to be more intelligent than others who make up my reference group." In order for someone to conclude that she or he is personally "intelligent," she/he requires a normative template to serve as a comparative standard. Indeed, for anyone to define the attributes that are unique to her or him personally (personal identity), s/he must have a norm, standard, or prototype to serve as a comparative template (see also referent informational influence theory [Terry and Hogg 1996]). This is precisely the role of collective identity.

The importance of collective identity for personal identity has surfaced in a variety of contexts in social psychology. Most directly for the present context, our own research (Usborne and Taylor 2010) indicates that, for real cultural groups, including one First Nations group, a clearly defined cultural identity is associated with a clear personal identity, which is then linked to self-esteem and well-being. In an Aboriginal context Chandler and his colleagues (Chandler and Lalonde 1998; Chandler et al. 2003) demonstrate that, in the case of Aboriginal Canadians, cultural continuity and control are important factors for well-being.

Hogg and his collaborators examine the role of group clarity in reducing personal uncertainty, and they provide evidence for the relationship between a clear collective identity and personal certainty or clarity. Clear categories provide individuals with behavioural scripts, locate them in the social world, regulate their expectations, and provide them with validation of who they are, what they do, and what they believe (Hogg and Mullin 1999). Hogg et al. (2007) find that not only does self-conceptual uncertainty motivate group identification but also that people prefer to identify with groups that are clearly defined. People turn to groups that provide clear and consensual prototypes that are best suited to uncertainty reduction (Jetten, Hogg, and Mullin 2000). Having a clearly defined group or collective identity would seem to facilitate the construction of a clear personal identity.

An example of how a collective, or cultural, identity might shape one's personal identity comes from McAdams's (2006) examination of the life-story narratives of highly generative Americans. He found that these individuals' life stories and, by extension, their personal identities reflected much more than their own efforts to make sense of their lives. Their personal identities were very much shaped by social and cultural forces, including the social norms, gender stereotypes, historical events, and cultural assumptions stemming from their cultural environment. In McAdams's case, a clearly defined "American" cultural identity appeared to guide the construction and understanding of participants' personal identities.

There is, therefore, some evidence to indicate that collective, or cultural, identity clarity is related to personal identity. The second important relationship for our model is that between personal identity and self-esteem/well-being. For this relationship, there is also some initial social psychological evidence. Pelham and Swann (1989) posit that the relative certainty of people's positive versus negative self-views is one contributor to their global self-esteem. Similarly, Baumgardner (1990) demonstrates that increasing self-certainty actually leads to more positive self-regard. Although a causal link between personal clarity and self-esteem has not been firmly determined (see Campbell and Lavallee 1993, for a discussion of potential causal mechanisms), we argue that it would be extremely difficult for an individual to develop personal (self-) esteem without the benefit of a clearly defined personal identity. Personal (self-) esteem is a form of self-evaluation that requires a concrete basis for engaging the evaluative process. An individual must know who she is – must know her own unique attributes – in order to arrive at an evaluation of the self. In this sense, personal identity is a necessary prerequisite for personal (self-) esteem. How can I know if I am worthy if I don't know who I am?

On the surface, research on implicit self-esteem (e.g., Greenwald and Banaji 1995) might appear to conflict with our arguments. Implicitly, research seems to imply that one does not need to acquire conscious knowledge of oneself before forming an evaluative reaction to the self. However, we argue that, even with implicit self-evaluations, some degree of self-knowledge, be it consciously or unconsciously held at the time of the evaluation, must have been available at some point. The information available to the individual at that point is what would allow her or him to engage in some form of social comparison, or self-evaluation process, to determine his or her level of self-esteem. In sum, we argue that a clear collective identity is associated with a clear personal identity, and that, by extension, a clear personal identity is the basis for the development of personal self-esteem and psychological well-being.

*Summary points*

Our focus on the primacy of collective identity and its relationship with personal identity and esteem runs counter to much thinking about the "self." The usual analysis focuses attention primarily on the individual and on her or his personal identity and esteem. Indeed, at least in the North American context, Gaertner, Sedikides, Vevea, and Iuzzini (2002) conclude that, in the case of self-definition, the personal self has motivational primacy over the collective self. We agree, in the sense that we do view personal identity as the pivotal aspect of the self for individual functioning and have no doubt that, in terms of an individual's conscious awareness and lived experience, it is most often the personal self that is evoked. Individuals from dominant groups, especially for whom group membership is not particularly challenging, may take their collective identities for granted (Ashmore et al. 2004). For them, cultural or collective knowledge would be so natural and engrained that it would not be necessary to consciously think much about their cultural or collective identity, and this would result in a primary focus on personal identity (Taylor 1997). In terms of the lived experience of the self, the vast majority of individuals probably experience it at a personal level.

However, in terms of psychological processes, we argue that, because personal identity and esteem are essentially derivative, it is impossible to form a clear personal identity without a clear collective identity to serve as a point of reference. Even if it is not experienced as such, collective identity has psychological primacy insofar as it affects the underlying process by which an identity arises, and this primacy has profound implications.

## COLLECTIVE IDENTITY, CULTURE, AND RELIGION

Each of us has a number of collective identities, as many as the groups to which we belong with which we share characteristics. These collective identities range from our ethnic, cultural, and gender groups to our work and leisure groups. Here, we want to focus on cultural (and, in some cases, religious) identity. This is not to imply that a person has only one collective identity that is the most important for him or her at all times or that a person's various collective identities exist in isolation from one another. However, we believe that cultural identity, and in some cases religious identity, is the most important and pervasive collective identity of all (Taylor 1997, 2002).

We recognize the very difficult and delicate theoretical debate surrounding the definition of concepts such as "racial identity," "ethnic identity," "cultural identity," and "minority identity." Here we use "cultural identity" to refer specifically to a socially constructed set of norms, values, and behaviours that has evolved into a guiding framework for group members. Indeed, some members of a particular ethnic, racial, or minority group may have one cultural identity, whereas others may choose to adhere to another, quite different, one. We see cultural identity as an individual's chosen cultural template, complete with the norms, values, and behavioural scripts that it prescribes.

We argue that cultural identity is the most important collective identity for most people, most of the time. We qualify this assertion somewhat by noting that, for some people, religious identity has the potential to be as important as cultural identity. We link culture and religion because both have the potential to be all-inclusive. Devout Jews, Muslims, Buddhists, and Christians do view their religion as a template for every facet of their lives, from the cradle to the grave. Thus, culture and religion *may* be synonymous in terms of their pervasiveness as collective identities. We emphasize *may*, however, because many people do not consider their religion to be central to every aspect of their lives. By contrast, their cultural identity is inescapable. I may be nominally Christian and, to a certain extent, follow Christian tenets, but my Western culture is pervasive. More broadly, when a society makes a sharp distinction between religion and secular culture, or between church and state, religion and culture may not be synonymous.

But why is cultural/religious collective identity so important? Surely we take our professional identity seriously, and, like it or not, our gender identity is very much a part of who we are. But our professional collective identity only provides us with a blueprint for job-related activities, and our gender identity is not always applicable. Indeed, there are many contexts, such as the workplace, in which it would be quite inappropriate to act exclusively according to our gender identity. Furthermore, both gender and professional identities are, for the most part, prescribed by the culture in which we live. Our cultural/religious collective identity equips us with a template for every facet of life, including family structure, child rearing, appropriate behaviour with members of the opposite sex and elders, how to cope with death, occupational structure and status, and explanations for the unknown – to name just a few. A cultural/religious identity provides its members with a shared history, and a set of broadly based valued goals, along with detailed informal normative information and scripts about how to pursue these goals defined by their collective identity. Cultural psychologists go so far as to argue that one's culture may even influence the very structure of the self-concept (Markus and Kitayama 1991), affecting an array of psychological processes (e.g., Kitayama et al. 1997; Rhee et al. 1995) as well as general reasoning about one's social world (e.g., Ji, Nisbett, and Su 2001; Norenzayan and Nisbett 2000). Thus, cultural/religious collective identity represents, for an individual, the most pervasive and all-inclusive type of collective identity.

The pervasiveness of cultural/religious identity is precisely what makes it so resilient. It cannot be destroyed at the "point of a gun,"– witness the failed attempts to assimilate Aboriginal peoples around the world. Nor, apparently, can culture be eradicated by positive inducements to replace one culture or religion with others that have more material resources to offer. Newcomers were attracted to the United States, a cultural "melting pot," where the streets were purported to be paved with gold. All that was asked of them was that they agree to have their heritage cultures "melted" away so that they could become culturally American. And yet cultural distinctiveness has maintained itself to the point that the United States now views itself as multicultural. Whereas older theories focused on the inevitability of assimilation, current theories focus on cultural relativity, diversity, pluralism, and multiculturalism (see Taylor, 1991). Indeed, Berry (2005) and other researchers examining biculturalism (e.g., Amiot et al. 2007; de la Sablonnière, Debrosse, and Benoit 2010; LaFromboise, Coleman, and Gerton 1993; Ryder, Alden, and Paulhus 2000) show that individuals flourish when they are successfully able to overcome the challenge of negotiating two or more cultural identities. What needs to be emphasized here is how fundamental culture is as a guiding template and as a foundation for collective identity and the self-concept.

Our theory of self makes very clear predictions in terms of psychological health and subjective well-being. Individuals with a clearly defined cultural collective identity, those whose cultural identity is clearly and confidently defined, internally consistent and stable, are poised to develop a healthy, functioning self. In other words, a clearly defined cultural collective identity is the necessary prerequisite for engaging in the process of defining a personal identity and, by extension, personal (self-) esteem.

With every culture or religion there are always some individuals who, for a variety of reasons, have not internalized a clear schema of their cultural or religious collective identity. However, there are also entire groups who struggle in a cultural collective identity vacuum. Specifically, disadvantaged colonized groups such as Aboriginal peoples have had their culture and religion destroyed and, thus, have no clearly defined collective identity to offer their members.

## CULTURAL VACUUM AND CULTURAL MISMATCH

Our analysis, which emphasizes the pivotal role played by a clearly defined cultural identity, directly challenges current theory and practice. The long-standing theoretical model designed to explain the legacy of failed interventions in Aboriginal communities is based on what we label a "cultural mismatch model." Our "cultural vacuum model" points in an entirely different direction with regard to developing constructive community interventions and programs.

Cultural mismatch models take a variety of forms, but all make the same basic assumption: identities are clearly defined. Although different theorists and disciplines use their own terminology, all refer to a mismatch between two or more cultures – a mismatch that individuals attempt to reconcile. Thus, we review the cultural discontinuity hypothesis, acculturation theories, the bicultural identity integration model, and identity integration theories – all of which reflect the basic assumptions underlying the cultural mismatch models.

The cultural discontinuity hypothesis is the cultural mismatch model that has been applied most directly to the Aboriginal context, especially as it relates to formal education. The mismatch theme is clear in Ledlow's (1992, 23) explanation for the academic under-achievement of cultural minority students: "Culturally based differences in the communication styles of the minority students' home and the Anglo culture of the school leads to conflicts, misunderstandings, and ultimately, failure for those students. The research focuses on the process rather than the structure of education and concludes that making the classroom culturally appropriate will mean a higher rate of achievement."

A number of prominent theorists promote and apply nuanced varieties of the cultural discontinuity hypothesis to Aboriginal communities. For example, Brady (1996, 11) cites Frideres (1987), who aptly summarizes the cultural discontinuity theory as applied to Canadian Aboriginal students:

> Schools, to a certain extent, reflect the dominant social values of society … Today then, the educational process instills the business creed into students, stressing the practical usefulness of education, competitive success and making students conform to middle-class standards. (Graham 1969) Any student unwilling to adopt and internalize this dominant value will find the education process frustrating and useless.

The solution in all cases of cultural discontinuity involves reducing the discontinuity by ensuring that Aboriginal culture is more prominently featured in Aboriginal institutions. The operating assumption is that there is a clearly defined Aboriginal culture and a clearly defined dominant culture and that the problem is that the latter has been forced on to an incompatible former. We would argue that this type of cultural mismatch is not the major issue; rather, the major issue is the existence of a cultural vacuum. For this reason, cultural mismatch solutions have not, and will not, be effective.

The mismatch concept has also figured prominently in the form of "acculturation theories" as applied to the context of Canada's multicultural reality and issues surrounding cultural diversity in general.

Newcomers to Canada, be they immigrants, refugees, or sojourners, all face the challenge of juggling at least two cultures, their heritage culture and the dominant culture of Canada. How that process evolves has been of great interest to social scientists, but all assume that newcomers are coping with resolving two distinct yet relatively clearly defined cultures – that is, the challenge is one of dealing with a cultural mismatch.

The most influential theorist in this tradition is J.W. Berry, who researches different acculturation strategies that newcomers might use to effectively cope with two distinct, and potentially competing, cultural identities. Berry (2006b) finds that newcomers and, indeed, established cultural minority group members who adopt what he labels an "integration" strategy, acculturate better and display higher levels of psychological well-being. Berry defines integration as a strategy whereby an individual maintains positive links with both his or her heritage culture and Canadian culture. Berry's research indicates that an integration strategy – as opposed to one that sees the individual focusing either mainly on Canadian culture or mainly on the heritage culture – is the preferred strategy. He agues that an integration strategy allows the individual to benefit from the support of two social networks (Berry 1990, 1997; Berry et al. 2006; Berry and Sam 1997). Berry would argue that integration would be the most effective acculturation strategy for Aboriginal individuals who, like newcomers, wrestle with two distinct cultures. Where we take issue with Berry is in the application of his theory to Aboriginal people. Newcomers face the challenge of resolving two distinct and relatively clearly defined cultural identities. However, because, due to the colonization process, Aboriginal people have to cope with an <u>unclear identity</u>, their major challenge is a cultural vacuum, not a cultural mismatch.

Bicultural identity integration theorists and, to some extent, cultural difference theorists who focus mainly on sojourners (Ward, Leong, and Low 2004) seek to build upon the acculturation model proposed by Berry (2006a) by exploring the role that individual differences may have on the course of the acculturation process (Benet-Martinez and Haritatos 2005). The bicultural identity integration model, for example, highlights two independent dimensions: the perceived *distance* and the perceived *conflict* between two cultures (Haritatos and Benet-Martinez 2002; Benet-Martinez and Haritatos 2005). The distance dimension is more cognitive than the conflict dimension and involves the apparent similarities or overlap between the "new" dominant culture and the heritage culture. On a cognitive level, then, the perceived distance between two cultures is linked to a sense of cultural isolation or stress.

By contrast the perceived conflict between two cultures refers to the tension between cultural identities. Individuals for whom the dominant culture clashes with their heritage culture experience a sense of contradiction as they are forced to choose between two competing cultures. Unlike the perceived distance dimension, the perceived conflict dimension has an emotional impact. Culture conflict can be generated by a poor mastery of the dominant culture's language, and it is also associated with the stress of being discriminated against. In these circumstances it is difficult for individuals to maintain a consistent and positive self-image or sense of belonging (Benet-Martinez and Haritatos 2005).

Interestingly, Benet-Martinez and colleagues have shown that individuals with a bicultural integrated identity often see themselves as members of a third cultural group, emerging as a combination of the two cultures. The two cultures are perceived to be compatible rather than mutually exclusive, opposing, or conflicting. Those with a poor bicultural identity struggle due to an inability to conceptualize their two cultures as a coherent whole (Benet-Martinez et al. 2002; Benet-Martinez and Haritatos 2005; Benet-Martinez, Lee, and Leu 2006; Haritatos and Benet-Martinez 2002).

Again, bicultural identity theories assume that individuals have two relatively well-defined cultural identities, and the focus is on how they resolve them. Our theorizing suggests that, in the case of Aboriginal people, the issue is more a question of dealing with unclear cultural identities than of resolving clearly defined competing identities.

The actual psychological process by which the integration of competing cultural identities unfolds is addressed in the form of a cognitive-developmental model proposed by Amiot and colleagues (2007). They view identity integration as a four-stage process. This neo-Piagetian-inspired model draws a parallel between the development of the self-concept from childhood to adulthood and an individual's multiple cultural identities. Several studies illustrate how an individual's self-concept becomes increasingly more complex as she or he matures from childhood into adulthood (Bidell and Fischer 1996; Fischer 1980; Harter 1999, 2003; Mascolo and Fischer 1998; Yan and Fischer 2002). Similarly, Amiot and colleagues argue that the process of integrating a new cultural identity evolves from a previously fragmented self-image into the formation of an integrated and coherent one.

According to these authors, identity integration is characterized by simultaneous and equal identification with both cultural groups (e.g., de la Sablonnière et al. 2010). Evoking two cultural identities at the same time may, at first glance, seem to highlight the conflict between them. In the early stage of categorization, an individual cannot integrate both cultures and so she or he chooses either the heritage culture or the new competing culture. However, when an individual reaches the final stage – integration – she or he manages to recognize the similarities between the two identities and is able to resolve any intra-individual conflict, allowing her or him to acknowledge the contribution from each culture to her/his self-concept. In other words, an integrated individual has succeeded in establishing consistency between different identities and identifies equally with two cultures.

A final phenomenon to which we need to draw attention in the context of the cultural mismatch theme is the extent to which members of a group choose to place themselves in a context requiring the resolution of competing identities. In this regard, both Berry (2005) and Ogbu (1992) make an important distinction between "voluntary" and "involuntary" groups. They point to the inordinate challenges that confront involuntary groups compared to groups who choose their fate. Immigrants choose, at least to some extent, to come to Canada. Aboriginal peoples did not choose to be placed in circumstances of competing cultural identities. Both Berry and Ogbu make the point that groups who struggle the most – for example, Aboriginal peoples and African Americans – are those who did not choose their bicultural circumstances.

Berry's and Ogbu's distinction is an important one, but even here the assumption is that members of involuntary groups are "caught between two worlds." Again, the assumption is that two clearly defined cultures lie at the heart of identity conflicts experienced by involuntary groups.

Our cultural vacuum theory builds on the rich legacy of cultural mismatch theory and research, as well as on the special plight of involuntary groups, but our conclusion is different. We argue that, where there are cultural differences and where those differences are involuntary (e.g., internal colonization and slavery) the end result is a cultural vacuum, not a cultural mismatch.

## IMPLICATIONS OF THE PRIMACY OF CULTURAL IDENTITY

Let's be clear about the implications of our cultural identity vacuum theory. We argue that psychological efficacy and well-being begins with a clearly defined cultural identity. A clearly defined cultural identity is what allows each and every member of a cultural group to develop a clearly defined personal identity. It is the process that allows individual group members to answer the question: "Who am I?" Once this question has been articulated the individual can answer the next question: "Am I worthy?" In short, personal identity clarity takes precedence over self-esteem and, by extension, psychological well-being.

Our analysis challenges current thinking. Programs designed to directly improve the self-esteem of struggling individuals will not succeed: individuals need to know who they are before they can develop self-esteem and, ultimately, achieve psychological well-being.

Our theory of the self-concept makes it clear that, without a clearly defined cultural identity, forming a healthy personal identity and, by extension, positive self-esteem is an overwhelming task. This is precisely what Aboriginal communities confront: colonization has led to a cultural identity vacuum for each member of every Aboriginal group. The result is that Aboriginal individuals cannot engage the basic processes necessary to form a healthy, functional identity.

Is our idea that colonialism has left Aboriginal peoples with a cultural identity vacuum far-fetched? After all, we see vivid, public depictions of First Nations, Inuit, and Métis culture everywhere. The Inuit inukshuk has become almost a national icon, from being the symbol of the Vancouver Winter Olympics to adorning gardens across the country. So how can we suggest that a cultural identity vacuum is not just "a" problem but "the" problem?

We turn for support to the celebrated Aboriginal writer Thomas King (2012), whose powerful narrative describes "the inconvenient Indian." As Joseph Boyden eloquently notes in his review on the cover of King's book: "*The Inconvenient Indian* is destined to become a classic of historical narrative. For those who wish to better understand Native peoples, it is a must-read. For those who don't wish to understand, it is even more so."

King captures Aboriginal identity by categorizing Indians into three types: Dead, Live (Invisible), and Legal. "You can find Dead Indians everywhere. Rodeos, powwows, movies, television commercials" (54). To this list we might add media events, political gatherings, and sporting galas. King's point is that modern depictions of today's Aboriginal people is really a resurrection of the stereotypical Aboriginal person from precolonial times: Dead Indians. All we are exposed to is a glorified image, usually involving traditional dress, that evokes a time when Aboriginal groups had a rich cultural identity that they had constructed to effectively tame and navigate the enormous demands of the country's geography and their own psychology. King describes Live, or present-day, Indians as invisible in the sense that they have no clearly defined cultural definition to set them apart. Only Dead Indians are culturally visible. Legal Indians, both dead and alive, are defined by politics and bureaucracy. They are a colonizer's construction and thus leave Aboriginal people in a state of bewilderment and frustration, not even having control over who is allowed to be Aboriginal. King's entire analysis, articulated with dark humour and irony, captures our theoretical point. Prior to colonization Aboriginal people had perfectly clear functioning cultural identities (Dead Indians). But today's Aboriginal peoples have had their cultural identity stripped away by colonialism and, thus, are left with no clear cultural identity (Invisible Indian), indeed there is not even clarity regarding who is or who is not an Aboriginal person (Legal Indian).

## CONSEQUENCES OF A CULTURAL IDENTITY VACUUM: ISSUES WITH COLLECTIVE SELF-CONTROL

The cultural identity vacuum that we are proposing as a direct consequence of colonialism has a number of serious consequences. It makes it impossible for each individual Aboriginal person to develop a healthy personal identity and, by extension, robs Aboriginal people of the capacity to develop self-esteem. It is important to elaborate upon each of these themes, but since earlier we pointed to collective self-control as the root cause of community dysfunction, we focus here on the link between it and a cultural identity vacuum.

The exercise of self-control requires that there be a well-defined long-term goal: goal-directed behaviour is impossible without a goal. And, of course the long-term goals that are deemed worthy of a lifelong pursuit are a product of our cultural identity. Quite simply, every culture spells out its priorities.

In order to ask people to pass up short-term pleasure there must be a powerful long-term reward on the horizon, otherwise why pass up immediate pleasure? First and foremost, then, self-control requires well-defined, highly rewarding long-term goals. Cultural identity involves a collective consensus about which goals are worthy. And, as mentioned earlier, you have to be willing to pass up on immediately pleasurable activities (e.g., a night on the town, rushing things on a first date, eating junk food) if you want to achieve worthwhile goals (e.g., passing an exam, establishing a long-term relationship, playing professional ice-hockey).

Healthy communities with clearly defined cultural identities provide group members with an array of long-term goals that are so important, so pervasive, and so deeply engrained in the culture that no young person can escape them. In non-Aboriginal communities, for example, the cultural ethos is clear. Education is paramount. It is deemed so important that there are laws requiring young people to attend school until the age of sixteen. The message is clear: sacrifice immediate pleasure for school success because your future depends on it. So a young person in Grade 7 is supposed to comprehend that he must slog through mathematics and literature today because fifteen years from now he will be poised to be successful. In Grade 7 your only focus is on the next hockey game, texting with your friends, and whether or not your parents will allow you to attend a party next Friday night. No Grade 7 student really understands why school is so important. But they all get the message. And the message comes clearly from the entire cultural group (parents, extended family, friends, neighbours, political and religious leaders) and indirectly from observing that adults who are "successful" are those with the most education. In fact, highly successful people with little or no formal education are so rare that they are singled out as having beaten the odds, often becoming the focus of magazine articles and interesting news stories.

The entire adult cultural community is sending young people the same message. Long-term school achievement is important, so important that we pass laws on school attendance that carry serious consequences for non-compliance. The entire community also provides a detailed roadmap regarding what subjects need to be mastered and precisely how this should be done, including a detailed "cookbook" about how to study, how to perform well on exams, and how to memorize and retain crucial information. This is what we mean by "it takes an entire community to raise a child." Long-term goals require immediate sacrifice, and without the support of the entire community, without a clearly defined cultural identity, young people would quickly choose partying, games, and immediate fun over "hitting the books."

Does this mean that every single young person dutifully passes up immediate fun for her or his schooling? Of course not. The majority will exercise self-control most of the time, but there will always be a small subset of young people who struggle with self-control issues. And, of course, this subset of young people sets off red flags throughout the community, which allots enormous resources to try and help young people who struggle with self-control issues. Our analysis places Aboriginal communities in a very precarious position. First, exercising self-control requires that people have a clearly defined cultural identity that specifies well-defined long-term goals. Aboriginal communities do not have a clearly defined cultural identity and, thus, no long-term goals to offer young people. Second, given the paucity of compelling long-term goals, most young people will have little incentive to exercise self-control. Any activity that offers immediate reward will be very attractive. Thus, there is nothing to counterbalance the lure of mood-enhancing drugs, fast vehicles, fast food, and reckless sexual behaviour.

Colonialism has destroyed cultural identities, leaving Aboriginal groups with no long-term goals and no motivation to exercise self-control. And since colonialism and a cultural identity vacuum affects every Aboriginal person, the challenge is one of collective self-control.

Our analysis is clear about where attention needs to be focused. Job one is for each and every Aboriginal group to craft a clearly defined cultural identity that will enable it to specify worthy long-term goals for every group member. Constructing a clearly defined cultural identity from the cultural vacuum left by the ravages of colonialism is a daunting task, and two corollaries must be kept in mind from the outset. First, a clearly defined cultural identity cannot and should not be imposed by non-Aboriginal forces: this is the task of Aboriginal groups themselves. Second, before the process of generating a clearly defined cultural identity can begin, we need to fully appreciate the social hurdles associated with the challenge. The only hope for developing a realistic strategy for identity construction and self-respect involves first carefully analyzing the current normative structure of Aboriginal communities. This is the focus of Chapter 6.

# 6

## The Normative Structure of Aboriginal Communities: When 80–20 Becomes 20–80

Aboriginal communities have, and are, confronting an array of social, medical, academic, and economic issues all of which revolve around collective self-control. Communities, in their long-term battle, have reached the point at which they are crying out for help. It is frustrating when those who might be positioned to help appear to be ignoring the plight of these communities. But perhaps even more frustrating, and ultimately more psychologically damaging, is living through cycles of rising expectations only to have intervention after intervention fail. Interventions can be massive, well-intentioned, welcomed, and fully funded, and yet they appear to have no constructive impact on the community. This is the reality for many Aboriginal communities. A typical story that appeared on page 1 of Canada's national newspaper underscores this point. The headline refers to a northern Aboriginal region that has "Canada's highest birth rate" and where babies are three times more likely to die. The article goes on to note that money has been spent and strategies exhausted but that little has worked. It concludes that "flying women out is a bandage solution and we've put so many bandages on the problem they won't stick to the sores anymore" (White 2010, 3).

Policy makers, educators, economic development officers, police officers, nurses, and social workers in Aboriginal communities are constantly frustrated, demotivated, and burnt out. It is not that these people have a harder job than anyone else, it is that conditions in the community never seem to improve. And if that challenges the sanity of those attempting to constructively intervene, what is the experience for those who are the victims of ongoing community crisis?

It is not easy to affix blame in these contexts. Political, economic, social, pedagogical, cultural, psychological, and, indeed, Indigenous interventions all seem doomed to failure. If communities themselves are struggling for answers, if non-Aboriginal interventions from a spectrum of disciplines, ideologies, and political agendas all experience the same lack of success, there must be a common fundamental flaw to existing programs.

Our analysis (see Chapter 5) leads us to the conclusion that Aboriginal communities suffer not a cultural mismatch but, rather, a cultural vacuum as a direct consequence of colonialism. The mission, then, is clear: Aboriginal communities need to engage in a process designed to articulate a clearly defined cultural identity. And that cultural identity needs to be defined by, and for, Aboriginal peoples. And this Aboriginally constructed identity must clearly define the long-term goals that the group values so highly that individual Aboriginal group members will forego short-term pleasure in order to achieve them.

Before describing the necessary steps for generating a clearly defined cultural identity, there remains one further issue to address: the normative structure of Aboriginal communities. The cultural vacuum in Aboriginal communities brought on by colonialism has dramatically affected the normative structure of communities. Only by understanding this normative structure can the process of building a clearly defined cultural identity be undertaken effectively.

We believe that there is a fundamental normative structure issue that renders the current range of intervention strategies ineffective. In this chapter we offer a theory of effective community functioning that focuses on the role of social norms. Our analysis focuses on the normative structure of an effectively functioning group and on normative features that may be barriers to constructive social change. We suggest that such a normative analysis may explain why non-Aboriginal solutions to the social issues confronting Aboriginal communities are doomed to failure, as is the application of traditional Aboriginal interventions. As a guiding framework, we use the "80–20 rule," which is evoked every time someone in any social organization feels frustrated at the disproportionate allocation of resources within their organization (Taylor and de la Sablonnière 2013).

## THE 80-20 RULE

Every group, organization, institution, community, or nation has a primary collective goal. The sports team strives to win games, the com-

*80-20 rule :*

pany tries to efficiently produce and market the best product, the classroom aims to educate, and a community's mission is to provide an environment that will maximize the quality of life for each and every community member. It stands to reason that the more members of a group that perform at the highest level, the greater the chances that the group will be successful in reaching its goal. Simply put, if 100 percent of group members are contributing positively to the group's goal, there is a very good chance the group will succeed.

But, of course, no group operates with 100 percent efficiency, and thus we introduce the 80–20 rule as a reality check. The 80–20 rule proposes that any relatively successful group, organization, or community involves 80 percent of its members functioning well, with 20 percent, unfortunately, not doing so well (Taylor and de la Sablonnière 2013). The fact is that, just as no individual is perfect, so no group is perfect. Every group will strive to have 100 percent of its members functioning effectively, but a group that can count on 80 percent of its members is likely to succeed. When the percentage of functioning members drops below 80 percent the group is flirting with danger. No wonder every group, organization, and community keeps a watchful eye on the effective functioning of its members and will take inordinate steps to ensure that the 80–20 ratio does not dip to 75–25 or 70–30. Every group is aware that to drop below 80 percent of effective functioning is to reach a tipping point that will ensure its destruction.

To the extent that the 80–20 rule is the pervasive pattern for all social organizations or groups, there are three critical categories of group membership that we must consider. First, there are the non-functioning, non-normative, demanding 20 percent; second, there are the, for the most part, well-functioning 80 percent; and third, there are the human resource workers within the organization or group, professional or otherwise, whose role is to help the 20 percent (Taylor and de la Sablonnière 2013). We need to examine each of these three categories of group members in more detail in order to ultimately arrive at a fuller understanding of the challenges confronting Aboriginal communities.

## THE HIGH MAINTENANCE 20 PERCENT

Who are the 20 percent in a social group, organization, or community who require inordinate attention? They are individuals who stand out as non-normative. They are the high-maintenance extended family member, the committee member who never completes work in time for the meeting, the disruptive or underachieving student in a classroom, the criminal in a community, or, in an international context, the nation that constantly requires support from others.

If we explore the conditions that give rise to the expression 80–20, we can intuit why such a rule would arise in popular discourse and why it would apply to so many social groups, ranging from families to communities to nations. Every group is comprised of socially defined formal and informal norms. These are beliefs, feelings, and behaviours that the group values, that it considers to be appropriate and "normal." These are crucial to every group if it is to achieve its goal. The importance of group norms to group success is gaining more and more appreciation, to the point at which we now accept as a given that even private companies have a "corporate culture."

To further facilitate effective group functioning, larger groups are organized into a set of roles. These roles are rationally related so as to efficiently achieve the group's goals. Companies have presidents, vice-presidents, production people, and salespeople; universities have administrators, professors, and students; sports teams have defensive and offensive specialists; and communities have political, economic, educational, and spiritual roles. Each role has associated with it socially defined rules or prescriptions (norms) that are expected to be followed. Indeed, group success depends on the people in a specific role strictly adhering to the norms of that role. Ideally, the entire social organization requires strict adherence to the overarching norms, as well as to the specific norms associated with each role, in order to maximize the smooth and effective goal-directed functioning of the group (Taylor and de la Sablonnière 2013).

If the majority of members in any social organization adhere to the norms, the organization has a reasonable chance of surviving and achieving some, if not all, of its goals. Failure to achieve its goals, ineffective social interaction, and, in extreme cases, chaos would be the inevitable result if many group members did not adhere to the socially defined norms. Imagine an organization, for example a school board that was designed to deliver formal education to young people in a region. What if no one in the organization, from board members to teachers to students, adhered to the norms regarding hours, class schedules, or curriculum content? What if there were no normatively defined qualifications for any positions in the system? In terms of more informal norms, what if there were no norms for professional interaction, appropriate speech, or dress. What if there were no norms regarding what teachers would or would not share with students about other students and teachers? What if administrators had no norms for class discipline or bullying or drug use? And what if teachers only paid lip service to genuinely caring about students?

In any reasonably functioning social organization, then, the majority of members adhere to the norms. All they require is sufficient feedback to reinforce their knowledge that their efforts are contributing to a positive outcome and to maintain their motivation to continue making a constructive contribution. The minority 20 percent that do not adhere to the norms are the ones that require attention. They require attention, first, because, by not following the norms, they are disrupting any collective effort that a social organization undertakes to achieve its goals. Second, the individuals themselves will suffer from being "out of step" and thus may be in need of assistance. The end result is that disproportional resources will be allocated to these non-normative individuals. The aim will be to bring them "back in line" so that they might integrate into the normative structure of the social organization and, thereby, contribute to, or at least not disrupt, the organization's collective goals (Taylor and de la Sablonnière 2013).

So in any classroom, it is the 20 percent of disruptive students, and those behind in their studies, who receive the lion's share of attention. Usually the attention is directed at helping the targeted students to behave more normatively in terms of classroom behaviour and academic performance. Similarly, it is the 20 percent minority of young people in a community who run afoul of the law who are the focus of inordinate attention. Their non-normative behaviour attracts the attention of the police, the justice system, parole officers, and social workers. Again, the aim is to redirect this minority of young people towards more normative behaviour. The same process operates in any organization. A family member with a drinking problem will be the focus for both the immediate and extended family, with a view to normalizing her or his behaviour. A large corporation will spend considerable resources on employees who are not performing adequately, while those functioning smoothly will receive far less monitoring and intervention. In any social organization, while 80 percent of group members function smoothly and require little maintenance, there are the non-normative 20 percent who require special and inordinate attention. Eighty-twenty is of course a mythical ratio, and the exact percentages will vary from organization to organization. Whatever the percentage, the inordinate resources directed at the mythical 20 percent have an explicit purpose: to transform that 20 percent into the 80 percent – that is, to turn non-normative group members into normative, contributing group members.

We need to emphasize that every individual participates in a wide variety of social organizations or groups. Someone may be part of a family structure, work hierarchy, leisure group, community, and nation-state. It would not be uncommon for someone who is targeted as a non-normative 20 percent minority in one domain to be part of the normative 80 percent majority in several other domains. That said, however, there are certain key domains that might be generalized to include several other domains. For example, a person who develops a serious gambling problem may well find that; with time, her non-normative gaming affects her family, work, and leisure group functioning such that she becomes non-normative across a number of domains. This is not to imply cause and effect in terms of domain generalization. The non-normative gambling may indeed be the cause of non-normative behaviours in other domains, but it is equally possible that non-normative behaviour arising in the work or family domain is what gave rise to the non-normative gambling.

*20% in one group, but 80% in another.*

The potential for cross-domain generalization is particularly important in the present application of our normative theory. Aboriginal communities, both First Nations and Inuit, seem to confront the same cluster of challenges in terms of domains. These include academic underachievement, underemployment, substance misuse, family violence, and poor physical and psychological health. We argue that collective self-control is an underlying issue. The implication is that, in Aboriginal communities, there is a high likelihood of non-normative behaviour across multiple domains (Taylor and de la Sablonnière 2013). Regardless, addressing non-normative behaviour in a single domain would be, by definition, a more manageable challenge than addressing non-normative behaviour in a wide variety of domains. Aboriginal communities, however, face the daunting challenge of non-normative behaviour across the full range of life domains.

## THE NEGLECTED 80 PERCENT

The 20 percent are a major preoccupation precisely because of the disruptive impact of their non-normative behaviour. Those who intervene to normalize the 20 percent receive attention not only because their mission is crucial to the effective functioning of the group or organization but also because successful normalization is the exception rather than the rule. Consider the frustrations that organizations express regarding how difficult it is to rehabilitate the 20 percent when issues such as violence, drugs, alcohol, delinquency, and underachievement are involved.

Forgotten in most analyses are the quietly functioning 80 percent. It is this 80 percent, perhaps precisely because they adhere to the norms, who, for the most part, are relegated to an unappreciated background role. But, from our normative analysis, their contribution is both pivotal and critical.

First and foremost, it is the 80 percent who define the normative standards that guide the entire process. It is the 80 percent of students in a classroom who, in the context of school culture, define, model, and exemplify the range of acceptable behaviour. For example, the respectful comportment of the 80 percent of students in the classroom, their study habits, and so on clearly define what behaviours are appropriate. And the 80 percent reinforce each other in terms of serving as constant reminders of the appropriate standards for behaviour. Of course, the 20 percent get singled out when their behaviour lies outside the normative boundaries of the 80 percent. When school and family resources are allocated to the 20 percent, the aim is to rehabilitate them so that they come to resemble the 80 percent. In this sense, the 80 percent are essential to defining the norms, both for identifying those in need of attention and for serving as the goal for any intervention strategy (Taylor and de la Sablonnière 2013).

Second, the 80 percent, or any subset of this normative majority, can put inordinate pressure on a non-normative individual. The classic social psychology experiments initiated by Asch clearly demonstrate how apparently normative members of a group can influence an individual member to comply with the group, even when compliance belies that person's physical senses. Milgram further illustrates how an individual member of a group will conform to what is asked by an authority figure, even if this entails violating universally defined moral behaviour. Finally, Zimbardo's experiments underline the extent to which individuals will conform to the normative expectations of a group-defined role. These experiments, which we describe in greater detail in Chapter 7, demonstrate the power of social influence when a number of group members, or a consensually defined authority, wish to pressure an individual member to conform to the group's norms. The 80 percent can indeed exert inordinate influence on the minority (20 percent).

There is no better example of the pivotal role played by the normative 80 percent than the 2011 Stanley Cup hockey riots that took place in Vancouver. The Vancouver Canucks lost a deciding game to the Boston Bruins and fans took to the streets, where a minority (20 percent) proceeded to wreak havoc. Seventeen vehicles, including police cruisers, were set ablaze, and there was widespread property damage. Besides the professional reaction of the police, the normative (80 percent) Vancouver citizens swung into action. First, there was a call to clean up the debris from the riot, and the next day ordinary citizens volunteered to clean up the mess. But that's not all. Citizens denounced the minority violence and used social media such as YouTube and Facebook to aid the police. The usually quiet majority (80 percent) aided police by posting photographs of rioters and generally took unprecedented steps to normalize the situation. Over 1 million photographs and one thousand videos were sent to police authorities. Clearly, the majority 80 percent served as exemplars for appropriate behaviour both in their contrast to the rioters (20 percent) and in their ability to reinforce each other with regard to establishing models for normative behaviour.

A third important function served by the 80 percent involves <u>support</u> and <u>encouragement</u>. What happens when the 20 percent non-normative members of a group have been defined and resources are directed at rehabilitating them? The 80 percent of normatively functioning group members will usually signal their tacit approval by not voicing any complaints. They may go further and offer verbal and behavioural support. Only rarely will they disapprove of attention being directed at the 20 percent. After all, the explicit purpose is to normalize non-normative behaviour so that the collective goals of the group can be realized. Thus, for example, the 20 percent of teenagers who are delinquent require inordinate attention from schools, parents, police, the courts, and social workers. Most of the time the focus on these young people is tacitly approved, and occasionally, when normative measures seem particularly effective, it is applauded. And, of course, the 80 percent will voice their opinion loudly if it is felt that the police, judicial system, or others are engaging in misguided interventions.

The importance of the effectively functioning 80 percent, the "silent majority," cannot be overestimated. They may be silent most of the time, but they serve as every-day role models for appropriate behaviour. They represent the group standard for effective functioning and, ultimately, for group success. They also apply pressure on those who are non-normative, and they support appropriate interventions to rehabilitate them. Normalizing the 20 percent is challenging enough: without the norm-setting 80 percent it would be impossible.

## THE INTERVENERS

Thus far we have identified the 20 percent who are non-normative and who pose a potential threat to the collective goals established by the group, the silent, functioning 80 percent, and the need to integrate the former into the latter. Specifically, those in the 20 percent need to undergo some form of attitude and behaviour change to ensure that they begin to move in the direction of the norms that are defined by the 80 percent. The interventions into the lives of those in the 20 percent are conducted by people who are specially trained to do so. These interveners may be police officers, court officials, social workers, counsellors, spiritual leaders, doctors, nurses, and/or therapists. They focus on those who are in the 20 percent on some dimension be it legal, mental health, physical well-being or other dysfunction. And where do these specially trained interveners come from? They come from the 80 percent. That is, they are a subset of the 80 percent who receive special training to focus on the 20 percent. And this indicates just how committed groups are to maximizing the number of its members who are functioning effectively.

Rehabilitating the 20 percent is so important that it is not only trained specialists who focus on the non-normative minority but also anyone who is in a position of authority. For example, CEOs, teachers, forepersons, and elected officials may find themselves spending an inordinate amount of time attempting to rehabilitate members of the non-normative 20 percent. Suffice it to say that groups are almost fanatical about maximizing the percentage of group members who function effectively.

## ELABORATIONS ON THE 80–20 RULE

Interestingly, in using the 80–20 rule as a way of understanding effective group functioning and change it becomes clear that it provides a relatively accurate portrait of how normal groups function. The actual percentages are mythical and were chosen largely for illustrative purposes. However, their relative magnitudes capture the actual functioning of groups. In other words, in a well-functioning group the behaviour of most group members conforms to the group's norms, with the result that these people invite little attention. However, there is usually a minority of group members who behave non-normatively. This non-normative behaviour will attract attention because it stands out relative to that of the normative majority. Moreover, the non-normative behaviour will, at the very least, be a distraction from group goals and may well be disruptive to effective group functioning. Thus, in the majority of cases the non-normative minority attracts a great deal of attention, most of which is directed at rehabilitating non-normative behaviour so as to render it normal.

The attention that the non-normative minority receives is purposive. Usually, it is designed to protect the group and its goals and, if possible, to redirect the behaviour so that it becomes more normative. Young delinquents receive attention from professional police officers and a court system designed to protect the community and, with the help of social workers, parole officers, and counsellors, to rehabilitate them. The non-normative 20 percent who disrupt classrooms, endanger their children, or drive under the influence have an array of professionals whose job it is to protect the community and/or to rehabilitate non-normative individuals.

Some group members are non-normative for a very short period of time and, with special attention, quickly rejoin the normative 80 percent (e.g., those who develop a curable physical or mental illness, or those who experience a short period of financial difficulty). Since every group functions more or less according to the mythical 80–20 rule, there are as many examples of short-term non-normative behaviour as there are groups. But notice how, in every case, the non-normative minority receives inordinate attention from specialists as well as the crucial support of the normative 80 percent. For example, in functioning communities, unruly young people who engage in a variety of destructive behaviours, from verbal disrespect to vandalism to more serious transgressions, receive a lot of publicity. In reality, 80 percent of young people are law-abiding, goal-directed, constructive contributors to their community and receive no attention. As we have said, it is the unruly 20 percent who receive by far the most attention from the media and a spectrum of professionals whose sole mission is to rehabilitate them.

It is difficult to appreciate the importance of the roles that are played by the seemingly quiet, fully functioning, underappreciated 80 percent. A few non-Aboriginal examples may help to underline both the importance of the 80 percent and the extent of the challenges faced by Aboriginal communities. These focus on the role played by the 80–20 rule with regard to how non-Aboriginal society copes with social change, and these changes are trivial compared to those thrust upon Aboriginal communities.

*Ex of 80%*

Television was an innovative technology that changed non-Aboriginal society in a variety of superficial, and not so superficial, ways. One of us remembers the introduction of a single channel and the excitement that, every few years, surrounded the addition of each new channel. Then came cable TV and access to three key American channels. Recently, of course, the introduction of satellites has led to an explosion of specialty channels and an accompanying information overload. For thirty years or so there were no clear norms about how much TV, and what type of programs, adults and their children should watch. It was only in the 1990s that people began to raise the issue of appropriate TV use, both in terms of what, and how much, children should be watching, and what they were missing while glued to it. Slowly norms evolved so that now a young person spending too much time in front of a TV, watching the wrong programming, or indeed never watching TV will evoke a disapproving response from others. Here we have the 80 percent, finally at work after thirty years. The fate of fast foods has followed precisely the same normative curve. Slow to be accepted, fast food chains came to play a dominant role in non-Aboriginal diets. Only recently have norms evolved regarding their appropriate use.

*Takes yrs to evolve norms*

The personal computer and access to the internet have followed the same path. Non-Aboriginal society is beginning to develop norms for its use, but they have not as yet been solidified. We are constantly wrestling with what privacy norms, and norms relating to the appropriate use of e-mail, might be appropriate. Finally, there is the recent explosion of cell phones. As yet there is no normative structure to their use. Proof of the need for norms is the fact that, at formal meetings and films, someone has to announce that cell phones should be turned off. Once norms have had time to evolve, there will be no need to tell people when and where they can and cannot use their cell phones. Proof of this may be found in Japan, where cell phone use has been established for much longer and among a much greater portion of the population than is the case in Canada. No one has to tell the Japanese when, where, and how to use their cell phones: enough time has elapsed to allow for norms to become clearly established.

These simple examples point to the extent to which an 80–20 normative structure allows groups and organizations to function effectively. Imagine the challenge for Aboriginal communities,  which are not slowly introduced to these changes but, rather, have them thrust onto their communities all at once in their full-blown state. With no time and experience to evolve a normative structure, it is little wonder that members of Aboriginal communities over-indulge in watching TV, with its LED flat-screen resolution, and eating junk food. Even these apparently trivial changes have a profound impact on the identity of Aboriginal youth and their general state of health. If non-Aboriginal communities take years and years to evolve an effective normative structure with the requisite 80 per-cent, why should Aboriginal communities be any different – espe-cially since they have not had the benefit of having been slowly introduced to these changes?

We are proposing that the 80–20 rule characterizes effective group functioning in any social context. Clearly, unless the majority of group members are acting normatively, the group will not be able to achieve its goals. Thus far, we have focused on norms common to every member of a group or organization. Most groups, however, are comprised of a complex set of interrelated roles, usually arranged in hierarchical fashion. The hierarchy is usually structured so that most group members occupy lower status roles, with the number dimin-ishing as one climbs the group hierarchy. Logically, the proportion of normative and non-normative group members should be equal throughout a group's entire structure. Thus, we would expect the 80–20 rule to apply as much to those in the role of vice-president as to those in lesser roles. However, as we ascend the hierarchy, the pro-portion of non-normative people should decrease. Theoretically, this diminution of non-normative people at the higher levels of organiza-tional structure would be due to the mechanism of promotion: in order to move up in the hierarchy, one must conform to the norms of the group. Logically, group members who are promoted within the group hierarchy are those who most diligently conform to group norms. It is unlikely that a non-normative person would be promot-ed unless the norm in question was of little importance. Thus, we would expect to find non-normative group members throughout all roles in a group hierarchy, but their proportion should be less the higher one rises in the group.

In a normative 80–20 structure, the role of leaders is of great importance: their position in upper-level roles affords them the opportunity to use their power to influence group members who are lower in the status hierarchy. As symbols of both organizational goals and normative behaviours, a leader's influence is top-down, and, while normative leaders serve to reinforce the goals and norms of an organization, non-normative leaders may have a significant impact on more than just the 20 percent from which they came. A position of leadership, and the power that accompanies it, provides an opportunity for non-normative leaders to change the normative structure at their level, which can, in turn, affect lower levels. Once the normative structure begins to change, the process accelerates as the number of non-normative people increases. Those at the lower levels of a social organization may then be influenced by their superiors to act in a non-normative way; thus, an imbalance at the top of the hierarchy causes a transfer of non-normative behaviour at lower levels. If the normative structure is inverted, so that non-normative group members no longer represent the minority, we suggest that the process of re-establishing an 80–20 structure will be instigated from the bottom-up. Those at the bottom may have less power, but they have the advantage of numbers. This size advantage makes it possible for them to regroup and engage in collective action such that, in the end, they may influence and initiate changes at the upper level of the hierarchy.

There is one final structural complexity in terms of the 80–20 rule that needs to be addressed. We have been applying our normative analysis as if there were only one set of norms operating throughout any social organization. In reality, as soon as an organization becomes larger than a handful of members, informal or formally designated subgroups will form. For example, in terms of our present focus, Aboriginal groups are among the important subgroups that comprise Canada as a nation. The larger group, Canada, will operate according to an 80–20 normative structure, but so will each subgroup, including provinces, territories, major cities, and Aboriginal communities. The issue is the relationship between the normative structure of the larger group and the structure of its subgroups. Clearly, the larger group's capacity to achieve its goals will be compromised to the extent that its norms and those of any particular subgroup are in conflict.

## WHEN 80–20 BECOMES 20–80

What can we expect when a group does not have the mythical 80 percent who are normative and a minority 20 percent who are non-normative? What happens when the normative/non-normative ratio is more like 50–50, 40–60, or, more dramatically, 20–80? These normative reversals will only occur when social change is sudden, dramatic, and affects every one of a group's goal priorities. Examples abound when we consider entire nations coping with the almost instant introduction of capitalism and democracy. Consider the catastrophic impact of slavery as Africans were suddenly kidnapped and forced from their culturally rich life to cope with a new role on a new continent. This is precisely what Aboriginal peoples face in their remote communities and reserves as well as in urban centres. No group has been forcibly coerced into widespread normative disruption more than Aboriginal peoples. The challenge they confront in terms of normative regulation needs to be addressed as our analysis reveals that the usual regulatory mechanisms that are applied within the non-Aboriginal 80–20 context will be completely ineffective in the Aboriginal 20–80 context.

The destruction of Aboriginal languages, cultures, and lifeways through the ravages of colonialism is documented in earlier chapters. The concrete, visible destruction that colonialism has perpetrated upon Aboriginal peoples' lives is appalling. But no less appalling is our growing understanding of colonialism's detrimental impact on psychological identity and the self, especially cultural identity (see Chapter 5). The norms that allow for the definition of a clear cultural and personal identity constitute the necessary psychological framework within which individuals can successfully navigate their lives and achieve a semblance of well-being.

Aboriginal communities struggle with pervasive social dysfunction, underemployment, and academic underachievement, along with physical and mental health issues that are unacceptable when compared to national standards. Repeated efforts both from within Aboriginal communities themselves and from non-Aboriginal interventions have been unable to successfully address these issues.

Our 80–20 analysis addresses three goals: first, it offers some insight into the magnitude of the challenge confronting Aboriginal communities; second, it points to precisely why many intervention strategies are doomed to failure; and, third, it suggests a direction for constructive social change.

## THE FAILURE OF CURRENT INTERVENTIONS

In the normal 80–20 scenario, there are a myriad number of interventions directed at the 20 percent of group members, depending upon the specific non-normative behaviour in question. What they all share, however, is resources, be they human or financial, directed at the targeted minority with a view to normalizing their non-normative behaviour. The underachiever, delinquent, violent offender, substance misuser, mentally ill, and physically ill are all targeted by trained professionals. Sometimes non-normative 20 percent group members are fully aware of their status and seek professional help themselves. Sometimes they are slow to acknowledge their non-normative status and thus do not immediately pursue help. And sometimes there is either no awareness of their own non-normative behaviour or there is complete denial, in which case professionals must do the targeting and implementing. In all cases it is the normative majority that tacitly defines the non-normative minority and supports the intervention.

In a 20–80 situation, without the crucial role of a normative majority, the rational basis of professional intervention collapses (Taylor and de la Sablonnière 2013). First, few will identify themselves as non-normative and seek help since there is no normative majority to serve as a reference group. Indeed, if anything, non-normative behaviour would, ironically, be the norm and hence there would be little incentive to change. Applied to Aboriginal communities, especially isolated First Nations reserves and remote Arctic Inuit communities, even services that are taken for granted are seen through a different lens in the context of an inverted 80–20 normative structure. For example, what could be more obvious than having a nursing station in a community? When residents have an accident or become ill, they go to the station, where a professional non-Aboriginal nurse will diagnose, treat, and, if necessary, medevac the patient to a hospital. The problem is that community residents have no normative context for knowing how, when, or whether to avail themselves of medical attention. Even in the non-Aboriginal context, the changing structure of health care has left most people confused and uncertain about when to go to the hospital, clinic, or family doctor, should they be fortunate enough to have one. In Aboriginal communities there is no normative structure associated with the use of health facilities. Not surprisingly, some residents demand help when none is needed, and many in dire need either do not seek help or seek it too late. Moreover, preventative health measures are not routinely observed. All of this because there is no long-term 80–20 normative structure to guide residents regarding the most effective use of a nursing station. If norms are lacking with respect to behaviour as concrete as physical health, other, less visible domains, such as psychological well-being and long-term goal setting, are likely to produce even more ambiguity.

The behaviour of students offers an instructive example. In most non-Aboriginal schools, attendance and class behaviour is more or less regulated. Those few who break the norms are dealt with through a variety of means, including after-school detentions and occasional short-term expulsions, with parental involvement for reinstatement in the case of serious violations. These remedial actions are directed at the minority 20 percent of students who transgress, and they are not always successful. Applying the same procedures to Aboriginal schools is doomed because their normative structure differs from that of non-Aboriginal schools. Arriving late to school, skipping classes, and missing entire days is so frequent that 80 percent of the students would be in detention every day. There is little incentive for school success since there is no clear relationship between academic achievement and employment status. This is because the vast majority of skilled and professional positions in the community are occupied by non-Aboriginal outsiders. Community jobs rarely if ever consider formal education as a criterion. Moreover, parents of students have little experience with formal non-Aboriginal education. Indeed, any experience they might have had, usually through the residential school system, is profoundly negative. There is a general sense in Aboriginal communities that education is important, but its importance is only recognized because it is a highly publicized non-Aboriginal societal norm, one that is defined and imposed by the powerful non-Aboriginal majority. In Aboriginal communities, there is no clear, concrete normative sense that formal education is directly relevant to Aboriginal lives. In short, the 80 percent have no shared norm regarding the fundamental importance of schooling. The result is that detentions and expulsions pose no threat to students, and there is no normative structure to reinforce non-Aboriginal notions of student conduct. No wonder non-Aboriginal disciplinary measures, when applied in an Aboriginal community, are destined to fail.

Equally problematic is the use of traditional Aboriginal procedures for dealing with non-normative behaviour. Aboriginal interventions are, in most cases, culturally more familiar and appropriate, leading

No norm on formal schooling

non-Aboriginal policy makers and Aboriginal leaders to have high expectations for their success. However, Aboriginal procedures for justice, healing, and child discipline, for example, all arose prior to European incursions, when Aboriginal groups truly controlled their own collective identity. Like any other organized group, Aboriginal groups evolved their own effective 80–20 normative structures. Regulatory interventions were directed at the non-normative minority with the full backing of the normative majority. These intervention strategies, which were developed in the context of a genuine Aboriginal 80–20 normative structure, cannot be successfully applied to the current 20–80 normative structure. Thus, culturally relevant Aboriginal-based interventions, without the benefit of an 80–20 supportive normative structure, face the same overwhelming challenges as do non-Aboriginal interventions. For example, with the ongoing failure of non-Aboriginal justice procedures, forward-thinking communities have begun to employ traditional Aboriginal justice circles. Community members comprised mainly of elders engage in dialogue with both perpetrator and victim to arrive at an appropriate resolution. Aboriginal justice circles evolved in the context of pre-European colonization, when a genuine 80–20 normative structure was in place. The justice circle was no doubt extremely effective in that context, but it is unlikely to succeed in the current 20–80 structural reality. The paucity of positive results is especially devastating, however, because, on the surface, it appears to reflect a failure of Aboriginal culture. Clearly, any cultural benefit is sabotaged by the lack of a functional 80–20 normative structure.

Functioning groups invest heavily in maintaining an 80–20 normative structure. They are fully aware of the dire consequences should the percentages slip to 75–25 or worse. Aboriginal communities are struggling with a 20–80 normative structure. No wonder all the best intentions and financial support has fallen flat. Any successful intervention will need to adopt a collective approach that addresses the need to reverse the current 20–80 normative structure of many Aboriginal communities. Because they were developed within a functioning 80–20 context, current non-Aboriginal intervention strategies tend to be individualistic. The 20 percent in need of support are relatively few in number and thus can be targeted one at a time, taking into account their individual circumstances and predispositions. Such an individualistic approach is not suited to a 20–80 context. When it is the majority 80 percent that needs to be targeted, a collective approach, not an individualistic approach, is what is needed. Specifically, interventions must focus not on the individual factors that are at work but, rather, on the collective experiences that might explain why the majority in the community share the same destructive characteristics. A 20–80 normative structure cries out for collective, not individual, strategies.

*Collective approach* [handwritten marginalia]

## ONE PERSON'S 80–20 IS ANOTHER PERSON'S 20–80

Our characterization of non-Aboriginal communities as 80–20, and Aboriginal communities as 20–80, raises an important question. Maybe we are describing two different cultural groups with different cultural norms, and what's wrong with that? Viewed this way, we would say that what we really have are two different communities, each of which is 80–20 but with the content of the norms for the 80 percent being quite different from one another. Worse, surely in describing non-Aboriginal communities as 80–20, and Aboriginal communities as 20–80, we are merely displaying a colonialist, ethnocentric attitude. Our communities are 80–20, and theirs are 20–80, only because we impose our norms on them and judge ours to be "right" and theirs to be "wrong." To cite a trivial but striking personal example, we were raised in a community in which the norms for eating required that we eat everything on our plate. The rationale was that not to do so was not only disrespectful to our parents, who prepared the food, but also wasteful. "People are starving in some countries, so eat up" was an often-heard mantra, even with respect to broccoli. Clearly, our 80–20 involved dutifully eating everything on our plate. Imagine the chaos and discomfort we created when we were guests in a culture whose 80–20 was just the opposite: You were *never* to eat everything on your plate. You always left some food to indicate the generous nature of your host. Needless to say, until we solved the 80–20/20–80 cultural difference, we ate until we nearly exploded and, in the process, did not effectively communicate our appreciation for the graciousness of our hosts.

*ethnocentrism* [handwritten marginalia]

Our example underscores how ethnocentric one can be when not vigilant about the normative structure of other cultural communities. In the context of Aboriginal communities, such an ethnocentric accusation would be warranted were it not for the fact that Aboriginal leaders and Aboriginal peoples generally are united in voicing the need to address the dysfunctions that they, themselves, believe are plaguing their communities. It is Aboriginal peoples themselves from coast to coast to coast who are beginning to speak out about a cluster of social norms that they want to see changed. These do not include a variety of norms of which they are understandably proud; rather it is those issues that we have labelled as collective self-control problems that they are anxious to change. Indeed, they are more motivated than anyone else to see concrete normative change.

Thus, our characterization of the normative structure in Aboriginal communities as 20–80 is meant to reflect the collective voices of Aboriginal leaders and people alike. Understanding the normative functioning of effective groups in terms of 80–20 emphasizes the nature and magnitude of the challenge confronting Aboriginal communities.

## CULTURAL MISMATCH AND 20–80

There is no shortage of programs and interventions in Aboriginal communities across the country. Moreover, these interventions range from economic, academic, and judicial to health-related, social, and psychological. Sadly, the vast majority of these initiatives have yielded disappointing results, to say the least.

The widespread failure of these interventions requires analysts to find a broadly based explanation – one that can apply to First Nations, Inuit, and Métis in every corner of the country. To date, it is cultural mismatch theory that has been offered to explain this failure (see Chapter 5). The fundamental idea behind cultural mismatch theory is that any time a non-Aboriginal intervention is imposed on an Aboriginal community it is doomed because Aboriginal cultures are fundamentally different from non-Aboriginal cultures.

The cultural mismatch explanation is appealing because it is consistent with colonial practices, its logic can be applied to any and all Aboriginal groups, and it seems applicable to all domains of dysfunction. In general, the cultural mismatch idea is wholly consistent with present-day initiatives shared by both Aboriginal people and non-Aboriginal governments. Popular labels such as "empowerment" and "decolonization" are evoked to rationalize land claims initiatives, self-government movements, and Aboriginal demands for more control over their institutions. For example, Aboriginal groups not only want their own schools but also their own colleges and universities, and they also want their own social services and legal procedures.

These demands by Aboriginal groups have at least two interesting features related to cultural mismatch theory. First, they all involve a push for further autonomy and control, made necessary by a colonialist legacy that robbed Aboriginal peoples of collective self-control over their own destiny. Second, the push towards autonomy is focused on making all of the institutions that touch individual life more consistent with Aboriginal culture.

Again, cultural mismatch theory is salient, and this is precisely why Aboriginal aspirations towards collective autonomy are shared by non-Aboriginal governments. Both have adopted cultural mismatch theory in order to explain the challenges confronting Aboriginal communities. Of course, negotiating autonomy will be a difficult process since non-Aboriginal governments and people have much to lose. However, the process is being engaged because both groups believe that non-Aboriginal processes and institutions are incompatible with Aboriginal culture. Hence the failure of all interventions to date to improve the quality of life in Aboriginal communities.

Our 80–20 analysis challenges this popular cultural mismatch explanation for Aboriginal disadvantage and dysfunction. And our challenge has important implications for developing an appropriate strategy for meeting the issues in Aboriginal communities. The cultural mismatch approach leads to a strategy that attempts to avoid imposing non-Aboriginal cultural practices on Aboriginal communities, insisting that, instead, Aboriginal-based programs are needed and that, luckily, everyone is on board with this. If this were true, then the empowerment and decolonization movements currently under way should be highly successful.

The very idea of a cultural mismatch presupposes that there are two clearly defined cultures at odds with each other. In Chapter 5 we propose that the real issue is not a cultural mismatch but a cultural vacuum. It is interesting to note that, when there are calls for more Aboriginal cultural content, the content alluded to is "traditional" Aboriginal culture. This being the case, what emerges in terms of educational curricula, justice interventions, and social services are values, practices, and symbols from precolonial times. There would appear to be no clearly defined present "cultural identity" to guide the process. For this reason, we question the basic underlying assumption of a cultural mismatch.

There is an aspect of cultural mismatch theory with which we entirely agree: Canadian society does have a clearly defined cultural identity rooted in the ideal of meritocracy, and imposing that identity on Aboriginal groups would indeed be inappropriate. We argue that it is not cultural differences or mismatches per se but, rather, the clarity of a modern cultural identity along with the existing normative structure in Aboriginal communities that needs to be addressed. Given the underappreciated role of current cultural identity and normative challenges, we argue that even culturally relevant programs will not succeed.

We are not in any way minimizing the reality or importance of cultural differences between Aboriginal culture and so-called non-Aboriginal culture. Indeed, there are equally important cultural differences among First Nations, Inuit, and Métis peoples. Just as there are cultural differences among First Nations groups, among Inuit from different regions, and among concentrations of Métis people. These cultural differences need to be respected.

But these cultural differences, as real and as important as they are, are not the only, or indeed the major, barrier to constructive interventions in Aboriginal communities. Rather, we argue, it is the 20–80 normative structure that needs to be addressed. Even in a healthy 80–20 structure maintaining an effectively functioning community is a challenge. Even with only 20 percent to rehabilitate, and with the full support of the functioning 80 percent, healthy communities invest significant human and financial resources in maintaining a healthy 80–20 balance. When a community is struggling with a 20–80 normative structure, the usual strategies simply will not work.

## TOWARDS A SOLUTION TO A 20–80 NORMATIVE STRUCTURE

The normative challenge that we describe is a daunting one, which perhaps explains why so many non-Aboriginal, and indeed traditional Aboriginal, interventions have been less than successful. Our normative analysis suggests where the beginnings of a solution might lie, but we need to underscore that what we propose is a framework for social change, not social change itself, with its accompanying cultural content. In other words, our focus is on the "how," not on the "what." We are not making recommendations about what values, priorities, goals, or lifestyles communities should adopt. These are rightly the exclusive responsibility of Aboriginal communities themselves. Rather, we are offering suggestions about how communities might stimulate change. These suggestions arise from a normative analysis, the genesis of which was stimulated by concerns that have been voiced by Aboriginal peoples across the country.

In non-Aboriginal society, the primary goal is to maintain an 80–20 normative structure. The non-normative 20 percent are routinely targeted to ensure that, at least, the percentage does not rise and, at best, that it is reduced. Such a maintenance process is challenging enough. For Aboriginal communities the objective is not one of maintenance but, rather, one of reversing a well entrenched set of dysfunctional norms.

While in a functional community the focus is on the 20 percent who are dysfunctional, in non-functional communities the focus, at least with regard to instigating social change, is on the 20 percent who are not dysfunctional. The functioning 20 percent in a dysfunctional community are pivotal in that they are the individuals who must instigate the monumental task of reversing a well-entrenched set of community norms. The first step is to identify and regroup those 20 percent of individuals who personify the desired set of new norms. The task of identification and regrouping is a difficult one since these individuals will not be found within one organization or strata of the community. The fully functional minority, precisely because of their non-normativeness, are not likely to maintain a high community profile. Indeed, they will usually do all they can to appear as if they adhere to the norms of the community. After all, on First Nations reserves and in remote Inuit communities leaving the community is not a realistic option since it requires abandoning family, friends, and a place that has served as the individual's point of reference for her or his entire life. Nevertheless, some do leave to pursue what they believe to be a more functional lifestyle, and often they work for the betterment of their communities from afar. But these individuals are critical members of their community's functioning minority and are, for the most part, lost to the mission of reshaping the normative structure of that community.

Unequivocal support for the functional minority in the community could, of course, come from non-Aboriginal institutions and the non-Aboriginal public at large since both espouse precisely the same norms. Unfortunately, a history of broken promises renders this possibility tenuous at best. Indeed, any demonstrable support could well backfire since it would be viewed as non-Aboriginal society imposing its will on Aboriginal communities. Such feelings are only to be expected from communities who have fought against a long history of colonialist policies directed at their assimilation.

As mentioned above, because fully functional individuals are sprinkled throughout all strata of Aboriginal communities, are motivated to maintain a low profile, and, indeed, may even have left the community, they are very difficult to identify and regroup. And even if key individuals can be successfully identified, getting them to agree to group together in order to redefine the norms of their community will be monumentally difficult. The task of identification and regrouping does have one factor on its side: communities have begun to talk more openly about the social problems they confront. Until recently, communities tended not to acknowledge the scope of their own problems. Non-Aboriginal institutions played a pivotal role in this denial process by placing themselves in a no-win situation. On the one hand, there was some recognition by non-Aboriginal people that the social problems in Aboriginal communities have their roots in failed colonialist policies that features blatant discrimination and assimilation. On the other hand, for non-Aboriginal institutions to make public pronouncements on the scope of the social problems in Aboriginal communities would appear as discriminatory in and of itself. This conspiracy of silence is slowly being broken as Aboriginal communities come to grips with the reality of their own past, and non-Aboriginal institutions are forced to confront their own role in the colonialist process.

Finally, the targeting of the "functioning" 20 percent is made more complex by the fact that individuals may be part of the 80 percent in one domain but squarely in the 20 percent in another. Initially, this might seem encouraging since the task is limited to identifying members of the functioning 20 percent in the particular domain that the community has chosen as its focus. But, as we noted earlier, there are some non-normative behaviours that tend to extend to most, if not all, other domains. In terms of domain specificity, we all know the family member who needs inordinate support but who has wonderful interpersonal qualities, or the unorganized, unpunctual co-worker who has amazing problem-solving skills. Unfortunately, many of the problems confronting Aboriginal communities extend into other domains. Problems with alcohol and drugs, or academic underachievement and underemployment, or indeed chronic malnourishment cut across all life domains. This harsh reality, however, is offset by our own personal experience in Aboriginal communities. An individual may have regular bouts with alcohol – bouts that affect both her/his family life and work efficiency. At other times, however, this same individual may well be a fully functioning constructive force. Not only might such individuals be able to contribute to constructive social change, but they might also serve as more realistic role models for those in the community who are pessimistic about their ability to change their own lives.

While it remains a daunting task at the community level, it is at least possible to think about identifying and regrouping a small minority of community members who might be willing to spearhead social change. Once the 20 percent is identified and regrouped, their main challenge would be to alter the norms of the 80 percent. Their goal would be to, over time, increase the number of well-functioning individuals beyond 20 percent, thereby reducing the number of people who fall into the dysfunctional 80 percent. The ideal would be a reversal of the 20–80 structure.

# 7

# Towards Constructive Social Change
# in Aboriginal Communities: Minority Influence

It has taken six chapters to document our theory regarding the challenges confronting Aboriginal communities. It has been a depressing journey. From colonization to collective self-control, a cultural identity vacuum and a 20–80 normative structure, it has become abundantly clear why over one hundred years of well- and not so well-intentioned interventions have fallen short. At this point, constructive change might look to be as difficult as trying to make a river flow back up a mountain.

We embarked on this journey with a simple philosophy: any strategy for constructive social change requires, first and foremost, *understanding* the root of the challenge. Our analysis uncovers profound social and psychological challenges that need to be addressed, and it enables us to appreciate why, to date, no meaningful, constructive change has been possible. There is no simple cultural mismatch that requires culturally relevant solutions. And there is certainly no room for clichés: "Why don't they just stop being lazy?" "Can't they see that booze is ruining their lives?" We cringe every time someone says: "Why don't they just ____?" There is no simple "just"; rather, there are normative structures, cultural identity, and collective self-control issues that require us to think differently. And that is precisely our mission here and in the chapters to follow.

Our intention is not only to appreciate the magnitude of the challenges but also to seek realistic and targeted solutions. Our solutions are targeted in that they are rooted in the specific social and psychological challenges discussed earlier. And, again, we need to emphasize that what we propose is a theoretical framework for social change, not the actual cultural content of that change.

In the next three chapters we propose three interrelated tools for addressing the challenges confronting Aboriginal communities. In this chapter we discuss the social psychology of minority influence. We argue that there is a minority of Aboriginal people in each community, the 20 percent, who have the psychological resources to potentially reverse the current normative structure. Understanding the functioning of minority influence will provide us with the guiding principles for constructive social change. In Chapter 8 we examine "zero tolerance." We argue that zero tolerance is a misunderstood policy and that, if applied correctly, it may provide a mechanism for changing entrenched destructive norms. In Chapter 9 we discuss a concrete community-based process that makes use of survey research. Because a survey research instrument can, under special circumstances, involve sampling every member of a community, and because there is the potential for in-depth feedback, we believe that, through its use, it is possible to instigate constructive, and indeed revolutionary, social change in very dysfunctional communities. In these three chapters, we argue that if we apply these interventions it is possible to reverse the current normative structure in Aboriginal communities.

MINORITY INFLUENCE

How do each of us, as individuals, know what to think, how to feel, and how to behave, or at least how we are supposed to think, feel, and behave? The physical environment offers few answers, except perhaps when to dress warmly, when to put on sunscreen, or when to avoid crossing a busy street. When it comes to important matters – our values, beliefs, and, indeed, our entire worldview – the only source of information is *other people*. Other people are our only source of information for answers to life's basic, and not so basic, questions. They, especially those who are members of our primary social groups, not only provide a source of information but also satisfy our need for affiliation. Humans are, after all, social animals, which is to say we need to have relationships with others, to connect, to belong. Most theorists describe humans as having two fundamental needs: "to get along and to get ahead." Our need for relationships with others gives others inordinate power over us. Because we need others, their values, beliefs, and norms matter to us. The more we conform to these, the more likely it is that we will be accepted and liked.

This does not mean that we blindly follow what others prescribe. But knowing what they prescribe certainly informs us of the consequences if we don't follow their agreed-upon judgments, their norms. And these consequences are not trivial. The group can pressure an individual to either get back in line or else face mockery, derision, and, ultimately, banishment from the group. Ask any high school student what it is like to be ostracized from a clique. The group can place inordinate pressure on us because it is the source of the information and affiliation that we need to successfully navigate our social environment.

We refer to a functioning community as being 80–20, where 80 percent follow the prescriptive norms of the group. The 20 percent who know the prescriptions but do not follow them come under tremendous pressure to become like the 80 percent. But there are always exceptions, and sometimes these exceptions lead us to ask: "Given the power of majority influence, how does it come about that sometimes the one influences the many?" How did Jesus, Gandhi, Martin Luther King, Nelson Mandela, and Hitler manage to change the thoughts, feelings, and actions of the majority? Admittedly they weren't working alone, but certainly it was a small minority who ultimately managed to change the majority.

These exceptions to the pervasive power of majority influence point to possibilities with regard to the challenges confronting Aboriginal communities. We describe Aboriginal communities as the inverse of the usual 80–20 normative structure. In functioning communities the majority 80 percent influences the minority 20 percent. How might it be possible for an Aboriginal community to have its 20 percent influence its 80 percent? How a minority in a community can influence a majority has become the focus of theory and research for a number of social psychologists. Their insights may well offer strategies for minorities in Aboriginal communities.

In non-Aboriginal societies the focus is usually on how the majority can influence the minority. At the heart of this process is what scientists refer to as "normative influence." Normative influence is a process whereby large numbers of people who share a common view regarding what feelings, thoughts, and actions are appropriate are able to influence the minority into conforming to their norms. For example, parents of teenagers worry constantly about peer pressure – that is, they worry that their teenager will not be able to resist the pressures from other teens to engage in undesirable behaviour. This worry is genuine because, when a majority attempts to influence a minority, the majority has tremendous power. The majority has the power to define the norms and, subsequently, to reward or punish every individual member of the group. The majority, then, has control over the feelings, thoughts, and behaviours of the entire group.

While majority influence is governed by the power of numbers, minority influence is governed by something else. Since the minority does not have the power of numbers they cannot force compliance on the majority. Consequently, the challenges faced by the 20 percent are daunting: not only must they resist the norms defined by the majority 80 percent but they must also find a way to influence the majority so that they change those norms. Research suggests that it is possible for a minority to influence the majority, but only under very specific circumstances. Here we discuss both majority and minority influence. We pay greater attention to the latter since it is the process that will be at the forefront of constructive social change in Aboriginal communities.

We begin our analysis with the "power of numbers" and discuss the research on the well-known and well-researched processes involved in majority influence. This positions us to define, describe, and appreciate minority influence and how it may be distinguished from majority influence. Applying the insights gained from looking at both majority and minority influence, we attempt to describe the concrete steps that Aboriginal communities need to take in order to transform their 20–80 normative structure into a constructive 80–20 structure of their choosing.

## THE PROCESS OF MAJORITY INFLUENCE

Norms are socially defined rules pertaining to what constitutes appropriate feelings, thoughts, and behaviour, and they clearly link social consensus to the definition of normal. Norms operate for every group, from the smallest to the largest. Thus, at one extreme, a couple may have their own norms involving pet names for each other and implicit rules about how often and when they should phone or text each other. At the opposite extreme, some norms apply universally. The norm of reciprocity, or turn-taking in informal conversations, may apply to all human interaction across all cultures. Every group operates with its own norms and, presumably, these group-based norms are designed, among other things, to support the group in the pursuit of its goals. For a company the norms may be designed to produce widgets, for the sports team they would be designed to win games, and for communities they would be designed to guide the community in providing a safe environment for members and the opportunity for them to actualize their full potential.

At this stage we need to make a distinction between two types of norms: descriptive and injunctive (Cialdini 2003; Cialdini, Kallgren, and Reno 1991; Miller and Prentice 1996). Descriptive norms involve the actual thoughts, feelings, and behaviours of the vast majority of group members. Injunctive norms refer to those thoughts, feelings, and behaviours that a group designates as highly desirable or ideal. Descriptive norms are what we as members of a group *actually* do, whereas injunctive norms are what we as members of a group *should* do. Both types of norms exert a strong influence on the behaviour of individual group members, although their relative domain of influence continues to be debated. Often descriptive norms and injunctive norms are mutually reinforcing: imagine a company whose injunctive norms support the value that "the customer is always right" and whose employees' actual normative behaviour is consistent with this. At times, of course, there will be a disconnect: the company's injunctive norms may specify behaviours that support the "customer is always right" value while the actual normative behaviour of employees supports a "maximize profit" value. The influence of norms on the individual will be maximized, of course, when the injunctive and descriptive norms are one and the same: a community whose members adhere to behaviours associated with maximizing the quality of life for all its members and who actually follow through with behaviours that are consistent with this will no doubt be a healthy community.

Both injunctive and descriptive norms place inordinate influence on the behaviour of individual group members. Thus, as our discussion of social influence unfolds, it may not always be necessary to distinguish between the two types of norms. However, at certain critical points in our analysis of norms in Aboriginal communities, the distinction between injunctive and descriptive norms will prove to be quite useful.

When the majority of group members adhere to a norm, be it injunctive or descriptive, this majority exerts inordinate control over individual members of a group. This is why theorists label this concept "majority influence." Majority influence is well illustrated by how easily individuals may be controlled by peer pressure. People tend to comply with the majority because they fear the negative consequences of non-compliance. Indeed, ignoring social norms can be costly in terms of popularity with other group members, and serious norm transgressions may well lead to exclusion from the group. Thus, out of fear of being rejected, individuals often prefer to change their attitudes and to comply with existing social norms. For example, many of us have experienced a situation in which we agreed publicly with a group even though we had, at first, disagreed with it. From everyday interactions, such as choosing where to eat with friends, to more important ones, such as selecting a new employee, we have all, at one point or another, complied with the majority in order to avoid negative repercussions.

The psychological experiment that pioneered the study of majority influence was conducted by R.L. Thorndike (1938). In his study, six students were assigned to participate in a group exercise that required them to arrive at a consensus in terms of their collective answer to a question posed by the experimenter. Each question had two possible answers. One question asked the six participants to "determine which of two newspaper headlines ha[d] the greatest social significance." Participants were individually asked their opinion regarding the question before they were placed in the group. Group cohesion was then measured after the group had discussed the question and arrived at a group decision. The results indicated that, within the group, the greater the number of students who agreed with the same answer, the more influence they exerted on the remaining students. The study was even able to predict the probability that an individual student would conform to the majority's answer to the question. It was estimated that, in a situation in which there was only one student who disagreed with the majority, there would be a 42.9 percent chance that the minority would be influenced by the majority. These results were the first to demonstrate the inordinate power of social influence.

The more well known, classic social psychology experiment by Solomon Asch (1955) offers an even more striking illustration of how much power the majority has over the minority. Asch's experiment demonstrates that, even when most members of a group make a clearly defined error in judgment, the members of the minority will still yield to the majority even though their common sense tells them to do otherwise. Specifically, with the help of students who were accomplices of the experimenter, "real" students participating in the experiment were asked to judge the similarities and differences in the lengths of different lines on a large wall-board. In the experiment, the accomplices, one after another, and upon instructions from the experimenter, firmly stated that two lines were of the same length, even though they were clearly and objectively very different. Although the disparity between the lines was blatant, the true participant in the experiment, who always answered last, was inclined to endorse the faulty responses of the majority. These results confirm, in a dramatic fashion, what Thorndike observed a decade earlier. From the results of Asch's experiment, it was clear that participants tend to conform by giving the same answers as the majority, even if the latter is clearly wrong. An unambiguous task, such as the one employed in Asch's experiment, points to an important group phenomenon: members of a group expect unanimity among all group members. Thus, when the majority of group members form a judgment about any issue, the minority of dissenting group members are under inordinate pressure to conform to the majority (Maass and Clark 1984).

Stanford Prison Experiment

Another dramatic experiment that demonstrates the power of majority influence is Zimbardo's (1982) famous prison experiment. His focus is on the extent to which individuals will conform to the normative expectations for those group members who occupy a specific role defined by the group. In Zimbardo's experiment, two groups were formed from a randomly selected sample of psychologically healthy undergraduate students. One group played the role of "prisoners" and the other the role of "prison guards." On the first day of the experiment, students assigned to the role of prisoner were arrested unexpectedly at their homes on suspicion of burglary or armed robbery. An officer advised them of their rights, handcuffed them, seated them in the rear of a police car, and drove them to the police station. Once at the police station, they were fingerprinted, a file was opened, and they were held in a detention cell. They remained in the cell until one of the experimenters blindfolded them and brought them to the mock prison in the basement of the university.

The prison used in this experiment was in the basement of Stanford's psychology building. The doors of the classrooms were removed and replaced with barred doors. The only furniture provided in the cell for each prisoner was a cot. A closet off the hallway was used as a cell for solitary confinement. Several rooms in the basement served as the guards' quarters. Once they arrived at the mock prison, the prisoners were ordered to strip in order to be sprayed with disinfectant. Afterwards, they were left naked for some time in a secluded room. Then they were given uniforms, identification pictures were taken, and they were escorted to their cells where they were ordered to remain silent. The guards, for their part, were summoned to an orientation meeting the day before the prisoners were arrested. Their assigned task was simply to "maintain a reasonable degree of order within the prison necessary for its effective functioning." No specific details were given regarding how their task was to be performed.

As soon as the experiment began, the members of each group, the guards and the prisoners, conformed to the norms for their respective roles. In fact, participants initially spent 90 percent of their time talking to each other about their group, clearly indicating the focus of their preoccupation. The pressure to show solidarity with their own group was so strong that each day the guards would try to generate new methods for affronting and harassing the prisoners regardless of how distressed the latter seemed to be. The prisoners, for their part, were more and more resistant to the guards' orders and became more and more depressed. The power of the norms for the members of the two roles was so strong that the researcher had to abort the experiment after a few days because it was becoming dangerous, both physically and psychologically, for the prisoners.

The results of this experiment clearly demonstrate that the norms associated with a role are a powerful determinant of behaviour. Here we have psychologically well-adjusted students randomly assigned to be either guards or prisoners, and the normative demands are so strong that they start behaving in ways that they would never have dreamed possible – to the point that the experiment had to be terminated for safety reasons.

Another classic case, when it comes to majority influence, is the famous conformity to authority experiments that were conducted by Milgram (1963). Following the Second World War, Milgram was distressed by the events associated with the rise of Nazi Germany, which he found to be incredible. How could one man, in conjunction with a few other top officials, induce so many to engage in atrocious behaviours that they would never consider performing under normal circumstances. Thus, he designed a simple experiment that was conducted at Yale, a reputable and prestigious university. Milgram engaged a thirty-year-old high school biology teacher to serve as an accomplice. The accomplice dressed formally and played the role of an "experimenter" who used his authority to influence another person to conform to his will. With the help of another accomplice, who played the role of a "student," the stage was set for the "experimenter" to test the power of authority to induce conformity.

When the real student participant arrived, it was explained that he would be playing the role of "teacher" in the experiment. It was further explained that students can learn effectively either by being rewarded for correct answers or by being punished for incorrect answers. So the real participant's task was, in his role as teacher, to ask a series of questions provided by the experimenter to the "student" seated in another room. If the student did not give the correct answer, the teacher was to administer an electric shock that would vary from "slight shock" to "moderate shock" to "danger: severe shock." The real participant was required to deliver a shock for each wrong answer, and the strength of the shock was to increase for each successive wrong answer. When stronger shocks were given, the student was in another room so the teacher was left to imagine the pain he was delivering to him. If the teacher questioned the experimenter about the possibility of stopping the experiment, he was simply told: "This is a scientific experiment, please continue."

Sixty-five percent of the participants in the experiment continued administering severe shocks to the student. If the shocks had been real, which for ethical reasons they were not, they may well have been lethal. Why did the participants conform to the experimenter's request, which required them to engage in behaviour that went against any reasonable person's definition of rational and moral behaviour? They didn't conform because the experimenter had the physical capacity to force them to administer shocks. Nor did they conform because a majority of their peers were pressuring them to administer shocks. They conformed because a legitimate authority, a scientist, was asking them to deliver shocks. Participants reasoned as follows: "No legitimate scientist would ever ask me to do something wrong, therefore there must be an important reason I am being asked to do this." And, of course, this is precisely the power of authority. When a group decides to place someone in a position of authority, then that person personifies the views of the entire group and thus speaks for the entire group. This is the ultimate in majority influence.

Recently, in quite a different context, social psychologists have reaffirmed the power of majority social influence to bring about behavioural change. Goldstein, Cialdini, and Griskevicius (2008) were confronted with a conundrum faced by major hotel chains across

North America. The hotels were anxious to be seen as contributing to a pro-environmental movement. Hotel management began by placing cards in the bathrooms of every hotel room encouraging guests to recycle their bath towels in order to reduce the amount of pollutants released into the environment. Although everyone claims that they support protecting the environment, very few guests bothered to recycle their towels.

Goldstein and his colleagues devised an experiment to get to the heart of the matter. They composed five different cards for the bathroom, all identical in size and format. All the cards asked guests to recycle their towels for the sake of the environment, but the message varied in terms of the inducement. On one card, the message was "Help save the environment" (Goldstein, Cialdini, and Griskevicius 2008, 476) and did not refer to any specific group. Critical for our focus on majority influence, one card noted: "Join your fellow guests in helping to save the environment ... 75 percent of the guests participated in our new resource savings program by using their towels more than once" (ibid.). Another card added: "75 percent of the guests who stayed in this room ... participated in our new resource savings program by using their towels more than once" (ibid.). The cards were then placed randomly throughout the rooms of a well-known hotel chain and the researchers kept careful records of the number of towels that were recycled.

The results were compelling. The card representing a standard environmental message had only a modest effect. However, the two normative cards, especially the one suggesting that 75 percent of the guests in *your room* had recycled, had a major impact: normative pressure, especially specific normative pressure (i.e., people just like you who stayed in your room), was powerful enough to change behaviour. These were the guests who actually recycled their towels.

Together, these experiments demonstrate the power of majority social influence in terms of placing pressure on an individual to conform to group norms. The power of the majority arises because individuals depend on the opinions of others, first, as a source of information and, second, as fulfilling their need to belong. The majority can indeed induce inordinate influence on the minority.

As we indicate in Chapter 6, every community aims to have 100 percent of its members conform to its constructive norms. No community actually reaches the 100 percent ideal, but if 80 percent are following the norms a community will function very effectively. If the

80 percent drops to 75 percent or 70 percent, with a corresponding rise in the percentage of those not following the norms, the community's effectiveness will be seriously compromised. In terms of majority influence, then, the 80 percent majority need to influence the non-normative 20 percent. The situation in Aboriginal communities is the inverse of what is experienced in most non-Aboriginal communities. Instead of being 80–20, Aboriginal communities can be characterized as 20–80. Aboriginal communities, then, do not have the luxury of being able to rely on the power of numbers to influence those few in the community who are not being productive members. Normative structures in Aboriginal communities are dysfunctional, and, thus, majority influence serves merely to exacerbate ongoing dysfunctional behaviours.

In these circumstances there are no clearly defined functional norms to guide individual behaviour. To take one simple example, even if school is scheduled to begin at 9:00 AM, it is not uncommon to find teachers arriving late, and students will frequently come late, if they come at all. Since the majority of students do not arrive at school on time, there are no clear norms in terms of punctuality. If a student is tired, it is normative to remain in bed for a few more hours and come to school late. This will not be easy to change. If the majority affects the minority, then it is the late, unpunctual students who establish the norm. Students will be guided by that norm and may well be held up to ridicule if they tend to be punctual. If punctuality is important for an Aboriginal community, we need to find a way for the minority of punctual students to defy the power of majority influence and somehow find a way to change the behaviour of the majority.

## THE PROCESS OF MINORITY INFLUENCE

Minority influence refers to the process by which a small number of people somehow convince the majority to change their normative behaviour. Given the demonstrated power of majority influence, minority influence is a daunting task. In the case of Aboriginal communities, what chance do the 20 percent have of dramatically changing the 80 percent? While the majority retains the benefit of numbers, the minority must resort to other strategies in order to have any hope of being influential. Research in social psychology demonstrates, interestingly, that it may indeed be possible for a minority to exert control over the numerically powerful majority. But only under very specific conditions.

One of the first experiments designed to demonstrate that minority influence is at least possible was conducted by Moscovici, Lage, and Naffrechoux (1969). Building on the famous Asch experiments, participants in Moscovici's experiments were shown an unambiguous physical stimulus. Each participant had to decide whether two slides were the same colour or not. In the context of this experiment there were two blue slides that only differed in their luminosity. The minority was comprised of two individuals (accomplices of the experimenter), and the majority was made up of four naïve participants. Although the two slides were clearly the same colour, the minority insisted that one was blue and the other green. The confidence and determination with which the minority presented their objectively "wrong" view influenced both the public and private responses of the majority. But if the minority were at all inconsistent in their responses, only modest influence on the majority was observed.

Clearly, in order to have an impact, a minority must be unanimous and determined. These results stimulated Moscovici and his colleagues to develop a two-step model of minority influence. In order for a minority to have an influence on the majority, they argue that: (1) the minority must induce a conflict (i.e., the minority must seriously question the norms of the majority with a convincing argument), and (2) the minority must be consistent, unanimous, and propose an alternative norm. Accordingly, the minority must be self-assured and consistent in its arguments in order to be persuasive. Even if people might doubt the value of the minority's responses at first, if the minority appears committed and convinced and is persistent in its discourse, the majority will begin to consider its point of view and eventually realize that the voice of the minority may contain a kernel of truth.

These initial experiments motivated follow-ups. In one experiment by Nemeth and Wachtler (1974), participants were seated around a table and asked to arrive at a consensus on a question concerning a case study they had read prior to the beginning of the session. It was observed that the minority had more influence when sitting at the head of the table rather than along either of its sides. Clearly, any act demonstrating confidence, including taking the seat of status at the table, coupled with maintaining a consensual confidence in opinion, will help the minority ultimately have an effect on the majority.

Hence, even though projecting strong convictions is crucial to influencing the majority, combining this with an authoritative action has greater success when trying to sway the majority towards the minority's point of view.

Media solution

Convincing the majority is no easy task. Face-to-face interaction, involving confederates of the experimenter, has yielded some positive results, but only in laboratory experiments in which the variables were tightly controlled. More recently, a ground-breaking field study conducted in Rwanda has shed some light on how community-wide attitudes and norms might be changed. Following the Rwandan genocide in 1994, the Tutsi population was nearly eradicated (75 percent were massacred in three months) and today it stands at 15 percent compared to 84 percent for the Hutu population. Even though these events occurred more than a decade ago, negative intergroup attitudes are, not surprisingly, still widespread. Paluck (2009) investigates the power of the media to influence reconciliation between the two populations. Specifically, the study explores whether a radio soap opera aimed at promoting values of reconciliation might have an impact on the majority of the population, which were not showing any interest in changing their attitudes. In Rwanda the radio is a major means of mass communication, and it is common for groups to gather around and listen to it. Interestingly, in Aboriginal communities it is FM radio that is the main vehicle for the sharing of information.

In her study, Paluck capitalizes on the importance of the radio and the popularity of its soap operas. She organized two groups of Rwandans, matched on a number of demographic variables, who were presented two different radio soap operas once a week over the course of twenty episodes throughout a one-year period. One soap opera focused on health issues (control group) and the other on the topic of reconciliation (the experimental group). It was observed that the radio program aimed at reconciliation did indeed have an influence on the majority attitudes in the community. The soap opera did not affect their personal beliefs about the group, but it did lead them to perceive the importance of having a norm that consisted of more positive intergroup attitudes. The fact that the media, through a popular soap opera, could modify people's perceptions, moving them in the direction of a more constructive norm, is instructive. In Aboriginal communities the challenge is how to dramatically change norms, and Paluck's study offers potentially important possibilities for meeting this challenge. Since it is such a difficult task to find effective ways for a small group of people, a "normative" minority, to have an influence on a dysfunctional majority, the use of the media – specifically, the creative use of popular programming – may be usefully applied in Aboriginal communities.

In a similar vein, Aarts and Dijksterhuis (2003) conducted a series of studies whose aim was to explore the role that the social environment might play in pressuring people to conform to social norms. To assess the power of situational norms, the experimenters chose environments that have rather strict behavioural norms, such as dressing formally in high-end restaurants and being quiet in a library. Their results demonstrate that the strictly defined norms for these situations are followed by virtually everyone. Minorities, challenged to change the behaviour of a majority, might well capitalize on such situational norms. Applying these findings to the challenges faced by a minority of Aboriginal members of a community might be useful. For example, luring community members into the school, church, or hospital, under any pretext, may pressure them to adhere to the powerful norms associated with these places.

Nevertheless, the minority 20 percent still does not have the benefit of numerical superiority and, thus must be especially vigilant in sending a well-formulated message that is simple and consistent. By comparison, majority members can afford to be inconsistent yet still exercise considerable influence on a minority. Because of their numerical superiority, the majority are often perceived as doing things the "right" way, regardless of the flaws, inconsistencies, and vagaries in their definition of "right." In fact, it is compelling for any of us to believe that if the vast majority supports something, they must be right. After all, "how could so many people be wrong?" In Aboriginal communities some leaders exacerbate this issue. As we noted, in a difficult 20–80 situation, dysfunction will be found at all levels, including among the formal leadership. This is especially problematic given the broad influence that their persona carries.

Thus, in order to be persuasive, the minority must be doggedly vocal, self-assured, and consistent in their argument. Faced with such a determined minority, the majority, while not under numerical pressure to comply, may begin to engage in what theorists label a "validation" process. The validation process is initiated when members of the majority 80 percent, as a group, begin to question and perhaps even doubt their own view. This self-reflection or validation process may gradually move majority group members, one at a time, towards the minority position (Moscovici et al. 1994).

The validation process (Moscovici et al. 1994) provoked by minority influence may be extremely difficult, but when it succeeds, it stimulates genuine attitudinal and social changes. That is to say, the changes are not a matter of mere superficial compliance in the face of overwhelming numbers, as is the case with regard to majority influence, but, rather, a genuine internalization of change. Once the validation process is set in motion majority group members will be motivated to carefully review their position compared to that advocated by the minority. The result is that more divergent and creative thinking will be stimulated (Mucchi-Faina, Mass, and Volpato 1991; Peterson and Nemeth 1996). Even if the minority's position is not immediately and automatically adopted, critical thinking may be activated and a careful review of alternatives may be considered. For example, if the 20 percent is sufficiently consistent and self-confident in arguing that education is necessary for children, it is possible that parents will begin to insist that their children attend school faithfully and take their learning seriously. Minority influence, lacking the power of numbers, has no guarantee of success. But when successful, the changes it promotes will, more often than not, be internalized and long-term.

We can gain a deeper appreciation for the validation process by considering our earlier distinction between injunctive and descriptive norms. Injunctive norms specify what group members *should* do, while descriptive norms specify what group members *actually* do. Now, the fact that injunctive norms focus on what members of a group "should" do means that they have a moral overtone. "Should" implies what is right or correct, which implies a moral authority that is absent from the definition of descriptive norms.

So the 20 percent minority may lack the power of numbers, but they are confronting the majority 80 percent with injunctive norms, and the moral overtones associated with them, with which the latter already agrees. The majority in an Aboriginal community face a normative disconnect: they endorse the injunctive, morally correct functional community norms, but, they actually behave in a normatively dysfunctional manner that is consistent with their descriptive norms.

Thus, our functioning minority 20 percent do have some leverage when challenging the majority 80 percent. They are asking the 80 percent to change their behaviour in a direction with which, at least at the injunctive level, they already concur. The majority, then, is being asked to engage in constructive behaviours, including healthy eating,

modest alcohol consumption, and gainful employment. The problem, of course, is that their descriptive norms are at odds with their
injunctive norms.

We have characterized the challenge in Aboriginal communities as
one involving a minority 20 percent of functioning community members converting a 20–80 normative structure into a functional 80–20
normative structure. Another way of characterizing this challenge is
to say that the minority 20 percent must convert the community's
injunctive norms into descriptive norms.

Despite the overwhelming challenge facing the minority 20 percent, there are, fortunately, historical examples to offer some hope and
guidance. A classic example that has all the elements we have underscored for Aboriginal communities is the Civil Rights Movement in
the United States, which set in motion a new epoch in race relations.

Until the late 1950s, the descriptive norms in the United States
involved mainstream (white) Americans and American institutions
systemically discriminating against African Americans. Meanwhile,
the injunctive norms for non-Aboriginal (white) Americans centred
on freedom and equality for all Americans.

How would African Americans, who represented but 10 percent of
the American population, influence the vast majority of Americans to
apply freedom and equality to them? Using non-violent protest, Martin Luther King implemented the minority influence processes we are
discussing in this book. King and his collaborators preached a simple
and consensual message: "I still have a dream. It is a dream deeply
rooted in the American dream. I have a dream that one day this
nation will rise up, live out the true meaning of its creed: we hold
these truths to be self-evident, that all men are created equal" (King Jr.
1963). The key sentence from a validation perspective is: "It is a dream
rooted in the American dream." King is reminding the majority 80
percent of white Americans that "all men are created equal" is central
to their own injunctive norms. So, even though civil rights leaders
were in the minority, and did not enjoy enough numbers to influence
the majority, they were in a position to challenge the majority with
the latter's own injunctive norms.

A parallel configuration in Aboriginal communities offers some
hope for the 20 percent minority. The functioning 20 percent are
attempting to persuade the 80 percent to adopt a new, functional set
of norms. The 20 percent do not have the power of numbers, but their
message may well stimulate the potential for change because the

majority's injunctive norms are in agreement with it. Community leaders are speaking publicly about the need for change and are, in essence, saying: "we need to convert our injunctive norms into descriptive ones; we need to shift from behaving according to our *actual* dysfunctional norms to behaving according to our functional *should* norms." For the minority 20 percent to influence the majority 80 percent is an enormous challenge, but the task is eased by the fact that their message is consistent with the majority's injunctive norms.

## IMPLEMENTING NORMATIVE CHANGE
## THROUGH MINORITY INFLUENCE

In functional communities, the primary goal is to implement and maintain an 80–20 normative structure. Unfortunately, majority influence cannot be applied in Aboriginal communities, where the challenge is not to maintain the current normative ratio, but, rather, to reverse it.

The challenges faced by the minority who favour a more constructive lifestyle are enormous: not only must they resist the norms as defined by the majority but they must also impose their will on the majority. It is, of course, important to realize that there are countless examples of non-Aboriginal communities confronting similar 20–80 challenges. How do you convince members of a community to change their eating habits when obesity has become the norm? How do you rally a community to take drinking and driving seriously? How do you address cyber bullying? These are all examples of there being a disconnect between a community's injunctive norms and its descriptive norms. So the challenge of minority influence is one shared by Aboriginal and non-Aboriginal communities alike. Sometimes the issues are the same, sometimes they are different. And, in Aboriginal communities, sometimes the real issue is a lack of financial resources and human capital.

The question for us is how minority influence might be applied to Aboriginal communities. Here, we present what we believe to be the three steps to successfully implementing social change through minority influence: (1) identify and regroup the minority members needed to implement minority influence; (2) define constructive new community norms; and (3) take action to implement these new norms.

*Step 1: Identify and Regroup the Minority*

The first step is to regroup a minority that is willing to face the challenge of instigating normative change in their community. Despite the fact that the minority 20 percent may share opposition to existing community norms, rarely do they constitute a viable organized formal or informal subgroup. This is not surprising as they are few in number and are scattered throughout the community. Moreover, being in the minority they tend to keep a low profile as the pressures on an Aboriginal person who is non-normative are extraordinary. This is an issue we have often discussed with Aboriginal friends from a wide variety of First Nations and Inuit communities. The conclusions reveal a frightening pattern. To put it plainly, a community member can be involved with violence, abuse alcohol and drugs, and engage in reckless sexual behaviour and yet not be ostracized. However, the Aboriginal person who does not engage in these behaviours and goes on to some academic or professional success may well be made to feel unwelcome. Many, many young people who have completed their education and then returned to their community to constructively apply their skills have confided that they were unprepared for the reception they received. Again and again they report how life-long friends and even extended family members pressure them to revert to a dysfunctional lifestyle. And when they resist, they are psychologically and socially ostracized from the community. Thus, to ask reform-minded individuals to come together and define themselves as such is to ask a lot. They are being asked to become visible and publicly vocal about social issues. They are being asked to bond together for the sake of a common purpose – a purpose that transcends their individual pain and the constant threat of exclusion from their own community.

Not only must this precious minority acknowledge the gravity of the current social reality, but they must also promote new, well-defined, and targeted norms. They need to understand that the root of the problem in Aboriginal communities is collective self-control and that the only solution to it is to create a clear collective identity.

The functioning 20 percent in a dysfunctional community is pivotal in that they are the individuals who must instigate the reversal of a well-entrenched set of community norms. Thus, the first step in dealing with any dysfunctional community will be to identify and regroup the minority of individuals who personify the desired set of new norms. The task of identification and regrouping is difficult since, as we have said, these individuals are scattered throughout the community and tend to keep a low profile. Indeed, most minority members will usually do all they can to appear as though they adhere to the norms of the community. After all, on First Nations reserves and in remote Inuit communities, leaving the community is not a realistic option for most.

Nevertheless, some do leave their communities to pursue what they believe to be a more functional lifestyle. They often take up positions in major cities where they can work for government or non-government organizations dedicated to addressing the issues plaguing Aboriginal communities. They are genuinely committed to the betterment of their community, and all communities, albeit from afar. These same individuals, however, are no longer available to be among the 20 percent within their own communities who might exercise their minority influence.

Unequivocal support for the functional 20 percent minority in the community could, of course, come from non-Aboriginal institutions and the non-Aboriginal public at large since both would undoubtedly espouse non-violence along with responsible drinking, sexual behaviour, and health practices. Unfortunately, the history of broken promises has instilled in Aboriginal communities a deep mistrust and thus rendered both non-Aboriginal individuals and institutions impotent as potential constructive partners. In fact, as we have said, any demonstrable support from the non-Aboriginal community could backfire since it would be viewed as non-Aboriginals once again imposing their will on Aboriginal communities.

In order to better understand minority influence, it is important to consider certain aspects of group composition. An outgroup minority, precisely because they are an outgroup, will have little persuasive impact on majority ingroup members. This has important implications in the case of Aboriginal communities. Non-Aboriginal members of an Aboriginal community are likely to be ineffective in promoting social change because they are associated with historical conflict and are not seen as trustworthy. The challenge for non-Aboriginal advocates of social change in Aboriginal communities is how to minimize their outgroup status and to take the steps necessary to gaining the trust of Aboriginal communities.

In contrast, the 20 percent in an Aboriginal community are not an outgroup, they are a subgroup of the ingroup and thus have a better chance of instigating social change in the community. Despite being judged as non-normative, and therefore different, the 20 percent are nevertheless similar in that they share their community's cultural heritage. This similarity provides them with leverage when it comes to instigating social change. They need to highlight this similarity by using labels such as "we" and "us."

Even if key individuals can be successfully identified, it will not be easy to get them to agree to form a group for the purposes of redefining the norms of their community. These are individuals who are used to keeping a low profile, and any regrouping for the instigation of social change will expose them to alienation from their community.

The task of identification and regrouping does have one thing going for it: communities have begun to talk more openly about the social problems they are confronting. Communities are coming to grips with the reality of their past, and non-Aboriginal institutions are being forced to confront their own role and responsibility in the process.

Finally, targeting the "functioning" 20 percent is made more complex by the fact that individuals can be part of the 80 percent in one domain and part of the 20 percent in other domains. Initially, this might seem unimportant since the task is limited to identifying members of the functioning 20 percent in one particular domain chosen by the community as its primary focus. But, as we noted earlier, there are some non-normative behaviours that tend to have an impact on many domains. Unfortunately, many of the problems confronting Aboriginal communities are those that extend to other domains. Problems with alcohol and drugs, academic underachievement, unemployment, and chronic malnourishment are all cases in point. This harsh reality, however, is offset by our own personal experience in Aboriginal communities. An individual may have regular bouts with alcohol yet, most of the time, be a fully functioning constructive force. This person could be a force for social change. Not only might such individuals be genuine contributors to constructive social change, but they could also serve as realistic models for others in the community.

We conclude that, while it remains a daunting task, it is at least possible to contemplate identifying and regrouping a small minority of community members who might be willing to spearhead social change. Once the 20 percent have been identified and regrouped, their main challenge will be to alter the norms of the 80 percent.

### Step 2: Define Clear Community (Cultural) Norms and Values

Once a 20 percent functioning minority is organized, it's initial challenge will be to redefine the norms and the values that define the community. This is a pivotal step because, in order to effectively change the majority, the minority must have a clearly defined, consensual message. This step is also crucial because, as we argue in previous chapters, the need for cultural identity clarity is at the root of both collective and individual well-being. A central component of cultural identity clarity is a shared knowledge of, and commitment to, the norms and values of one's group. Aboriginal communities need to ask themselves: What are our values and long-term goals? What are the norms that support our values and long-term goals? It is not sufficient to point to destructive norms that need changing; rather, it is necessary to espouse a set of constructive values, long-term goals, and norms that will serve as the core for a positive community and cultural identity.

In terms of concrete action with regard to defining norms, values, and long-term goals, it will be necessary to convene a working group comprised of the minority 20 percent. Any attempt to define an exhaustive, all-inclusive list of values would be unrealistic. Instead, the group would need to choose a specific focus. For example, if education should be the chosen target, the working group might consult Aboriginal school teachers, parents, and elders within an education-related working group. They could meet initially to brainstorm about what would be needed in terms of defining the community's values and developing a community identity in terms of education. They might generate a preliminary list of concrete educational values, goals, and normative supportive behaviours. After having developed this preliminary list, they could meet with other community members to further solidify and clearly define the values, goals, and norms. What would be hoped for, ultimately, would be a clearly defined *short* list of what would constitute a functional and healthy set of interconnected values goals and norms in support of education. The list could then serve as the basis of a simple message that would guide the minority 20 percent as they set about to instigate constructive normative social change in their communities.

Generating a clearly defined set of values is a major challenge. However, if the exercise unfolds step by step, domain by domain, it might be manageable. Moreover, arriving at a consensus may not be overly difficult. The issues are dramatic and their constructive counterparts are easily articulated. We need to underscore, however, that the choice of domain and subsequent choices of values goals and norms is the right and prerogative of the community – in this case, the functioning 20 percent minority. Thus, we need to reiterate that the examples used here are for illustration purposes only: they are not designed to in any way suggest priorities or content.

## Step 3: Implementing Social Change

Once the regrouped minority has established the community's guiding principles, they are poised to become publicly vocal about their values, goals and norms and to begin implementing social change. At this point, they need to develop concrete ways of promoting these values, goals and norms among the majority of community members. In other words, they need to put forward a series of strategies that will be employed, separately or simultaneously, in order to instigate change. In the coming chapters, two of these strategies are proposed and discussed: zero tolerance and the use of survey research. However, it is important to note that there may be other effective strategies that could be implemented if the minority believed that they could also help to clarify the group's collective identity.

No matter how organized and committed the 20 percent minority might be, they are challenging an 80 percent majority. The minority's message is guaranteed to provoke resistance from the majority. It is important that the minority be prepared for this and not become discouraged by it. As research indicates, the first reaction of the majority will be to dismiss the minority's message. Dismissal or denial is only natural when someone is told that their behaviour is wrong. If, for example, as a shared norm the minority wants to promote the idea that parents need to pay more attention to their children, especially in terms of helping them with their school work, the majority of parents will feel doubly threatened: not only are you not a good parent but you also aren't competent enough to help your children with their school work. Such a statement will almost certainly be met with denial. However, even in the face of denial, if the minority is consistent and confident in their message, majority members may begin to doubt their own position, at which point the validation process begins.

Movement towards the minority position is assumed to depend on the behavioural style of the minority – that is, how it orchestrates its verbal and nonverbal cues in presenting its arguments. Inconsistent behaviour will fail to bring any change to the majority's attitudes and norms. For example, if the 20 percent minority are promoting the idea that education is essential for the future of Aboriginal communities but their own children are not attending school regularly, then the impact of their message is likely to be lost.

Thinking positively, what the minority is hoping for is a snowball effect. As more members of the majority defect and take on the new functional norms, the less the minority is a minority and the less the majority is a majority. Indeed, the voice of a majority member who has defected can be more persuasive than a minority voice.

CONCLUSION

Minority influence represents the first step towards constructive community change because it involves identifying the people who will regroup and begin instituting that change. This will not be an easy task, nor will it be easy for the minority to regroup and start working together towards a common goal. They will face resistance and, at times, will feel isolated from members of their own community. One hopes that, as their message begins to take hold, their challenge will become easier, and they will see real change occurring.

# 8

# Zero Tolerance

Our analysis of minority influence is designed to mobilize community action towards clearly defining a new, constructive set of values,
long-term goals, and normative behaviours. If minority mobilization
is to have any hope of success, it must have a well-articulated implementation plan to change the existing behavioural norms.

In normal circumstances, how does a community, institution, organization, or any group deal with behaviour that is inappropriate? They
punish it. Arrive late for school, you get a detention. Get caught using
drugs, you might get suspended. Engage in bullying and authorities
and parents may rally to offer counselling. Acts of violence will lead
to serious repercussions. It is quite simple: the more serious the transgression the more serious the consequence. Or, to add a touch of complexity, you make the consequence fit the nature of the transgression:
counselling is sometimes more appropriate than expulsion, and education is sometimes more constructive than a detention.

Sometimes none of this works. Sometimes the inappropriate behaviour seems to be occurring more often. Then what do you do? You
introduce a "zero tolerance" program, where the "zero" is meant to signal that a group is serious about regulating the undesirable behaviour.
Walk into most schools and the walls will be festooned with glossy
posters proclaiming: "Zero tolerance for bullying or violence or drugs
or any other frequently occurring destructive pattern of behaviour."
The problem is that zero tolerance has become a popular, overused
buzz-word, and this has often rendered the concept meaningless and
its implementation void.

So what is a genuine zero tolerance program? The concept of zero
tolerance was designed for situations in which a particular destructive

behaviour has become so prevalent that it compromises the effective functioning of the group. For example, it is designed for situations in which school violence has become so frequent and normative that no one feels safe. It is designed for situations in which drugs have become so prevalent that it renders the entire community dysfunctional. It is designed for situations in which the normal 80–20 normative structure of a functioning group is compromised. Genuine zero tolerance is contemplated when the anti-normative 20 percent rises to 30 or perhaps 40 percent. We describe Aboriginal communities as 20–80, implying that dysfunctional behaviours are so pervasive that they have become the norm. Never was there a situation more in need of the benefits that a genuine zero tolerance policy may have to offer. However, such a policy needs to be well understood and well implemented in order to be effective.

What is unique about a genuine zero tolerance program is that it violates the most fundamental principle of justice: equity (or the meritocracy). The equity (meritocracy) principle states quite simply that every person should be rewarded or punished according to his or her behaviour: the better the performance, the greater the reward; the more serious the transgression, the more negative the consequence.

In modern society there are two policies that purposely violate equity, and that is why both are so controversial. The first is "affirmative action," or its Canadian equivalent "employment equity." Women, members of identified minority groups, and certain categories of physically or mentally challenged persons will be given preference when it comes to hiring and promotion. Equity is explicitly violated since targeted group membership, rather than ability and effort (equity, meritocracy), are partial determinants of success. The rationale for violating equity is the explicit attempt to redress a legacy of systemic discrimination that has been perpetrated against members of these targeted groups, itself a violation of equity. The point is, equity is such an important and fundamental societal principle that even a rational deviation from it is bound to be controversial.

The second policy to violate equity is zero tolerance, the focus of this chapter. The violation of equity (meritocracy) in the case of zero tolerance calls for serious consequences for all, including very minor, transgressions within a designated behavioural domain: bring a potential weapon to school, be it a plastic knife or an automatic rifle, and you will be expelled. There is no attempt to apply equity in the sense that the severity of the consequence is not commensurate with the severity of the transgression. Even a minor violation results in the maximum publicly announced penalty. Like affirmative action, zero tolerance is a serious policy for serious challenges.

We contend that, if implemented correctly, zero tolerance, like "minority influence," can have a constructive impact on the normative structure of Aboriginal communities. There are two reasons for the careful analysis of zero tolerance: (1) it violates equity, which means that it is certain to be received with great scepticism; and (2) it has been evoked so frequently that its meaning and import have been lost.

Zero tolerance is defined as a "law, policy, or practice of not tolerating undesirable behavior, such as violence or illegal drug use, especially in the automatic imposition of severe penalties for first offenses" (*American Heritage Dictionary of the English Language* 2013; see also *Canadian Oxford Dictionary* 2004). Specifically, zero tolerance is the policy of applying laws or penalties to even minor infringements of a code in order to reinforce its overall importance and to enhance deterrence (*West's Encyclopedia of American Law* 2005). In the context of education and school attendance, a zero tolerance policy might dictate that all students be given the same severe punishment for being late to class, irrespective of the degree of their lateness. Thus, a student who is three minutes late would receive the same harsh punishment as a student who is two hours late.

Zero tolerance might at first glance appear draconian, especially to the vast majority of people who operate in a functioning community in which the vast majority of students are relatively punctual, with only a usual few who are habitually late. However, in a community in which 80 percent of students are always late, often very late, pedagogy grinds to a halt and desperate measures are needed. In Aboriginal communities, zero tolerance might be the only viable strategy that authorities have at their disposal to reverse a dysfunctional normative structure. Zero tolerance has proven to be very successful in similar contexts – for example, in some schools in inner cities in the United States where violence has become so prevalent that normal classroom activity has been completely compromised. What makes zero tolerance unique is its focus on norms, which is what is at the heart of our analysis of potential constructive social change in Aboriginal communities. Thus, we argue that zero tolerance represents a potentially effective tool for enabling functioning, legitimate authorities to reverse a community's dysfunctional norms. Moreover, since changing undesirable norms are at the core of zero tolerance policies, it could represent one of the first steps towards constructive social change.

We begin by describing how norms are maintained in a typical functioning community and then contrast this with the reality of Aboriginal communities. We then elaborate on the policy of zero tolerance, including how it originated, its successes, and the hard lessons learned from existing zero tolerance programs. Finally, we address how zero tolerance might be concretely applied in Aboriginal communities, using school attendance as a concrete example. Specifically, we propose four steps for successfully implementing a zero tolerance policy.

## MAINTAINING NORMS

In Chapter 7, we underscore that functioning communities operate with an 80–20 normative structure, with 80 percent adhering to community norms and 20 percent not adhering to them. Forgotten in this simple analysis, we argue, is the crucial role played by the "silent majority" (80 percent) who support and maintain the 80–20 normative structure. The 80 percent are also careful to ensure that the normative structure maximizes the chances of the community meeting its goal of offering its members the highest quality of life possible. As such, the 80 percent are constantly monitoring the normative structure to make sure it does not deteriorate to such compromising proportions such 75–25 or even worse. The 80 percent also constantly work to, if possible, increase the ratio from 80–20 to 90–10. To achieve such an objective, norms have to be clearly spelled out and well-defined. It is essential that people know how and why they have to behave in a certain way in various social contexts.

In a functioning community, there is an array of norms that touch all the dimensions of community life. Whether it is work, school, or leisure, community members must follow the norms that are promoted by the majority in order to be successful. When some people deviate from the established norms or behave in a non-functional way, the majority will refer to that norm and remind the minority to act in accordance with it. In most cases, when a minority does not act in accordance with the established norm, the consequences are proportionate to the gravity of the deviance. For example, if a student does not come on time to school for the first time, she might get an informal warning from the teacher. Usually, the student understands the message and will come to class on time the next day. If she does not, however, the next time she is late for class she might be asked to visit the principal's office. If the same student is again late another day, her parents might receive a phone call from the principal. When all of these interventions have failed, the student might get expelled for a few days. Eventually, she might even fail her school year. This pattern of increasing consequences for persistent violation of norms is how the majority makes sure that the minority "stays in line." In an 80–20 normative structure, or in a relatively successful community, this mode of functioning is usually quite efficient. So, as often happens, when a small offence occurs, the punishment associated with it is usually small and serves as a reminder of the norm, thus ensuring that the 80–20 normative structure is smoothly maintained.

However, what happens when a person engages in non-functional behaviour, such as arriving late for class, but there are no clear attendance norms? Specifically, how can functional behaviour be reinforced when most students, and even teachers, do not adhere to basic functional behaviours? These questions symbolize one of the recurrent challenges Aboriginal communities face daily in their communities. The lack of norms and support from a functional 80 percent is the most significant obstacle that these communities confront. Moreover, this is precisely why well-meaning non-Aboriginal interventions, which presume an 80–20 normative structure, are doomed to failure.

Since there are no clearly defined norms that are shared by the majority of people in the community, and no 80 percent majority to support the implementation of constructive social change, only a drastic intervention, such as zero tolerance, has any chance of succeeding. It is for this reason that we suggest that this strategy be implemented and reinforced. When only a minority of group members share clearly defined norms, the goal is to find an effective way to transfer these to the majority members. Zero tolerance represents a possible and powerful solution that may be well adapted to the reality of Aboriginal communities.

## THE ORIGINS OF ZERO TOLERANCE

Over the years, zero tolerance has become a popular label to indicate that certain behaviours are not appropriate. Rarely do people fully understand the genesis of zero tolerance as a serious policy designed for dire circumstances. Thus, people are surprised when loosely and inappropriately applied zero tolerance policies are basically ineffective.

Genuine zero tolerance originated with Wilson and Kelling's (1982) "broken window" theory. They argued: "One unrepaired broken window is a signal that no one cares, and so breaking more windows costs nothing" (30). And, further: "Serious street crime flourishes in areas in which disorderly behavior goes unchecked" (32). The key ideas for the broken window theory of crime originated in part from the results of an experiment that was conducted in 1969 by Stanford social psychologist Philip Zimbardo. In his experiment, Zimbardo arranged for a car without licence plates to be parked with its hood up in the Bronx in New York. Within a mere ten minutes, ordinary citizens began dismantling the car. Once valuable parts were taken, people passing by began to vandalize it, and within twenty-four hours it was totally destroyed (Zimbardo 2008). When a small crime goes unchecked, according to the broken window theory, this leads to more serious crimes. This is when it becomes necessary to punish even small crimes. And this requires implementing a zero tolerance policy, which means punishing both minor and major crimes equally.

The link between Zimbardo's experiment, the broken window theory, and genuine zero tolerance policies is that they all operate in circumstances in which there are no clearly defined norms and, thus, in which collective self-regulation is impossible. The second link is that they all emphasize, not severe transgressions but, rather, the smallest of norm violations. Intuitively, the tendency for policy makers is to focus on the most serious manifestations of a problem. With genuine zero tolerance, attention focuses on lesser manifestations of a problem in order to avoid their escalating into more widespread and serious transgressions (Goldstein 2001).

In terms of specific application, zero tolerance was first employed by US president Ronald Reagan's administration when it initiated the War on Drugs in the early 1980s (West's Encyclopedia of American Law 2005). Next, the actual phrase "zero tolerance" was used in the *Lexis-Nexis* national newspaper in 1983, when the US Navy reassigned forty submarine crew members for suspected substance abuse (Skiba and Peterson 1999). In 1986, zero tolerance became the actual title of a program developed by US attorney Peter Nunez to impound boats carrying drugs (Skiba 2000). By 1988, this program reached national attention, and US attorney general Edwin Meese authorized customs

*[margin handwritten note: No defined norms = of collective self-regulation]*

officials to charge, in federal court, anyone crossing borders with even the smallest amount of drugs (Henault 2001; Skiba 2000).

Following this, the Drug-Free Schools and Campuses Act, 1989, was implemented throughout the American school system. The ultimate goal was to eradicate drug and alcohol possession and their use on school grounds and college campuses. Zero tolerance policies were highly encouraged because educational agencies and institutions of higher learning were at risk of losing federal financial support if they were not applied. In sum, zero tolerance as a policy was developed in the United States and grew out of federal drug enforcement in the 1980s (Skiba and Peterson 1999).

Zero tolerance, however, really took off several years later with the Clinton administration's introduction of the Gun-Free Schools Act, 1994. This act requires that any student in possession of a weapon be expelled from school for no less than one year and be referred to either the criminal or the juvenile justice system (Skiba 2000; Skiba and Peterson 1999; Webb and Kritsonis 2006).

To appreciate the zero tolerance policy, we need to reflect on the social context in its initiation, development, and implementation. It is important to recall that zero tolerance, as a strategic intervention in schools, was first designed to counter widespread non-normative behaviour. In this context it was rare to find a student who did not carry a weapon or who did not have an alcohol or drug problem. In short, these schools were experiencing an epidemic of non-normative behaviour, and zero tolerance was applied to send the strongest possible normative message.

In these schools, where the usual 80–20 normative structure was inverted to a dysfunctional 20–80 one, the success of zero tolerance policies was almost instant. For example, in Henry Foss Senior High School in Tacoma, Washington, 133 fighting incidents were reported in 1989-90 and 195 in 1990-91 (Burke and Herbert 1996). That number was dramatically reduced to twelve reported incidents in the first semester after applying a zero tolerance policy, and it dropped to four fight-related incidents for the entire 1992-93 school year. Such dramatic success was also observed in other contexts. Litke (1996) reports the case of Lacombe Junior High School in rural Alberta, which faced a sudden and pervasive violent climate in the mid-1990s following a series of changes to its student population and its teaching and administrative personnel. Violence and bullying suddenly became a major problem, and the school successfully addressed the situation by

implementing an anti-violence program that included a zero tolerance policy for harassment, violence, and the formation of crowds.
Feda (2008, 91) reports very positive results for "the first quantitative
measures of zero tolerance policies and physical assault in an educational setting" (91). The Fedora study found a lower risk of physical
assault on educators in settings in which a zero tolerance for violence
policy was enforced. Other researchers concentrate on the effect of
zero tolerance on bullying (Twemlow et al. 2001), returning to the
broken window theory of crime, which holds that no offence, even a
minor one, will be tolerated. They distinguish their offerings from traditional zero tolerance policies because their interventions address
the cause of the behavioural disturbance as well as entailing the traditional zero tolerance consequences of immediate suspension. Thus,
the goal continues to be to address all unacceptable behaviours, but
recent recommendations for school violence prevention programs
usually emphasize the need for complex interventions that combine a
number of strategies along with a zero tolerance policy (American
Psychological Association Zero Tolerance Task Force 2008; Stader
2006).

In sum, in an environment in which violence and drugs represents
a major, pervasive, and persistent problem, zero tolerance is an effective strategy for reversing the normative structure in that it reinstates
functional norms and behaviour. What a zero tolerance policy accomplishes initially is the articulation of extremely clear guidelines and
norms: no violence, no drugs, no exceptions. As a result, students
begin to question their own and each other's behaviour and to
encourage each other not to deviate from the "new" norms. This
is precisely what happened at Henry Foss High School. Students
reminded each other and themselves of the consequences of not following the zero tolerance policy. If they got caught, the consequences
of zero tolerance outweighed the "gains" associated with their dysfunctional behaviour. A sense of community emerged from the
common goal of reducing violence and creating a new positive environment (Burke and Herbert 1996).

Zero tolerance has also been applied to some extent in Canada, but
national procedures or guidelines concerning zero tolerance policies
on drugs have never been established, largely because education is
provincially/territorially regulated. In 1993, the Safe Schools Policy on
Violence and Weapons, introduced by the Scarborough School Board
in Ontario, represented Canada's first zero tolerance policy (Lipsett

1999). According to Shannon and McCall (2000), several provinces (the Atlantic provinces and Ontario) followed suit and either recommended or required zero tolerance policies (i.e., automatic suspension for serious offences). However, the strategy has changed since then, and, in Canada, strict zero tolerance policies are no longer common official disciplinary strategies. The Ontario government put an end to its zero tolerance policy in 2007 as a result of the pressure it received following two years of student complaints to the Ontario Human Rights Commission. Many schools in Canada, especially private ones, still enforce a loosely defined zero tolerance policy on drugs, violence, and bullying.

It has been over twenty years since zero tolerance policies were introduced into the school setting, and several schools all over the United States and Canada have adopted them, citing their effectiveness (Burke and Herbert 1996; Holmes and Murrell 1995; Schreiner 1996; Skiba 2000). Certain unfortunate events, such as the 1999 Columbine massacre, have since made these policies even more socially relevant. However, even before these high-profile tragedies occurred, zero tolerance policies in schools were gradually spreading across the country, not only for weapons or drugs (Skiba 2000; Webb and Kritsonis 2006) but also for substance abuse (Kumar 1999), fighting (Petrillo 1987), uttering threats (Borsuk and Murphy 1999), and swearing (Nancrede 1998; Skiba 2000). This new policy, which punished all offences severely, took hold quickly in the 1990s and, within months, was also being used to solve various issues in other domains, including environmental pollution, trespassing, sexual harassment, racial intolerance, and homelessness (Skiba and Peterson 1999).

Given the reported successes of zero tolerance policies it is surprising that they have not been adopted everywhere. Clearly, we need to address the criticisms associated with these policies.

*Why not adopted everywhere?*

*↓ controversy*

## CONTROVERSIES SURROUNDING ZERO TOLERANCE

The media attention surrounding zero tolerance policies not only underlines its strengths but also its problems. Specifically, the implementation of zero tolerance policies received negative national media attention when seemingly "trivial" events that occurred in schools led to controversial suspensions or expulsions. For example, in Columbia, South Carolina, in October 1996, a sixth grader was suspended for bringing a steak knife to school in her lunch pail in order to cut her chicken. She noticed that she had a knife and, before using it, asked her teacher for permission. The police were called and the young girl was questioned and suspended for eleven days even though she never took the knife out of the lunch box (Skiba and Peterson 1999). Another highly publicized case occurred in Pennsylvania, where a five-year-old male kindergarten student came to school on Halloween in a firefighter costume that included a five-inch plastic axe. According to the Deer Lakes School District, the plastic axe violated the school's weapons policy and the principal called the boy's parents. This student was subsequently suspended for a day. Some controversial Canadian cases have also received media attention: near Lockeport, Nova Scotia, an eight-year-old boy from Ragged Island Elementary School was suspended for saying "bang" while pointing a breaded chicken finger at a classmate. Also in Nova Scotia, at Georges P. Vanier high school in Fall River, a snowball fight cost four students a controversial one-day suspension.

There are countless examples of bizarre school events that have led to suspensions or expulsions in the name of zero tolerance. Skiba and Peterson (1999) compiled seventeen well-documented cases that illustrate how zero tolerance may fuel controversy. Lacking a full appreciation for the appropriate context for zero tolerance, these sensational stories undermine the power of the policy. The suspensions described in these stories are interpreted by the media as ridiculous overreactions and, as a result, provoke widespread public ridicule. This negative media attention was seemingly substantiated when several cases of expelled students were brought to court. In these court cases, it was argued that the process of zero tolerance was "unfair" because it violates the fundamental societal norm of equity. Specifically, it was argued that zero tolerance is unfair because even small, and at times seemingly silly, transgressions are treated as if they are capital offences. No wonder zero tolerance policies have been so controversial. It often seems unfair to administer the same harsh punishment to someone who committed a minor offence as to someone who committed a major offence. This argument has also raised civil rights concerns (Skiba 2000). Although the goal of zero tolerance programs is to send a clear message that certain dysfunctional behaviours will not be tolerated, Skiba and Peterson (2000) argue that it is unclear whether they have been successful.

The notion that zero tolerance policies provide a carte blanche for authority figures contributes to their controversial status. There is genuine concern that zero tolerance policies enable authority figures to repress non-normative behaviours without being required to justify their subjective judgments of what constitutes an offence (Marshall 1999; Wacquant 1999). The essence of a genuine zero tolerance policy involves imposing a harsh, predetermined punishment regardless of extenuating circumstances. Most of the time controversies arise when people misunderstand the desperate context within which these policies are applied.

Does this mean that zero tolerance policies should be discredited and therefore discarded? As with any other policy, there are always two sides to consider. On the one hand, supporters of zero tolerance argue in favour of people's safety and well-being and highlight its preventative value. They believe that the implementation of zero tolerance policies guarantees equal treatment for every child. On the other hand, critics of zero tolerance argue that such inflexible disciplinary policies have detrimental results. They claim that school boards lack common sense and judgment when applying zero tolerance policies, and they cite such absurdities as a child's being expelled from school for bringing a plastic knife in her lunchbox to support their position.

## IN SUPPORT OF GENUINE ZERO TOLERANCE

Despite zero tolerance's checkered history, we believe that desperate conditions require desperate measures and so argue in favour of its implementation. Specifically, we argue that, when the culture of an institution such as a school is dysfunctional to the point at which it presents a reversed 80–20 normative structure, zero tolerance might be the only intervention that is capable of restoring a functional normative structure. From our analysis of zero tolerance in both the United States and Canada it is clear that it is inappropriate when there is no normative imbalance. However, its strong message may be precisely what is needed in environments in which the normative structure is dysfunctional.

To understand the difference between a successful and an unsuccessful application of zero tolerance we must return to the roots of the policy and remember why it was implemented in the first place. The controversies that arise from the application of zero tolerance programs within non-Aboriginal society underscore the fact that zero tolerance is an extreme intervention that can *only* be effective in the context of a reversed 80–20 normative structure. Zero tolerance is reserved for precisely those conditions that are common in Aboriginal communities, or Henry Foss High School, or the myriad inner-city communities in which conditions are desperate. In a school in which violence, bullying, and drugs are rampant, most students meet school boards' and teachers' appeals to common sense with mockery and derision. Out of fear for their safety, those few who support such measures don't dare voice it. The vast majority of students in such situations have too much invested in the existing dysfunctional normative structure. They feel in control of their environment, and several earn money and respect by taxing weaker students or selling drugs. Even those not benefitting visibly know their position in the structure and have found a quasi-comfort zone. These students have no interest in supporting change and will undermine it at every turn.

In a reversed 20–80 normative structure the application of a strict zero tolerance policy makes eminent sense. Initially, schools that evoked a zero tolerance policy were those in which violence had become the norm. For these schools, taking another minor step to curb the violence, a step just like the hundreds that preceded it, was simply not going to work. When 80–20 becomes 20–80, the aim is not simply to reinforce an existing norm gone awry but, rather, to overturn a socially destructive norm. This is why a genuine and literally applied zero tolerance policy makes sense: no violation, even a minor one, can be tolerated because, if it is, the entire intervention will fail.

Our first encounter with a successful zero tolerance policy was in the context of disadvantaged inner-city high schools in the United States, where problems of violence and drug use had become so prevalent that teachers were more preoccupied with discipline than with teaching. Every high school confronts problems related to drugs and violence, but they are usually not the norm. In most schools, the majority of students go about their academic business to a greater or lesser extent, while a few are highly disruptive. In some schools, however, drugs and violence extend beyond the few and become the norm. When this happens, an atmosphere of crisis and resignation permeates the school. Faced with such a normative crisis, a school principal, instead of attempting yet another procedure to regulate the problem, might introduce a zero tolerance policy. This policy would be simple, extreme, and unyielding, and the consequence for any violation, even a minor one, would be immediate expulsion.

Again, what makes a zero tolerance policy especially noteworthy is that, on the surface, it violates societal norms of equity and justice. In both our formal justice system and our everyday world the punishment is supposed to fit the crime; the more serious the offence, the harsher the punishment. Zero tolerance violates the norm of equity by pronouncing that, in a particular domain, the same severe consequence will follow both the smallest and the most extreme offences. Thus, the implementation of a genuine zero tolerance rule is a serious undertaking. The hope is that its imposition can be revoked once the message has been understood and a more normative state restored.

Since the 1980s, in the United States zero tolerance drug and weapon policies have been reinforced not only nationwide but also within the majority of schools. This is largely due to the implementation of the Free Schools and Campuses Act, 1989, which applies zero tolerance policies across the country. In total, reports show that more than 80 percent of the schools in the United States employed a zero tolerance policy (US Department of Education 2001). For many of these schools a zero tolerance program was inappropriate, but they did not have much choice as their funding was dependant on their adoption of these policies (Casella 2003). This alone may explain why zero tolerance is so controversial: it was applied ubiquitously irrespective of social context or necessity. It is, therefore, not surprising that zero tolerance policies have been widely criticized in the literature (Skiba and Peterson 2000).

Let's return to the example of the little five-year-old boy, his Halloween costume, and his small plastic axe. In a context in which there are no major concerns with violence it would be very difficult for the students, the teachers, and the parents to understand why he was punished so severely. Where the normative conditions in a school are functional, immediate expulsion of the five-year-old would seem like an unfair over-action to a child's harmless Halloween costume. Costumes like his are commonplace and are sold at every corner store, and the boy is only in pre-school. How can it be possible that a five-year-old intended to hurt people with his small plastic axe? It wouldn't occur to either the parents or the child that the costume would be offensive or cause any trouble. Why would it? Taken out of context, these cases seem ludicrous and can lead to a lack of confidence in those in charge of an important institution such as a school. As many researchers point out, in many schools there is no need to apply a zero tolerance policy because there are very few instances of violence. In these contexts, when the normative structure is a functional 80–20, zero tolerance policies are often regarded as nonsense.

*Normative imbalance = last resort*

By contrast, in a context in which there *is* a normative imbalance, people can easily explain the rationale for a zero tolerance policy: it is used when all previous interventions have failed. Research shows that students in schools forced to implement zero policy programs understand its objectives and the norms it promotes. It is all right to violate equity when a group has a severe structural problem. Zero tolerance has been shown to significantly decrease violence in schools that had severe problems (Burke and Herbert 1996; Litke 1996; Stader 2006). These schools were in the same position as Aboriginal communities in the sense that only a small proportion of their population were functioning effectively. In these schools, the norms were to carry weapons and to engage in violence as a means of resolving everyday conflicts. It is only in these contexts that zero tolerance has been successful in terms of lowering violence levels and, consequently, in reversing the 20–80 normative structure.

Why is zero tolerance successful when other interventions are not? Precisely because equity is violated to the point at which even minor transgressions receive the severest of penalties. When the majority of people treat undesirable behaviours as normative only a dramatic change in the rules and contingencies will be sufficient to make them take new policies seriously. If minor transgressions are ignored, the new rules will be ridiculed and the undesirable behaviours will continue unabated. Expel a student for bringing a plastic knife to school and you instantly have every student's attention: zero means zero – deal with it!

The controversial aspects of zero tolerance now make sense. Most people live in relatively functioning communities. An intervention that violates equity and punishes people severely for miniscule transactions seems ludicrous and is not acceptable. Most people have no idea what it is like in communities in which undesirable and destructive behaviours are normative. Under these conditions only a policy as radical as zero tolerance has any chance of reversing the norms.

## APPLYING ZERO TOLERANCE IN ABORIGINAL COMMUNITIES

Zero tolerance shares some similarities with minority influence in the sense that it needs to be applied consistently. Knowing that self-control – and, more specifically, collective self-control – is at the centre of constructive change, we link these concepts with the application of a zero tolerance policy. With zero tolerance the aim is to re-establish what the community defines as "functional" behaviours so that they again become normative. We suggest that the normative array of dysfunctional behaviours in Aboriginal communities is due to a lack of collective self-regulation. Academic underachievement, alcohol and drug abuse, risky sexual behaviour, violence, and poor nutrition all have in common a lack of self-control, a tendency to give in to immediate gratification rather than to engage in the pursuit of more important long-term goals. We also turn to the concept of collective self-control to underscore the fact that, in Aboriginal communities, self-control issues are so prevalent as to be normative.

In order for an individual to exercise self-control, she or he must have a valued long-term goal that defines "clear and consistent standards" (Baumeister and Heatherton 1996, 2). In order to exercise collective self-control, a community must have a clearly defined identity that defines its long-term goals and the behavioural norms that support them. If a clearly defined set of norms is not supported by the entire community, then it is certain that individual community members will struggle to regulate their own behaviour.

In Aboriginal communities the normative structure does not support behaviours consistent with exercising self-control. Nothing short of changing the entire normative structure in the community will work. Such a dramatic community change requires a dramatic policy. A genuine zero tolerance policy might well be one of the first steps towards clarifying valued norms, enforcing their consistency, and providing the contextual conditions in which self-control can become normative.

What are the necessary steps for applying a genuine zero tolerance in a community? First, in terms of Aboriginal communities, the one advantage is that most of them are isolated and self-contained. Thus, there are no boundary confusions, and it is not easy for community members to come and go: the community is well–defined, responsibilities inescapable, and results clearly visible. Second, zero tolerance requires targeting a specific norm that needs to be changed. There are any number of norms that might be chosen, but for illustrative purposes we focus again on formal education and the enduring challenge of school attendance.

*Step 1: Awareness of the Lack of Normative Support*

Any inspired community members who are determined to implement a zero tolerance program need to be acutely aware of the obstacles they will confront in terms of social support. Although the community is well aware of the need for normative change, and although leaders are speaking out openly about the need for such change, implementing it will not be easy.

It would be tempting for those about to introduce a genuine zero tolerance policy in Aboriginal communities to model their strategy after the experiences of certain schools in the United States and Canada. However, there are major differences between the two settings, and these need to be appreciated. In an inner-city school context violence may become normative among students, but it is not normative for the school board, the principal, the teachers, students at other schools, or members of the wider community. A principal's introduction of a zero tolerance policy will usually have the full support of all these stakeholders (Burke and Herbert 1996; Litke 1996). And as we have seen earlier, even the students, at some level, understand why a zero tolerance policy might be necessary.

In contrast, Aboriginal communities do not have the benefit of such widespread social support for normative change, especially among community leaders, local institutions, and society at large. Most of the social problems and behaviours that violate the injunctive norms of Aboriginal communities cut across all strata. They are not limited to a definable subset but, rather, affect young and old, rich and poor, and men and women. Education, employment status, or family connections offer no immunity. Indeed, the role of leaders is a particular challenge when it comes to attempting to implement normative change. They are just as likely to be normatively dysfunctional as is anyone else in the community. Indeed, they are often the least motivated to implement fundamental change as they have often been extremely successful within the dysfunctional normative structure. If we take, for example, the school attendance issue, it is common to see adults sending their children to school late and going to work late themselves, sometimes even skipping a few days.

Non-Aboriginal institutions and the wider public would be 100 percent supportive of any reasonable program to change the normative structure of Aboriginal communities. Unfortunately, such support may not only be irrelevant but also a distinct liability. A legacy of colonialism has meant that non-Aboriginal motives are simply not trusted in Aboriginal communities.

Because social and normative support might be weak in Aboriginal communities, it is extremely important that the minority implementing the zero tolerance strategy be both strategic and transparent about their goals. They will, for instance, have to convince the school principal and the school board of the benefits of applying a zero tolerance policy in the school.

### Step 2: Identify One Pressing Issue

The second step in applying a zero tolerance policy is for the instigating minority to strategically choose the issue they wish to target. There are a number of factors to consider. First, it must be an issue of genuine concern to the community and not one imposed from outside. Second, with so many potential issues to target, there is always the fear that too many will be selected. One zero tolerance program at a time is challenging enough; multiple programs might dilute the constructive impact of each. Third, it is important to choose an issue that is manageable. For example, alcohol abuse is a core issue in many communities, but it may not be a good first choice for a zero tolerance program. The alcohol abuse issue is so complex and layered that it needs to be addressed after the community has had some experience with the realities of zero tolerance. We chose school attendance as our illustrative example because it is easily measured, easily monitored, and is likely to at least have the backing of school authorities. The simple decision about what behaviour to target for the implementation of a genuine zero tolerance program is more complex than it seems. There are many challenges, and a genuine zero tolerance policy is a very invasive intervention strategy.

We would suggest that a subgroup in the community comprised of the functioning 20 percent decide which issue needs to be targeted. To do this, it might initiate informal consultations with community members about what should be the targeted issue. Should it be drugs? Should it be school attendance? Should it be violence in the household? This way, community members will be aware that action will soon be taken on one of the issues they have been discussing and will feel that they have had some personal input. The chosen issue should be the one that is uppermost in the minds of most community members as this will facilitate its implementation. Once the issue has been identified, it is important that the minority sit down and think about what behaviours will and will not be tolerated. Clear and detailed rules are extremely important to an effective zero tolerance program. Once these behaviours have been identified, details about the imple-

*[handwritten margin notes: ① Issue of concern  ② One issue only  ③ Manageable]*

mentation of the new zero tolerance policy can be communicated to community members. For example, if school attendance is the chosen issue, it could be decided that, without exception, nobody, can come to school late, not even a minute late. The consequences of violating the new rules must also be developed. In the case of a student's being late, for instance, he/she could be sent to the principal's office for an all-day, in-school suspension and given school work to complete.

Even when thoughtfully implemented, no zero tolerance policy will be effective without the support of key stakeholders. Aboriginal communities, for the most part, cannot be expected to provide that support without a good deal of campaigning. A successful program will require some effort to increase community and stakeholder motivation and involvement beforehand. This is one of the most important steps in instigating a genuine zero tolerance policy.

*Campaigning for O tolerance*

Another central consideration regarding self-regulation is the management of attention. In fact, Baumeister and Heatherton (1996, 4) note that "most models of the cognitive control of behaviour begin with attention because noticing something is by definition the first stage in information processing." A well-applied zero tolerance policy aims to increase attention in two different ways. First, before the implementation of the policy, a special effort is made to communicate information about certain target behaviours. This serves to increase the community's attention to the problem and creates a dialogue about why it needs to be addressed and the advantages of doing so. Second, during the policy enforcement period, the consequences of not following the new norm, which must be applied without exception, will be a powerful tool for maintaining sufficient attention to help prevent self-regulation failure.

### Step 3: Inform All Community Members about the Up-Coming Zero Tolerance Policy

The third step in implementing zero tolerance is to inform the school and the community about the targeted issue as well as about the behaviours that will not be tolerated. This step should take place over a period of time, at least a month or two, in order to let parents and community members adjust their attitude before enforcement. The zero tolerance policy, we believe, should be highly publicized through the use of posters, at community meetings, and on FM radio. This is extremely important because it creates the expectation of change while publicizing the importance of the problem and the gains associated with normative change.

It is also essential that the community be fully aware that even the slightest transgression will lead to a serious, well publicized, consequence. A massive failure on the first day of implementation would not auger well for success. For example, we would not want the suspension of students from their class to be a secondary gain for them in the form of a "holiday." Choosing an appropriate serious consequence for being late is crucial. It may, for example, require students to spend a significant amount of time in the library after school, where they will be required to produce products that are pedagogically relevant.

*Don't want punishment to be a "holiday"*

When the (20 percent) minority, in collaboration with the school, inform the parents and the community members about the behaviours that will and will not be tolerated, it is important that they clearly explain their choices. If one wants to focus on school attendance, for instance, it will be useful to explain to parents that, contrary to the beliefs in the community, succeeding at school is directly related to better and more meaningful jobs and higher salaries (Canadian Labour Congress 2005). If community members understand why a program is implemented and what behaviours are associated with it, half of the work is already done. Once implemented without exception, the zero tolerance policy acts to reinforce the new functional norms and, thereby, serves to support constructive normative change. In our example, zero tolerance is successful when the vast majority of students attend school every day and on time. At that point, it would be important to replace the zero tolerance program with a more equity-driven attendance policy.

*Revoke zero tol. for equity*

A concern raised by experts in the field of self-regulation failures merits our consideration. Simply put, self-regulation failures are normal and to be expected (Baumeister and Heatherton 1996). Not being aware that failures are normal, people often revert to their undesirable behaviour the first time they give in to temptation. For example, if a person's goal is to lose weight, he may perceive slipping up and eating a piece of cake as a self-regulation failure, and this may lead to a general lapse of vigilance in terms of his diet. If the person is aware that occasionally giving in to temptation is normal, he is more likely to resume his diet after having eaten that piece of cake. Thus, it is essential that a zero tolerance policy not be implemented in such a way that "failures" to conform allow for no possibility of resuming the tar-

*"Temptation" is normal*

geted behaviour. So if school punctuality is the focus, lateness needs to be punished severely but not permanently. Expelling the student for a lengthy period of time would not be a good choice. A lengthy, meaningful detention might be better because it would allow the student another chance to conform. This is also why we argue that it is necessary to inform all community members about the upcoming zero tolerance policy, so that people have a chance to "start practising," with occasional failures, before it is officially implemented.

A second caution involves the psychological stress that new self-regulation behaviours produce. "One cannot regulate everything at once [and] a person can become exhausted from many simultaneous demands" (Baumeister and Heatherton 1996, 3). This is a reminder that a community would not want to become overly ambitious in terms of implementing several zero tolerance policies simultaneously. It is best to introduce a single, well-defined behaviour as a target for a zero tolerance policy. To the extent that the policy produces the desired results there are certain to be spin-off effects. For one thing, it provides visible evidence that a community can implement change, and, more generally, it serves to show the community that it can control its own destiny. The success of a well-defined zero tolerance policy, especially if it is focused on an achievable goal, can be empowering and thus continue to inspire positive change within the community.

*Step 4: Applying Zero Tolerance*

The fourth, and last, step in implementing zero tolerance involves its application to the chosen issue. When confronted with widespread socially destructive behaviour, many institutions in Aboriginal communities have evoked some form of zero tolerance policy. Unfortunately, they are rarely implemented rigorously and, as a result, have simply served as a superficial reminder that a particular behaviour is not valued.

The people who implement a zero tolerance policy without a complete understanding of its genesis and rationale often feel uncomfortable having to punish a small crime to the same extent that they punish a much bigger one. It is hard to refrain from using common sense when punishing a transgression. This is perfectly understandable because it seems to run counter to our deeply ingrained sense of equity. When people begin questioning a zero tolerance policy in terms of equity, it is an indication that the initial reason for applying

it has either been forgotten or has become unclear. It is important
that the goal continues to be clearly defined: it is essential to respect
a zero tolerance policy until the dysfunctional 20–80 normative structure has been replaced with a functional 80–20 structure. Only after
this has been achieved can zero tolerance be dismantled and an equi-
ty-based system be reinstalled. Consistency and rigour in applying
zero tolerance is the key to success.

## CONCLUSION

Although zero tolerance may at first seem controversial in that it violates the fundamental value of equity, it is a promising short-term
policy for enabling Aboriginal communities to initiate constructive
social change. If rigorously implemented in combination with minority influence, it can reverse the normative structure in Aboriginal
communities. It is entirely consistent with self-control and collective
self-control processes as it aims to promote clearly defined long-term
goals and the norms that support them.

# 9

## Survey Research as a Vehicle
## for Constructive Community Change

Many of our children and youth are in crisis. We need to work with
parents and community members to provide a solid foundation.
Mary Simon, President, Inuit Tapiriit Kanatami, October 2006

The minute you set foot in an Aboriginal community these days, you
feel an inescapable optimistic, mission-oriented vibe. The decolonization process is in full swing everywhere, but especially in the field
of education. Aboriginal communities are retaking ownership of an
institution that has long been the symbol of colonialism – the school,
that large structure that, both literally and figuratively, dominates the
community landscape.

Gone are the days when non-Aboriginal curricula, teachers, schedules, and standards defined every detail of the school experience. Aboriginal input, from process to content, is making a tangible difference.
The call for a more culturally relevant pedagogical experience for Aboriginal students has moved from "hope" and "wish" to visible changes in
curricula and the offering of culturally appropriate materials. And these
have all been integrated into a new educational philosophy revolving
around Aboriginal identity, Aboriginal language, and Aboriginal experience. These are heady times, and everywhere there are new education
acts and Aboriginal initiatives fuelling the feeling that success is just
around the corner. Finally, the decades of dramatic academic underachievement are receding, and increased levels of achievement and
pride are beginning to define a new era.

It is, therefore, with great reluctance that we are forced to come
to the following conclusion: these culturally relevant, Aboriginally
based academic initiatives will all *fail*! And their failure will have a

profoundly demoralizing impact on all communities. Aboriginal as well as non-Aboriginal people have always been able to explain away the academic underachievement of Aboriginal students by pointing to the impact of colonialism. The negative repercussions of colonialism are often evoked to explain the frightening dropout rate in Aboriginal communities (Chapter 3). According to the misguided cultural mismatch model, failure is to be expected when you import and impose a non-Aboriginal curriculum on communities in which there is no respect for or knowledge of Aboriginal culture. But what will the response be when expectations have been raised for an Aboriginally owned and designed curriculum and nothing improves? This will result in a devastating blow to the functional integrity of Aboriginal culture. And failure is inevitable since the real issue has to do with a cultural identity vacuum, not a cultural mismatch. Thus, even if Aboriginal communities take control of formal education, there is as yet no clearly defined Aboriginal worldview to serve as a guide.

*Colonialism as a past excuse*

*Reason for failure; cultural identity vacuum*

The new culturally relevant educational blueprints being implemented across the country need not fail. But they will only succeed if *students arrive at school every day, all day, on time, well-rested, well-fed, and eager to learn.* It doesn't matter how good or how culturally relevant a curriculum might be, it will be useless if students do not show up. And this is the enduring issue. Dropout rates are off the charts, and those who do attend school do so only sporadically. And even the regular attenders lack the sleep and requisite nutrition to function effectively. This is a prescription for failure for any pedagogical program that might be implemented in Aboriginal schools.

How, precisely, do we get students to attend school every day with a commitment to learning? There is much the school can do, and much the education bureaucracy can do, but the real issue is to solicit the cooperation of each and every parent. We do not literally mean "parent," of course, since everyone in a community shares in the parenting process, from elders to extended family members to older siblings: what we need to do is solicit the help of the entire community.

We also need to emphasize that we are in no way targeting parents and guardians as convenient scapegoats for the attendance woes confronting Aboriginal schools. What we *are* doing is focusing on an untapped resource and hoping that it will come to the rescue. We need everyone in the community to help address the challenge. The fact is that, in every Aboriginal community, there has been and continues to be a profound psychological divide between the formal school and the community.

## BRIDGING THE PSYCHOLOGICAL DIVIDE: THERE ARE NO SHORT-CUTS

There are certain social realities unique to Aboriginal communities in Canada that make a genuine partnering with parents and community members especially challenging. Borrowing strategies from the experiences of non-Aboriginal school boards, or tweaking existing initiatives, will not suffice. Nothing short of a concerted, collective national strategy that is specifically designed to meet the unique challenges that Aboriginal community members face is needed. And this is true not only for the school attendance issue but also for every challenge a community prioritizes.

The usual strategies for initiating community change involve information campaigns coupled with community meetings. These are ineffective. Information campaigns such as FM radio broadcasts and colourful posters, of which there are an inordinate number, do not engage community members – they simply alert or, at best, inform them. Community meetings only attract those community members who are already committed to the goals of the meeting, not the majority who are the real targets of a community change program.

Simply put, the usual practices of engaging the community in genuine change have not, and will not, work. And this is equally true for non-Aboriginal communities. We have witnessed a number of heavily funded initiatives designed to promote social change in poor, non-Aboriginal, disadvantaged communities in major metropolitan centres in Canada. These are communities in which the vast majority do not avail themselves of badly needed mental health, social, employment, or educational services. To address the issue, a building may be furnished with kitchen facilities, computers, and professional counsellors. The only people who avail themselves of these services are those few from the disadvantaged community who are exceptional in their commitment to a well-articulated goal. The vast majority do not pursue the resources offered.

The solution is obvious: regardless of the issue, a one-on-one non-threatening exchange with each and every community member is required. It sounds simple, but it isn't. If a constructive series of face-to-face conversations were that easy, the problem would have been solved long ago. You cannot simply knock on someone's door and expect to be received with open arms and a willing attitude. The trick is to have the "right" person with the "right" reason do the knocking.

## ENGAGING AN ENTIRE COMMUNITY WITH SURVEY RESEARCH

There is no simple way to engage in a dialogue with everyone in a community, especially in a face-to-face context that is welcoming and unthreatening. Surprisingly, we have found that survey research, an exercise that seems at first glance to be cold, formal, and remote, can engage community members. Survey research is a professional undertaking that is usually used as a fact-gathering exercise, designed to inform and promote evidence-based policy initiatives. Indeed, Aboriginal communities are now receiving a tsunami of surveys on every conceivable topic.

In our experience there are unique features to conducting survey research in Aboriginal communities that make it the perfect vehicle for engaging everyone in the community. First, if the topic of the survey is one that is a genuine preoccupation for the community, then, with a little effort, participation can be extensive, including those community members who are usually reluctant to become engaged. For example, we have been able to work with communities that were successful in having 90 percent of adults complete a one-hour survey. That means that 90 percent of the community has at least been engaged to the point of sitting down for an hour to offer their views on a topic.

Second, when the survey is not the usual information-gathering exercise but, rather, a stimulus for community change, its questions can take a different form. We can ask questions that are designed to elicit "positive community norms." To take a simple example, if asked "Would you prefer to be healthy or ill," virtually everyone will choose the healthy option. In terms of our focus on education, almost everyone will answer "definitely agree" to a statement such as "Education is important." Now we have 90 percent of community members endorsing the importance of education, and yet the attendance figures and parental support for school success are notoriously lacking. Every community member must then confront the disconnect between the clearly articulated shared community positive norm regarding the importance of education and her or his own lack of tangible behaviour in support of that norm.

Finally, a traditional survey always has a feedback component. Usually the results are fed back at a community meeting or provided to a specific organization in the community. We propose a different strategy. Armed with survey results depicting positive community norms about education, trained community members would visit each and every home. Positive community norms provide just the right stimulus to facilitate home visits whose purpose is to engage parents in the process of supporting their children's formal schooling. Who is going to refuse a community member who knocks on the door and opens with: "Remember the survey on education you were kind enough to complete for us? Well, I'm here to share a few of the results with you. Although we've already talked about these on FM radio, I have some pictures with me that I'm sure you would like to see."

## DOES A SURVEY PROCESS REALLY WORK?

In order to answer this question, we describe an ongoing intervention process that we have already initiated in several First Nations and Inuit communities across Canada. For these interventions, there was a consensus that the priority issue should be school success and, more specifically, school attendance. The focus of the intervention was determined by a group of Aboriginal leaders from five communities across the country who met face-to-face on two separate occasions. This elite group brainstormed about priorities for possible constructive interventions. A variety of topics, such as alcohol, drugs, and violence, received serious consideration, but there evolved a consensus among all group members that "school success" was the necessary base from which to build strong, goal-directed communities.

## TOWARDS SCHOOL SUCCESS IN ABORIGINAL COMMUNITIES

Our call for a completely new, collective approach to addressing the widespread academic underachievement of Aboriginal students through surveys, requires, first, that we present a detailed analysis of the hurdles that have thus far created such a profound psychological divide between formal education and the community. Our analysis emphasizes the need for an innovative, collective, community-based intervention strategy. There are two themes that need to be addressed: (1) community members' own experiences with formal education and (2) the normative structure of Aboriginal communities.

*Community Members' Own Experiences with Formal Education*

There are four very good reasons parents and guardians in Aboriginal communities feel a deep disconnect with formal education: experience, trust, feelings of inadequacy, and the importance of education. Since these distancing factors are all related to the impact of colonialism, they are common to virtually all First Nations and Inuit parents across the country.

EXPERIENCE

It is one thing to ask parents to prepare their children for school when they themselves have had extensive experience with the educational institution to which their children are being exposed. It is another to do so when parents have not had much personal experience with formal education and when whatever experience they have had does not correspond to that of their children. This is what is being asked of Aboriginal parents. They have typically had little experience with formal education, and schooling has changed dramatically in Aboriginal communities. Because they lack first-hand knowledge and experience, it is both unfair and unrealistic to expect Aboriginal parents to know how to support their children in the context of formal education.

This issue is made more complex because Aboriginal parents may know about the visible aspects of schooling but have no knowledge of its deep structure. They may know about different teachers for different subjects, report cards, when school begins and ends but not about the hidden structures that lie at the heart of formal education. Here we cite two basic examples because too often educators make vague allusions to the difficulties their students are experiencing without clearly articulating the process that lies at the heart of these difficulties.

Formal education is, by design, cumulative. Entire curricula, and individual lesson plans, are constructed in a progressive fashion: students need to master A so that they can understand the next unit, B. Thus, A and B are not discrete units of information: without knowledge of A, it would be impossible for a student to master B. A basic understanding of this premise is necessary for any student if she or he is to be successful. Now, if units of knowledge were separate a student could master A, skip B and C, and then master D with little difficulty. But because units are progressive, a student cannot skip any of them without being frustrated in her attempts to learn any subsequent units. This is, of course, why parents with in-depth experience of formal education will do everything in their power to ensure that their child never misses a class: the student would not only miss that class but also experience difficulty with all subsequent classes.

Our second example revolves around a fundamental misunderstanding that we hear from many, often inexperienced, non-Aboriginal teachers in Aboriginal schools. They make such remarks as: "Aboriginal students never ask questions in class, they never seem interested, they always act bored." These educators are seeing disinterest when what they are witnessing is precolonial cultural differences.

Traditional Aboriginal learning involved acquiring skills that were immediately relevant to daily survival. Traditionally, young Aboriginal boys and girls spent all day, every day, growing up surrounded by their extended family. This means the teacher-student ratio was perhaps ten adults for each child. And what was every member of the family doing? They were all contributing to survival, coping with the climate, hunting and fishing, preparing clothes and food, and staving off the elements. Children learned by observing and listening and copying their many adult role models. And this is the key point: they were always learning because they were always surrounded by the adults who were their teachers. Because what they were learning was necessary for survival, it had to be taken very seriously. Learning was not a game, it was crucial to the maintenance of life. Make a mistake while hunting and there may be no food for the family. Make a mistake while sewing and hard-to-find skins might be wasted or the clothes might not adequately protect people from the elements. The essence of Aboriginal learning, then, was that children grew up learning by quiet, careful observation, and only when, after considerable practice, they had mastered the skills would they be allowed to participate in the pursuit of group survival.

The culture of formal school learning is totally different. First, school is not, as in traditional Aboriginal learning, a 24/7 preoccupation. Students are only in school for six or seven hours a day. Second, the same group of adults does not do all the teaching. Each classroom sometimes has fewer than ten to twenty students, and there is only one teacher, one role model. This makes the teacher-student ratio ten students per one teacher rather than ten teachers per one student, as in traditional Aboriginal learning.

But the biggest difference is that, in the culture of formal school learning, the school is a place to practise for real life. Unlike traditional Aboriginal learning, school learning is not about life and death. It is a place to learn by practising and preparing for adult life. The pressure is not ensuring survival but passing exams and assignments. Real-life pressure comes later on, when the student has to earn a living, raise a family, and cope with life's challenges. School is where young people practise until they learn the skills needed to survive in adult life.

This means that school is a place where the student can, and should, make mistakes, and ask questions, and try new solutions and ideas. Making mistakes, and being corrected, is how the student learns. Students should not be shy about asking questions. Traditional Aboriginal learning, with its multiple "teachers" for every child, did not require the child to compete for attention. In today's classroom of one teacher to many students, the student needs to seek intellectual and developmental information by asking questions. Teachers expect this and use the student's questions to teach the whole class. What teachers value the most in this practice environment is effort. They do not expect students to know everything. They want students to try, to ask questions, to make mistakes, to stumble, and then to try again. The formal school culture is built around the idea that intellectual effort and curiosity leads to questions and mistakes in the classroom but that, once the student leaves the school environment and enters the real world, he or she will have mastered the skills needed to succeed.

When students do leave the protected environment of school and enter the real world, the skills they have acquired are crucial. Companies want to hire the best trained airline mechanics, and they want painters who will not spill more paint on the floor than they get on the wall. The NHL wants only the best hockey players. And you and I want the best medical specialist if we encounter a health crisis, and we want the best legal or financial advice if we run into problems in those areas. So, even though school is a place for the student to practice, it is serious practice.

Does this mean that young people should stop learning the Aboriginal way and concentrate exclusively on formal school learning? Absolutely not. Aboriginal learning is designed to teach young people the skills needed to succeed in life, just as is formal school learning. Aboriginal learning is important for every Aboriginal person and is a life-long process. But for those hours that a young person is in the formal school culture, they should be trying hard, making mistakes, and asking questions.

Parents and guardians may well be motivated to support the school-ing of their children, but a history of colonialism and the recent ar-rival of formal education in Aboriginal communities have rendered parents uncertain about how to go about doing this. Especially lack-ing is an understanding ·of the deep structure of the pedagogical process, which is, for the most part, invisible.

## TRUST

Asking Aboriginal parents to partner with the school is especially diffi-cult considering their own personal experiences with formal education. Very few Aboriginal parents would describe their school experience as positive. Those who were subjected to residential schooling can hardly be expected to have any trust in formal education. But this is but the tip of the iceberg. Although younger parents might have attended formal schooling in their own community, the assimilation agenda may well have precluded there being any Aboriginal cultural content in the cur-riculum. As well, with the growing disciplinary problems in schools, parents must be wondering what goes on inside the biggest building in their community. All of these factors combine to create a barrier between parents and the school.

## FEELINGS OF INADEQUACY

If parents lack experience, or their own personal experiences with for-mal education have been demeaning, it is only to be expected that they might feel uncomfortable partnering with the school. Every encounter they have with the school likely leaves them feeling ashamed. Often parents are forced to engage with the school because of a problem with their child and this can be a demeaning experience at the best of times. These feelings are exacerbated by Aboriginal people's historical experience with formal schooling. Even a casual encounter with school personnel regarding how well their child is doing will be intimidating as it will involve talking with trained non-Aboriginal educators whose knowledge and experience often remind parents of their own inadequacy. Anyone would try to avoid an insti-tution that evokes feelings of inadequacy, and successful partnering will require breaking this cycle.

## IMPORTANCE OF EDUCATION

Parents have a multitude of responsibilities, and they apportion their time accordingly. To date, formal education is not central for "getting ahead" in life. Few jobs in the community reward education directly. For example, employees working side by side might be paid the same wage yet have dramatically different levels of formal education. In the vast majority of job postings in an Aboriginal community, there are no formal education-level requirements listed. Just listing a formal education requirement with each advertisement would raise awareness of the importance of formal education. What is the incentive for students and their parents when succeeding at school is not rewarded? The result is that parents do not place a premium on formal schooling and direct their parenting skills elsewhere.

### The Normative Structure of Aboriginal Communities

Addressing Aboriginal parents' experiences with formal education is challenging enough, but a second challenge involves the normative structure of most Aboriginal communities. Here we adapt the 80–20 rule to the specific context of education.

In order for any group to succeed each group member must contribute in her or his own way: in a community, leaders must lead, parents must parent, and so on. It is unrealistic to think that every community member will perform his or her role perfectly, and here is where the 80–20 rule is evoked. As we have said, in every well-functioning community, 80 percent of community members perform well but 20 percent do not. Realistically, if a community can maintain at least an 80 percent rate of effective functioning, it has a good chance of succeeding.

So the 80–20 rule describes the normative structure that can be found in every successful community. Why is this normative structure so important for understanding the lack of parental involvement in Aboriginal communities? Aboriginal communities do not have the benefit of an 80–20 normative structure. Indeed, some Aboriginal leaders would say that their communities are not 80–20 but 20–80. The precise percentages are not important. What is important is recognizing that the normative structure in most Aboriginal communities is such that the usual interventions *will not be effective*. And this is because there are not enough highly functioning role models to support the difficult rehabilitation of the 80 percent.

For example, imagine a small classroom of ten students in which the usual 80–20 rule is operating. This means that eight of the students will be performing well in terms of attendance, completing assignments, passing exams, and behaving in a cooperative manner. Two of the students might be disruptive, with irregular attendance and poor exam performance. These two students will be the focus of the school counsellor, who will have individual sessions with them in an attempt to redirect their behaviour. The counsellor has some hope of success since the two troubled students do not really want to be "weird," and the behaviour of the other eight students in the class makes them feel out of place. But the eight model students help the counsellor offer the troubled students a concrete set of classroom behaviours that will lead to success. The eight students are living daily proof that success is possible and are real-life examples of what behaviours lead to success. Under these circumstances the counsellor has at least a chance of rehabilitating the two non-normative students.

What if instead of 80–20 our classroom had a 20–80 normative structure? That would mean that only two of the students are performing well while eight are not. In such a situation it is the majority eight students who will establish the norms, not the two well-functioning students. The teacher faces an uphill battle when trying to establish discipline in a classroom in which the normative structure is 20–80 rather than 80–20.

Our normative 80–20 analysis has important implications for encouraging parents to partner with the school. In the absence of an 80–20 structure parents have no normative support and no clearly defined models for guiding them with regard to how best to support their children. This means that the usual outreach efforts to involve parents simply will not work. If 80 percent of parents in each community were already partnering fully with the school, it would be relatively easy to encourage the remaining 20 percent. But when 80 percent of parents, for very good historical reasons, are not participating fully, and have few models to follow, promoting a partnership with the school will be a daunting challenge.

Our 80–20 normative analysis is not designed to paint a discouraging portrait but, rather, to serve as a reality check. Simply put, the usual outreach efforts will not succeed because they are designed to be effective in the context of an 80–20 normative structure. This is especially true of interventions that build on traditional Aboriginal solutions in an attempt to regulate behaviour. Healing circles, for example, arose prior to European colonization, when Aboriginal communities operated effectively with their own 80–20 normative structure. They were not designed to be effective in a 20–80 normative structure. It is this reality that leads us to conclude that all non-Aboriginal-, and indeed all Aboriginal-, based interventions will ultimately fail, despite good intentions and commitment to pedagogical initiatives designed to serve the needs of students. However, an awareness of the 20–80 normative structure puts us in a position to design interventions that will succeed in engaging parents in the formal education process.

Specifically, we need to think differently about the challenge. Every constructive intervention designed to address each community challenge, including school success, is based on the assumption of an 80–20 normative structure. These are *individualistic* intervention strategies in that they individually target the few (20 percent) for rehabilitation. However, when the structure is 20–80, what is needed is a *collective* intervention strategy. We now turn our attention to just such a strategy.

## SURVEY RESEARCH AS A VEHICLE FOR CONSTRUCTIVE SOCIAL CHANGE

Engaging parents in the education of their children is a universal challenge. As we have seen, the challenge in Aboriginal communities is particularly great, and the usual methods will not succeed. Inviting parents to school meetings, organizing workshops, and a host of other well-intentioned efforts will simply not suffice.

We propose to use survey research as a collective intervention strategy whose aim is to instigate a partnership between parents and the school. Usually, community-based research is designed to objectively document a situation. The evidence-based results may be used by community leaders to address an important issue, they might be used to seek funding and support to solve a community problem, they might be used to document the relative success of a community program, or they might be used to document the need for financial support to initiate a new program. We propose to use survey research for a new and unique purpose: stimulating a community into constructive social change in general and addressing the issue of school attendance and school success in particular.

*Conducting Survey Research in Aboriginal communities:*
*Lessons Learned*

The impetus for this novel use of survey research arose from the fundamental differences we experienced when applying survey research in the context of Aboriginal communities. The very first research survey in which we were involved was in an Aboriginal community whose focus was to protect its Aboriginal language. The purpose of the survey was to provide an opportunity for every adult in the community to share their language experiences, voice their opinions, and specify the role that parents and the school should play for ensuring that young people remain fluent in their Aboriginal language.

The survey had a number of features that are relevant to how we wish to use research surveys to meet the present challenge:

1  The survey on language was genuinely community-based. It was instigated by the education committee in the community, which was pressured by parents to address the question of language loss.
2  The survey design followed state-of-the-art procedures for maximizing its objectivity and, thereby, its credibility. For example, questions about language use were designed by a team of community members and researchers. The questions were prepared in one language and then back-translated into other languages relevant to the community. Respondents provided their answers on standard rating scales that were amenable to powerful inferential statistical analyses.
3  In most community-based surveys, the research aims to have a 10 percent representative sample complete the survey. Remarkably, and as an indication of community interest and cooperation, virtually every member (over 90 percent) of the community over the age of fifteen completed the survey instrument. Such an inclusive survey ensured that every voice was heard and that every voice had equal weight.
4  The survey process yielded a number of outcomes beyond the immediate results. The survey raised awareness and interest in the entire community regarding the value of their Aboriginal language and how fragile its status might be in the future. Beyond this, it facilitated attendance at community meetings about language and allowed other community organizations to reflect on their language policy. Finally, it provided a basis for organizations

to seek funding for projects designed to promote the development and use of the Aboriginal language.

### Survey Research as a Vehicle for Change

Our novel method calls for conducting a community survey, which is to be completed by every adult in the community. Completing a survey on formal education and the needs of students is an engaging process for community members. Moreover, by surveying every adult in the community, every voice in the community is heard, making it a fine exercise in democracy.

But most important, our community-based survey research exercise is designed to change the 20–80 community norms so as to positively affect school attitudes, improve school attendance, and increase graduation rates. In order to stimulate this change in norms from 20–80 to 80–20, our survey research process has three key features. First, we ask the opinions of respondents using a standardized response format that lends itself to statistical analysis and, thereby, ensures that every respondent's voice has an equal weight in the conclusions derived from this analysis. Second, we seek to survey every adult in a community. Most surveys select a representative sample of a population, whereas we seek to survey the entire population.

The third feature of our survey is pivotal for engaging parents. Unlike traditional surveys, our survey includes a number of questions that are designed to focus not on the usual problems surrounding formal education but, rather, on potential *positive norms and attitudes* regarding education in the community. For example, it is likely that virtually all respondents will provide a resounding "yes" to a question such as: "Is education important for young people today?" Similarly, we would expect community members to respond positively to a statement such as: "A parent is the child's first teacher." The point is that, rather than focusing on the problems associated with education, we focus on the positive. If community members do respond positively to these items, and if every community member is surveyed, then we have, as a starting point, a positive norm that is genuinely community-wide.

So far, we have administered the survey instrument to community members in several First Nations and Inuit communities across the country. The percentage of community members who have completed the survey research range from 74 percent to 86 percent, and the final percentages are certain to be higher. We will probably never reach our ideal of a 100 percent response rate, but to date the only people we have missed are those who for a variety of reasons (e.g., health, postsecondary study) are out of the community for an extended period of time.

We attribute the success in obtaining such large community samples to our Aboriginal partners in each community. They have a deep knowledge of their community and are creative and relentless in ensuring that everyone is surveyed. Our community partners share the view that "education," despite evoking negative experiences, represents an important and inescapable issue for every member of every Aboriginal community. They were also unanimous in their belief that respondents should not be paid to complete the survey, even though the final survey required at least half an hour of their time. An added challenge is that many communities are "surveyed-out," and often respondents are paid between twenty-five to fifty dollars to complete a survey. Our community team members did not believe that we should pay our respondents to complete the survey as they wanted community members to offer their views out of a genuine community commitment. Despite all these hurdles, the success rates are extremely high, meaning that, when the results reveal an endorsement of our positive norm questions we can conclude that they genuinely reflect the views of the entire community.

### The Social Psychology of "Positive Norm" Survey Questions

Our positive norm questions (e.g., Is education important for young people today?) are designed to serve as a starting point for changing community norms relating to student attendance. Two well-researched processes in social psychology that inform our survey strategy are: (1) the foot-in-the-door phenomenon and (2) the power of social norms. Both processes operate best when attempting to encourage people to engage in socially constructive behaviours that they seem reluctant to undertake. The foot-in-the-door technique involves making a small request of someone that they are certain to agree to and then, later, making a much larger request. If they agree to the small request, people are very likely to agree to the larger request later. The teenager who wants access to the family car would be best to ask for permission to use the car for a quick trip to the store before asking to borrow it for the entire weekend. Because the parent has already said "yes" to a smaller request, for the sake of consistency it only makes sense for him or her to say yes to the larger request.

In an early experiment (Freedman and Fraser 1966), householders were visited under the pretense of promoting safe driving. They were then asked to sign a petition, a small request to which they easily agreed. Two weeks later, the same householders, as well as others that had not been visited previously, were solicited to fill a bigger request. This time, the householders were asked if they would be willing to put a large sign promoting safe driving on their front lawns. Many of the householders who had agreed to the first request during the initial visit were inclined to accept the second request, whereas those who had not received the initial visit were far less accommodating. The small request requires little effort, but it builds commitment to the object of the request and to the person doing the requesting. When the bigger request comes, it is difficult to say "no": nobody wants to be inconsistent.

*[handwritten margin note: Experiment Foot in door]*

The foot-in-the-door technique has been applied successfully in a variety of domains, from encouraging respect for the environment, to addressing drinking and driving, to raising money for any number of worthy causes. Furthermore, there are studies to suggest that a survey research instrument can be used to set the foot-in-the-door principle in motion. For example, a survey research instrument was used to activate people's thinking about registering as organ donors, and this influenced their willingness to later become actual organ donors (Brug et al. 2000; Carducci and Deuser 1984; Carducci et al. 1989). Similarly, studies have shown that surveying individuals about politics prior to an election increases their tendency to vote on election day (Granberg and Holmberg 1992; Greenwald et al. 1987). Even a short survey simply asking people if they plan to vote on election day has been found to increase the voting rate (Granberg and Holmberg 1992).

*[handwritten margin note: Survey to set foot in door ie smaller 1st request]*

Clearly, a survey instrument is the perfect mechanism for initiating a foot-in-the-door process that might later lead to substantial change. When our respondents take an hour to complete a survey on education, and endorse positive norm items such as "education is important," they have already made a small commitment. The foot is in the door. The actual results from our surveys in two communities indicate that the foot is planted squarely in the door. In both communities over 90 percent of respondents strongly endorsed statements such as "education is important" and "a parent is a child's first teacher." We are now positioned to have parents agree with a more substantial commitment to support their children's education.

#2    The power of social norms is another important mechanism underlying behaviour change. Norms are what most people say or do in a particular situation, and they are extremely important sources of information with regard to guiding an individual's behaviour. Whenever there is even the least bit of uncertainty about what to do, an individual will turn to norms. When an individual is uncertain about how to vote, what to wear to an event, whether or not to drink alcohol, or whether she should throw her litter on the street, she looks to what others do, especially others who are similar to her. Norms, or what others define as "normal," will have a potent influence on how an individual chooses to behave.

When we add what social psychology teaches us about the power of social norms to our foot-in-the-door, we are poised to make a larger request of our community respondents. If everyone in a community completes the survey, and if everyone endorses the item "education is important," then we have a clearly defined positive community norm regarding the perceived importance of education. The problem, of course, is that community members are not encouraging their children to attend and perform well at school.

How do we use the positive norm information obtained from our survey, along with our foot in the door, to engage parents in the education process? Unlike traditional surveys, in our survey it is the feedback process that is key. Specifically, we begin the process of changing the normative structure by feeding results of the positive norm questions to the community – results that reveal a positive norm regarding education and in which every member of the community has had a voice. This then serves as the stimulus for making a collective change in education. As we have seen, the results from two surveys already completed indicate that over 90 percent of community members believe that education is important. Parents may well be positively inclined to better support their children's education when they know that it is not only they but everyone in the community who believes in the importance of education.

In Chapter 7 we describe a classic experiment conducted by Cialdini and his colleagues (Goldstein, Cialdini, and Griskevicius 2008; see also Cialdini, Reno, and Kallgren 1990; Cialdini and Goldstein 2004) that illustrates the potential for our feedback process. Cialdini was confronted with a conundrum faced by major hotel chains across

North America. The hotels were anxious to be seen as contributing to a pro-environment movement. They began by placing cards in the bathrooms of every hotel room encouraging guests to recycle their bath towels. At first, very few guests responded to the bathroom cards by recycling their towels. Cialdini found that adding a "positive norm" to the bathroom card (75 percent of guests who have stayed in your room recycled their towels) was all it took to get guests to recycle their towels.

This elegant experiment speaks directly to our use of survey research. We have a socially progressive value (environment/education) that everyone says they support, but they do not follow through with concrete behaviours (recycling towels/encouraging children to attend school). Clearly, if we can present parents with survey feedback showing that everyone in the community supports education, this should encourage individual parents to begin taking concrete steps to support their children's education. Presenting a parent with survey results indicating that 90 percent of people in their own community believe that education is important should be a powerful normative incentive for her/him to take constructive action.

*Survey feedback*

ENCOURAGING PARENTAL SUPPORT
THROUGH SOCIALLY CONSTRUCTIVE NORMS

Having completed a survey with virtually every adult in the community, and having included socially constructive foot-in-the-door questions on the survey, we are positioned to use the results to encourage change through normative influence. Concretely, how is this achieved? We share the results of the positive educational norms with the community through the usual mechanisms: community meetings, meetings with key community groups and organizations, FM radio, and occasionally on local community television. But, more important, the key results will be presented through a personal visit on the part of a trained community member to every family in the community. The rationale for the visit is to share the results of the survey. The results will demonstrate that everyone in the community judges education to be important, everyone in the community believes that a parent is the child's first teacher, and everyone in the community believes parents can and should support their child's education. The trained community member will present these results and then note how community consensus is at odds with the current reality of school attendance and school success. Parents will then be asked about their willingness to engage in realistic goal setting for their child's attendance and daily school experiences for the next three months. The concrete goals negotiated by the community member and parents will be recorded on a one-page survey and each will keep a copy. The understanding is that the community member will return in a few months, at which time the goals will be reviewed, adjustments made, and new goals specified. This follow-up process will continue every few months until all key goals have been met, and it will be replicated for every home in the community.

What needs to be underscored is that the community members who conduct the home interviews are required to do far more than merely ensure that respondents indicate their goals for the next three months. In fact, they receive training in interviewing that approximates the currently popular and highly respected five–stages-of-change model proposed by Prochaska, DiClemente, and Norcross (1992). These three conducted an in-depth analysis of the entire "self-help" professional therapy and social intervention literature and noticed that social change involves five discrete stages. These stages move from the "precontemplation" stage, where people do not acknowledge they have a problem, through to an "action" stage and finally to a "maintenance" stage, where people take the necessary steps to consolidate their new, constructive behaviour pattern. A key feature of the model is that the interviewer must accurately evaluate a person's stage before advocating for change. Asking too much from a person will only backfire and sabotage any movement towards constructive change. Thus, our community members who make home visits will need to be trained to conduct home interviews so that they can maximize the chances for motivating parents in a constructive direction,

The last, but vital, feature of the survey research process is capacity building. Building capacity among community members occurs at all stages of the process, from the development of the survey research instrument to the completion of the survey to the feedback process. The whole philosophy behind our approach is that, at all stages, the process is led by trained community members and not by members of the research team. The end result is that, in one way or another, everyone in the community is involved.

In terms of our experience with feeding survey results back to the community and capacity building, we have found that there are understandable challenges. What needs to be appreciated is that survey research is a long-term, ongoing process, and the fact that community members are involved at every stage augers well for capacity-building objectives. However, it is not always easy to regroup key members of the community. Often, the key community members who will lead the feedback process are overly busy with a multitude of community tasks. Because of their skill and their positive attitudes towards work and addressing community challenges, they are often called away when pivotal meetings are scheduled for the project. As we have often noted, the non-Aboriginal expression "if you need something done, ask the busiest person" has its limits. For talented Aboriginal community members, the demands are limitless.

## BEYOND SURVEY RESEARCH

Our survey process is designed to meet the challenge of dramatically changing an entrenched set of dysfunctional norms. While a survey strategy is perfectly suited to changing norms regarding education in a community context, there are other methods that can be used to achieve the same end and that, in different circumstances, may be more appropriate. Critically, any other method must also target everyone in the group, must highlight positive group norms, and must allow for constructive one-on-one feedback designed to instigate positive norm change.

Imagine a group of Aboriginal students who have moved to a metropolitan centre and who are struggling with adjusting to postsecondary education in their new challenging environment. To help with their adjustment we have experimented with replacing surveys with having students keep a detailed and structured daily diary (Kachanoff et al. 2013). Specifically, each student chose two school days and kept a detailed diary for those two days. We used the information to produce a "group profile" of how the students spent their time. No information about individual students is revealed, only the group profile. Sleeping, school work, and social activities occupied most of their time, as we might have expected.

The students are presented the group profile at a group feedback session. They are not told what to look for; instead, they examine the profile, talk about it, and come to their own conclusions. The discussion takes the form of: "we seem to do a lot of X, and maybe we need to do more of Y." The point is that, like the survey, the diary reveals the reality of the group norms, and, through discussion and comparison, the group of students is positioned to collectively change some of their personal habits. Not surprisingly, a consistent theme is: "We need to do a bit more organized studying and stay away from wasting time." This form of norm change exercise may be well adapted for use among secondary students in Aboriginal communities, where more constructive school habits need to be reinforced. In this case it is the students themselves who are instigating the process in a constructive and informed manner.

Now imagine a group of secondary students wrestling with their Aboriginal identity and what that means in the context of modern technology and the cultural onslaught from the dominant non-Aboriginal society. We have found that just having a student write about his or her identity dilemma has a constructive effect (Huberdeau, Cárdenas, and de la Sablonnière 2014). The exercise seems to offer self-insight and clarify some of their cultural identity challenges.

Following our survey and diary strategy, each student might write freely about his or her identity challenges. A group profile depicting recurrent themes could be compiled and presented to the students as a group. Again, no individual student's writings would ever be displayed. What is presented is a group-based profile of themes. The students would not be told what to conclude but, rather, would be left to draw their own conclusions and construct their own strategies for resolving identity issues.

## THERE ARE NO SHORT CUTS

We conclude with what we view as the essential ingredients of any successful intervention whose purpose is to change group norms. The group must decide what norms it deems necessary to change. Group members must then make a small statement of commitment (e.g., in a survey or a diary) that can be used to produce a believable, objectively based group profile. They then need to confront the disconnect between the group profile and their desired behaviour. And nothing short of a one-on-one non-threatening, constructive dialogue with each and every group member will be required to support constructive change.

There are no short cuts, but the benefits begin immediately. It is community members who choose the issue, who elicit the small commitment, who present the group profile to group members, and who engage in the one-to-one dialogues. Every step is a challenge, but every step is constructive in and of itself.

# 10

## Towards Constructive Change in Aboriginal Communities: From Theory to Implementation

In this the final chapter, we attempt to review our analysis of the challenges confronting Aboriginal communities, which led logically to a whole new approach to generating effective solutions. Our review is especially important because we have introduced a large number of inter-related concepts that only when woven together point the way to solutions that can offer a degree of optimism.

In order to guide our review of the different concepts we have described in detail over the past eight chapters, we offer a schematic representation of them and the links between them. We review each of the boxes in our diagram in turn. However, rather than repeat what we have described in the separate chapters, we focus on real community experiences to illustrate the concept in question. Sometimes a story can get to the heart of the matter.

COLONIALISM

We, as non-Aboriginal Canadians, interpret colonialism as a historic event that involved direct exploitation as well as a misguided policy of assimilation. We understand the travesty of residential schools, but we take some solace in the fact that they no longer exist and that our government has apologized on our behalf. Colonialism, then, is a thing of the past. Or is it?

Spend time on First Nations reserves and remote Inuit communities and the vestiges of colonialism are everywhere. We arrive at the airport, and, after greeting everyone – and we mean everyone – it's off to the school. The school dominates the landscape, and it looks like any school you might see in metropolitan, non-Aboriginal Canada.

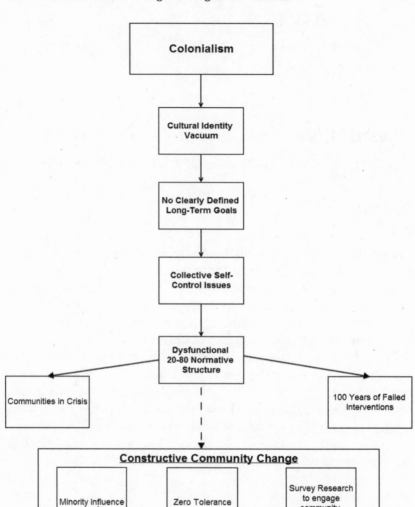

Figure 10.1   Proposed links among concepts leading to community challenges and proposed steps for constructive community change

All the superficial trappings are there, including the administrative offices, the classrooms, and the gym. Someone might have integrated an element of Aboriginal design into the building, and there are certain to be Aboriginal artefacts on the wall or a large stone carving or canoe in the foyer. Beyond that there are mostly non-Aboriginal teachers and administrators. Even in schools in which the Aboriginal language is very strong, and a few Aboriginal teachers can be found, the non-Aboriginal languages dominate and the Aboriginal teachers are confined to teaching in the primary grades. And here comes the yellow school bus to pick up the students. We are dumbfounded! To walk from one end of the village to the other takes ten minutes. Aboriginal experience is rooted in the natural environment and all the challenges of its weather. Why would Aboriginal children need the city dweller's crutch to escape the natural environment? Why a yellow bus? And yet, because non-Aboriginal schools have yellow buses, so must small remote communities. The whole school scene is as non-Aboriginal as you can get. Vestiges of colonialism?

*Vestiges of colonialism school buses*

Pre-school children have their own non-Aboriginal influences. In southern cities when teachers take pre-schoolers on an outing they attach them to a colourful chord so that they can safely navigate the crowds of people on the sidewalks and avoid the dangers of traffic as they cross busy streets. Here we are in a remote community, writing this chapter, and what do we see out the window? In a village with no sidewalks, few roads, and only occasional vehicles, there is the pre-school teacher leading her charges all attached to the requisite chord. She is leading them across village ground where there is more chance of running into a caribou than a dangerous vehicle. And the chance of a child getting lost in the village is zero. Colonialism is alive and well.

But we are now looking over class lists in order to schedule some testing. The first thing we notice is how many students have the same last name. We quickly realize that there are three main extended families in the community. What's up with that? Aboriginal friends quickly fill you in. These would originally have been three independent families who lived a nomadic life in rhythm with the animals, fish, and seasons. If the three families wanted to unite into one group they would have done so, but they preferred operating independently with only occasional contact. One of the first acts of colonialism was to regroup the families into settlements or reserves so that they could be managed more effectively. Besides, regrouping was needed for purposes of economic exploitation and schooling. That single colonialist act of grouping families continues to have a major impact on community life. Those who belong to the dominant family occupy the important positions and profit from being members of that family. Merit, in the form of education, skills, training, and experience, is not the fundamental value: it is family name that counts. Colonialism is alive and well.

The colonialist attitude, and the resulting dependency it creates, is everywhere. Aboriginal communities are flooded with non-Aboriginal junk food, television, music, computers, and videos. In mid-winter young people are dressed like hip hoppers from inner city Chicago, with low-slung pants, piercings, and colourful hair. The "gangster" look is all the rage.

Non-Aboriginal people design and build everything in the community, including all the infrastructure and specialized vehicles needed to navigate the terrain outside the communities. Even simple maintenance is a non-Aboriginal business. We remember boarding a twin otter plane in a community where we were joined by two young non-Aboriginal men who were meeting for the first time and laughing about a coincidence they had just discovered. Both worked for competing security companies in the same big city in the south. One had just finished checking the alarm at the small bank in the community, a task that took fifteen minutes and no special tools. The other had just checked the alarm at the new municipal office building, another fifteen-minute task. We had joined in by this time and wondered aloud at the exorbitant cost of sending someone so far to perform such a simple task. "Couldn't someone in the community perform this task," we asked. Both looked at us as if we were from Mars.

Such situations are common. As we write the present chapter we are seated in the kitchen of a small village hotel in the company of three veterinarians from the South. They are here at great expense to administer rabies shots to dogs in the village. This is an Aboriginal community whose identity is rooted in the land and its animals. So why fly a team of veterinarians all this way to administer a simple shot to village animals? Colonialism is alive and well.

Sometimes the vestiges of colonialism are emotionally raw. We remember that, long before residential schooling and its related exploitations made their way into public discourse, we often taught classes to Aboriginal teachers in their own community. At that time any discussion of the social issues plaguing Aboriginal communities was taboo. At some point, we, and our Aboriginal co-teacher, concluded that these issues needed to be addressed. We took the plunge with the following introduction: "To understand our students and how they think about school we need to talk about some difficult matters. So when we put our cowboy hats on it is a signal that we need to talk about some difficult things." The hat depersonalized the experience, but the flood-gates were opened. One middle-aged student cried as she recalled how, in the very classroom in which we were seated, years ago she had been banished naked to a snowbank for uttering a word in her Aboriginal language. That was only the beginning. We even had a husband and wife in our class who spoke about the early colonialist days for the very first time: neither had known of the other's trauma. To this day, as we travel through airports in isolated communities, someone is bound to step up and laughingly ask us to take our hats off. Colonialism is emotionally alive and well.

Let us not deceive ourselves into thinking that the ravages of colonialism are a thing of the past, with only lingering vestiges to deal with. A new era of blatant colonialism is upon us. The current non-Aboriginal mantra, led through government policy, is "northern development." Nowhere is this more obvious than in the renaming Department of Indian and Northern Affairs: it is now the Department of Indian and Northern Development. How exactly does this "Northern Development" process work? First, you explore and find a valuable resource to be mined. Next, you open a mine and make the pitch that it will create jobs for Aboriginal people. Finally, you pay off adjacent Aboriginal communities in the form of company dividends. Sounds politically correct until you examine the effects on Aboriginal communities. First, the jobs available to Aboriginal people are at the lowest level and require a certain lifestyle and commitment to work so that, ultimately, the mine is very much a "foreign" operation in every sense of the word. And then there are these large dividends that the community receives just for being located close to the mine. The results of these payoffs are disastrous. Everyone in the community talks about and waits for their cheque from the mine: no need for skills training here. The minute the cheque arrives the entire community is mobilized into action, buying expensive vehicles, household items, and the latest technology, often heading to the big cities to hit the malls and casinos. In one community a group of friends couldn't even wait for the scheduled flight and so chartered their own plane to the city. Dividends shut down communities for days as the extended party takes over. Moreover, thievery increases dramatically because everybody knows that people are walking around carrying wads of money. In one community the residents chose to use the dividend money for the collective good and built a new community centre and small engine repair shop. This decision positively affected the entire mood in the community, but, unfortunately, the following year residents voted to take the cash for themselves.

These colonialist practices virtually guarantee that communities will continue to adopt a passive and demotivated attitude. Colonialism is indeed alive and well.

## CULTURAL IDENTITY VACUUM

We argue that, when there is a vast power differential between colonizer and colonized, the cultural identity of the latter is totally destroyed. This is precisely the reality for Aboriginal people: colonialism produced a cultural identity vacuum that brought about the complete destruction of Aboriginal identity with nothing offered to replace it. Our argument is not easily made. After all, First Nations and Inuit people tend to live in their own communities and to appear physically distinct from other people. Moreover, many wear symbols of their Aboriginal heritage, some speak their own Aboriginal language, and when they speak English they have a distinct accent. How can people who tend to live together on their own and appear so different not have a distinct culture?

The question of Aboriginal cultural identity is one we have had the privilege to discuss with a wide variety of First Nations and Inuit groups across Canada. Often these discussions take place in the context of courses given in the community for Aboriginal teachers, some of whom teach in or about their language, others of whom teach Aboriginal culture classes. These are hardcore, culturally committed Aboriginal people who are insightful, thoughtful, and rightly proud of their Aboriginal cultural identity.

Any discussion usually begins with a quick and confident consensus that "sharing" and "independence" are the primary Aboriginal cultural values, along with close family connections and an emphasis on children. They realize very quickly that these are values that every cultural group espouses. What group doesn't value family, especially children? Very quickly, our Aboriginal group comes to realize that the values it is using to describe its people are not unique but universal.

Especially revealing in terms of a cultural identity vacuum is the focus on the distant past. Today, there is a renewed pride in Aboriginal identity, a pride that is evidenced by a revival of Aboriginal languages, Aboriginal ceremonies, Aboriginal dance, and Aboriginal drumming. What is revealing about this revival is that the entire focus is on central cultural elements that were prominent *prior* to European colonization. This is understandable from two points of view. First, many of the revived cultural elements are those that were outlawed by European colonization. Thus, their resurgence is symbolic of the decolonization process. Second, the last time there was a vibrant Aboriginal cultural identity was prior to European colonization. So naturally this is the era that is targeted as the source of the current revival. There is no current cultural identity to which a group can point.

The other North American group experiencing the same phenomenon, for the same reasons, is the African-American community in the United States. Their proud African cultural identity was destroyed by slavery. Years ago we were working in poor, urban, African-American communities. At that time, and as part of the civil rights movement, there was a determination to change the group's label from "negro" to "black." We argued that soon there would be a groundswell to change from "black" to "African American." Are you crazy? Blacks in the United States have never even been to Africa. Our response was: "True, but that was the last time they had a clearly defined cultural identity. Slavery left them with a cultural identity vacuum. The starting point for rebuilding a cultural identity must begin with the last time the culture was intact." And so for them, as for Canada's Aboriginal peoples, cultural pride begins with the historical elements that symbolize a well-defined cultural identity.

We have on more than one occasion been involved in some of the more poignant realities of a cultural identity vacuum. Often we would travel with Inuit colleagues and friends from the eastern Arctic, one of the few regions where Inuktitut remains a vibrant language, to the Western Arctic. Inuit friends would be full of anticipation upon landing in the western community and rush to embrace and share with their fellow Inuit. Exuberance dissipated instantly when our friends' greetings were met with vacant stares. Our Inuit friends, who were fluent in Inuktitut, realized that their fellow Inuit only spoke English. Thus, we were faced with the devastating reality that we, as non-Aboriginal people, could converse much more easily with Inuit in the community than they could. Many a tear was shared, and years later that initial encounter remains for our friends a defining moment.

*[handwritten margin note: African American cultural identity vacuum]*

## NO CLEARLY DEFINED LONG-TERM GOALS

Modern, non-Aboriginal society is in the throes of cultural change. Once upon a time the non-Aboriginal trajectory was clear. You pursued education and training with vigilance, obtained an entry-level job commensurate with your training, established yourself, climbed the ladder of success, got married, had two and one-half children as well as a dog and a station-wagon, and lived in the suburbs. Times have changed. People change jobs more frequently, and many work on contract instead of for a large private or public-sector institution. And now every non-Aboriginal person needs a gaggle of experts from tax specialists to financial planners to computer savvy fixers to help her or him navigate modern complexities. All the while there is flex time, part time, and, with the "BlackBerry," no time.

In terms of relationships, the idea of having a partner for life and growing old together has unravelled. Divorce and common law are the norm, with children learning to adjust to multiple extended families, which creates havoc on important holidays.

But really, not that much has changed. The basic long-term goals remain solidly entrenched. Education and specialized training are carefully monitored, highly competitive, and are the "ticket" for advancement. Equity, what you bring to the table, is what determines your pay, status, advancement, power, and station in life. Non-Aboriginal people still strive for long-term stable relationships, it's just that life has become more complicated.

Some cultural groups pursue non-Aboriginal long-term goals with a vengeance, and the results are visible. In our own personal academic environment, the Jewish community stands out. This is a culture that reveres formal education and both wants and expects all young people to pursue it from the cradle to the grave. So successful were young Jewish scholars that, despite constituting a small minority of students, they came to dominate the most prestigious professions, including medicine, law, and science. Their dominance was so visible that we are ashamed to say that, for a period of time, our academic institutions discriminated against Jewish students.

We found a similar example when we were conducting research in a poor inner-city community populated by academically underachieving white, black, and Latino students. The sudden arrival of Hmong refugees to the community was enlightening. Despite being poor, having escaped outrageous violence in their home country, and being unable to speak English, within one year they collectively dominated the school academically. Most of the students lived in a crowded room with an "uncle," who was really an adult who took care of them since most of them had lost their parents in the revolution in Laos. Their long-term goal was education, which, in their minds, was the vehicle to upward mobility and the "good" life. We remember one day saying to a group of African-American students in the cafeteria: "So, one day these Hmong guys are going to own their own businesses. What do you think of that?" Their response was a casual shrug and the comment: "As long as they pay well." While the African-American students coasted, the Hmong students paid more than lip service to their desire to achieve a long-term goal.

If non-Aboriginal Canadians, the Jewish community, and Hmong refugees from Laos and Thailand seem to have culturally defined long-term goals, Aboriginal communities do not. On the surface and in terms of rhetoric Aboriginal communities seem like any small community. For the most part, however, this is not the case. All of the basic infrastructure jobs are held by non-Aboriginal people, construction to electricity, banking, retail, and transportation. Aboriginal people tend to have government-funded jobs related to governance of the community. In other words, they have no real incentive to worry about goals that require a long-term commitment to education or training.

We have already noted that the dropout rate before completion of high school may be as high as 70 percent. The same is true for training programs for skilled labour. Students wander in and out of these programs, few complete them, and those who do are not likely to be employed. Some are employed to satisfy an agreement to hire a certain percentage of local talent and then told to stay home.

Why there seems to be no long-term goals is obvious given the lack of culturally defined opportunities. So Aboriginal teachers teach, but often without qualifications; administrative positions are held by those without even a high school education, and certainly their salary is not dependent on either training or education. The problem is not that Aboriginal people are under-qualified for many positions – that is to be expected at this early phase of dramatic social change. The problem is that, even within a more restricted range, there are no opportunities. With no contingencies there is little incentive for long-term planning.

One of our favourite people at the first Aboriginal school with which we partnered was the centre director. She occupied a lofty administrative position and began taking courses to grow into the job; however, half way through left her post to work at a lesser position as a receptionist at the hotel. We were demoralized and grumbled to Aboriginal friends in the community: "What a shame to invest all that training only to have her leave." The answer we received has stuck with us ever since: "We may have lost her to the job, but she is not lost to the community. Her training follows her everywhere." The pattern is not what you would expect. People don't leave one job for a better one. Instead, what would be expected in terms of education and training, people not only move, but move in terms of status: not only from low to high, but from high to low and everything in between. Another of our favourites was a young man who left his community to become the first certified Aboriginal airplane mechanic in the entire region. He returned to his community and was immediately employed by the airline company. Fast-forward five years and he is working in the community garage: more pay, fewer midnight shifts, and zero stress. The point is that there is no linear "getting ahead" trajectory but, rather, fluctuating job domains and status and no apparent long-term goals.

Once in a community we were encouraged to learn that there was a person who could really help our Aboriginal team with conducting some surveys there. Eddie worked in the municipal office, which is where we found him. Just as we had been told, he was personable, intellectually quick, and thrilled at the survey prospect. Right then and there we gave him an introduction to the necessary training. Further training was scheduled for 10:00 AM the next morning, but, when the time came, there was no sign of Eddie. We bumped into him in the street after lunch, and he was as amiable as the day before but clearly a little foggy with drink. Later when we mentioned this to the person who recommended Eddie, she casually noted: "Yeah, he is in a fog most of the time." Another talented individual with no mission.

In fairness, many high-achieving Aboriginal people are stretched to an unreasonable limit with work, family, extended family, and community responsibilities. Our closest Aboriginal friends in the community might be the principal of, or teacher in, the school – a major challenge in and of itself. But you can be sure they are also the stabilizing force within their extended family and, thus, will be called upon to deal with crisis after crisis. Beyond this, they will sit on every committee in the community and have to respond to endless demands. Finally, as Aboriginal educators, they will be called away to represent the school board on any matter touching Aboriginal communities.

These special community members are in the minority and are under tremendous pressure. They are placed in an inordinate number of highly responsible positions and expected to perform at the highest level. We remember vividly attending a board meeting of Aboriginal and non-Aboriginal educators where we ultimately "lost it." The Aboriginal board was under attack by non-Aboriginal education "specialists" for being slow in terms of curriculum development. We immediately asked the non-Aboriginal director of the mathematics curriculum at a large metropolitan school board, hypothetically, how long it would take him to orchestrate a board-wide change in the math curriculum for Grade 3. He was proud to announce that within seven years he and his professional department could assemble the competing math programs, review them, including their pilot test results, make their choice, and implement the new program. We went ballistic: "How do you expect an Aboriginal school board that has zero materials in the Aboriginal language to choose from and therefore has to create them from scratch, no trained curriculum developers, no trained teachers, and no professional staff to have an intact curriculum in no time?" The fact is that all of the planning, developing, training, and teaching will be done by a small group of overextended Aboriginal personnel who will be asked to do everything – and that's to say nothing of the one hundred other challenges and non-Aboriginal attacks these same few individuals will be required to address. No wonder the few role models, who do have well-defined long-term goals, are burned up and burned out.

The impression created by the lack of long-term goals in an Aboriginal community is not so much chaos as fluidity and flux. People are not on any planned trajectory, be it getting ahead, getting along with others, or, indeed, pursuing traditional Aboriginal activities. Time is fluid, and deadlines, work time, sleep time, and wake time appear as mere suggestions. You constantly look for the signs that point to a dedication to a long-term goal. In non-Aboriginal society, commitment to excellence is glorified: Michael Jordan, Wayne Gretzky, and Sidney Crosby, we are constantly reminded, practised their skills more than their competitors, and, as youngsters, they had to be dragged off the court or ice to have a meal or get some sleep.

This form of goal obsession is not to be found in Aboriginal communities. Young people sleep until noon. If asked, their family members will say they were out late, which is the norm, and need their sleep. Indeed, when we conduct one-on-one testing in a school we always have a gym mat handy. Often the nine-year-old child is so tired he or she can't think, so we borrow a trick learned from many teachers who face similar realities. We invite the child to have a nap on the mat, and the student is delighted to get some sleep. Upon awakening the child is happy and eager to perform on the tests. Where was the child all night?

## COLLECTIVE SELF-CONTROL ISSUES

When, because of a cultural vacuum, there are no long-term goals that a culture holds as sacred, self-control issues will be pervasive. Self-control requires people to say "no" to immediate temptation so that they might achieve a long-term goal. Passing up an immediate reward is difficult enough at the best of times: even if we want to be in shape to run a marathon in eight months, it is hard to pass up that chocolate cake in front of us and eat our vegetables. But imagine how quickly we will pounce on that chocolate cake if we don't have the long-term goal of running a marathon. It's no contest: immediate reward will win out every time.

Another way to view self-control issues is from a "time" perspective. Humans are unique in that they have the mental capacity to live in the present but reflect on the past and contemplate the future. Long-term goals require people to focus on the future, and the evidence would suggest that people who do so enjoy the best mental and physical health. Of course, being too future oriented can have its problems too. But in terms of quality of life, it would seem that it is people rooted in the present who encounter the most difficulties. These are the people who tend to prefer immediate gratification and have little or no concern for the future. Self-regulation requires long-term goals that can provide a focus for people's future orientation.

Examples of collective self-control challenges abound in Aboriginal communities. We spend much time in schools and so see it constantly. The number of actual school days per year is determined by provincial governments, who typically offer school boards a range from which to choose. Aboriginal school boards tend to choose the minimum, and so the school year might begin with 180 days. The minute spring arrives, and the weather turns warm and the days become longer, school is abandoned. Goose hunting is the order of business, and make-believe class outings. Students roam the community until three or four in the morning, and roaring ATVs make you think of the Indianapolis speedway. School and work are forgotten.

Ice hockey has become a passion in Aboriginal communities. Tournaments abound and, of course, entail complex logistics since communities are remote and travel complicated. Schools and workplaces empty for every tournament, sometimes for an entire week. And there are more unfortunate interruptions. Every death in a community involves everyone else, and community members are frequently lost on the land or in accidents. Add school events to this list and the number of actual school days, and indeed workdays, is reduced dramatically.

So maybe there are no collective, long-term goals to be found in domains related to non-Aboriginal culture, such as education and work. But what about traditional Aboriginal activities? The news is not good here either. Are there skilled hunters and sewers to be found? Absolutely, and we have had the good fortune to accompany them on hunting expeditions. Their skill is astonishing. But they are few in number, and there are even fewer among the younger generation. Moreover, all too often expeditions are an excuse to get out on to the land and be able to party away from prying eyes. It is not uncommon for the older generation to go out on a weekend hunt, leaving teenagers home with a fistful of money. For most, traditional skills are no longer a life and death issue but, rather, a passionate hobby – a hobby that, with snowmobiles and modern hunting equipment, is becoming more and more expensive. Traditional activities carry none of the long-term planning and slow, committed learning of skills that were once required. Today, traditional skills no longer require culturally defined long-term goals that are essential for community functioning.

*Skills now a hobby*

When there are no compelling and clearly defined long-term cultural goals, immediate gratification is a "no brainer." And thus the litany of collective self-control issues. Everybody knows that the days following payday and the issuing of welfare cheques are a write-off. When we teach courses in the community we see that the priorities are junk food, parties, flirting, sleeping in, playing bingo, gambling (lottos and scratch tickets), and so on. There are no long-term goals to put the brakes on these immediately enjoyable activities. Having a job as a teacher is not dependent on completing this or that particular course. No one is thinking of education as a career but, rather, as an interesting alternative. And, of course, classes are free, books are free, travel to take courses in another Aboriginal community is free for the teacher and dependents, and living and food are free. And if something comes up back in your own community, you just pack up and fly home.

Regular students are under no pressure to perform. Their job status is totally independent of education and training, and there are an abundance of extremely well-paying jobs in the community that are not linked to amount and quality of education. Indeed, school boards are so desperate for role models that they invent incentives for performance, about which the few students who pay attention to these matters laugh quietly. We have had dozens of conversations across the country with just such students, who say, for example: "Oh yeah, if I want a trip to the big city to go mall crawling I just dash off a quick essay on some feel-good topic, and they enter it in a contest and away I go."

One of the controversial domains associated with Aboriginal communities is the highly visible casino. Let us be upfront about where we stand. We are not big fans. Casinos teach, preach, live off, promote, and symbolize the quick fix, the get–something-for-nothing ideology that is the epitome of immediate gratification. And non-Aboriginal governments are collaborators in their promotion of gambling, lottos, and the "free-lunch" ideology that exacerbates the lack of commitment to long-term goals and the exercise of self-control.

The counter-argument, of course, is that casinos offer Aboriginal communities a genuine economic opportunity both as a moneymaker and as a source of employment. Imagine our discouragement, then, when we visited a casino only to notice that, while there were large numbers of Aboriginal people gambling, there were no Aboriginal employees. After some discussion it was revealed that, at the outset, the staff was overwhelmingly Aboriginal. However, as time went by Aboriginal employees were replaced with non-Aboriginal people. Why? Because Aboriginal employees were unreliable, both in terms of being punctual and in being committed to work once on the job. This, of course, is the narrative that reverberates throughout First Nations and Inuit communities across the country and is heard from all educators and employers. The portrait is a clear example of the extent of collective self-control issues.

To conclude our observations on collective self-control, we take a step back and return to our link between collective self-control issues, "time," and the broader non-Aboriginal society. <u>Self-control is all</u> <u>about time: immediate gratification is all about now,</u> about the present, while long-term goals are all about the future. Those who live in the present are not focused on the future consequences of their actions, and this is not a recipe for success in any of life's important domains (see Chapter 3).

Despite our focus on the undesirability of adopting a "here-and-now" perspective, we would be remiss if we didn't acknowledge that an overzealous "future" orientation can also be psychologically unhealthy. Sometimes we do need to stop and smell the roses. We remember a non-Aboriginal colleague who was as ambitious and competitive an academic as you would ever want to meet – the ultimate future-oriented, middle-aged go-getter. Now he was also a wine connoisseur who enjoyed several glasses of the best every day. After a spirited tennis match one day we sat down at the club lounge, where he ordered Perrier water. We looked at him and said, "What, no wine today?" He responded: "No, in order for me to stay ahead of my younger colleagues and work the long hours fully focused, I have had to reduce my intake of wine to one glass a day." For him to give up his one passion besides work was a bit extreme. You can't live your whole life in the future or life will pass you by. So, as much as we lament the here-and-now focus associated with collective self-control challenges, we are not suggesting that people adopt a 100 percent focus on long-term goals. But we are suggesting that a reasonable balance might be in order.

## DYSFUNCTIONAL 20–80 NORMATIVE STRUCTURE

Anyone in an Aboriginal community who decides to focus on a long-term goal and exercise self-control will not find support for their mission – quite the opposite. We argue in Chapter 6 that effectively functioning communities require at least an 80–20 normative structure: the majority 80 percent of community members function constructively, with only a minority 20 percent not doing so. The problem for Aboriginal communities is that, symbolically, they can be characterized as 20–80, with only 20 percent functioning effectively while the majority are engaged in a cluster of non-normative behaviours related to self-control issues. It is this dysfunctional normative structure that poses such a challenge for any community member who is motivated to change any important aspect of her or his life.

Growing up as teenagers in non-Aboriginal society, we, along with 80 percent of our friends, had a running battle with our parents about curfews. Week days we had to be home early, say 8:00 PM or 9:00 PM, and only if we had finished our homework were we allowed to go out. On weekends we might bargain for 11:00 PM or, on very special occasions, midnight. We all knew one or two classmates who did not have a curfew, and of course we would use that as ammunition to bargain for more time: "Yeah, but Marie-Eve is allowed to stay out later," to which would come the reply: "If they decided to jump off a cliff, would you jump too?"

The 20–80 normative structure in Aboriginal communities makes the idea of a curfew meaningless. Eighty percent of young people are free to be out as late as they choose, and so by the time they get to bed there is no chance of them getting up in time for school the next day. The one or two students who do have a curfew imposed on them face real social problems. They may do well in school, but they are teased, mocked, and ostracized by the other students – a devastating experience for a young person in a small isolated community who has nowhere else to turn.

Once, in frustration, the mayor of a small community imposed an 11:00 PM curfew for all young people. A horn would blow and the police would tour the community to gather up any young person not in his or her home. This generated instant entertainment for young people. They would lay low until 11:00 PM and then taunt the two police officers before running away in pure glee. The few young people who were rounded up would be taken to their home, and fifteen minutes later they were back in the game.

We often teach courses to adults in Aboriginal communities and are constantly amused when new, non-Aboriginal, teachers come to offer a course. The adult students never arrive on time and the punctual teacher will often find the entire school locked up because no one showed up to open the doors. Once class does begin, the adult students will one by one randomly wander out of the class to grab something to eat, make a phone call, or chat with someone who has popped their head in the door. Most often the adult student will have received a phone call about some calamity at home and may disappear for a while to address the issue. More serious interruptions are frequent and usually involve accidents, sudden illnesses, and dramatic domestic situations. This is the normative reality for both adults and young people in the classroom environment.

And this normative structure is what makes it such a challenge for someone to pursue a long-term goal and exercise self-control. In any domain – be it work, school, or interpersonal relationships – any individual motivated to change will feel that she has embarked upon a lonely quest.

## COMMUNITIES IN CRISIS AND FAILED INTERVENTIONS

The end result of colonialism – a cultural identity vacuum, a litany of collective self-control challenges, and a dysfunctional normative structure – involves community after community stumbling from one crisis to another. We have detailed these challenges, so now we refer to examples of how each new non-Aboriginal preoccupation seems to bring Aboriginal communities even lower.

It wasn't that long ago when non-Aboriginal media were all over the pollution issue, to the point that it became customary for radio stations across Canada to include a pollution index along with the weather forecast. We remember heading to a small community in the High Arctic and reflecting about the purity of the air and how maybe that explained why the colours were so crisp and well-defined. What did we learn? Pollution was even worse in these remote communities. Why? Some complicated scenario involving prevailing winds that suck up urban southern pollution and send it north: A new crisis to deal with.

And more recently, global warming is the universal preoccupation. And wouldn't you know, again isolated northern communities are feeling the pinch, with glaciers melting, waterways opening up, and ships from different countries wondering about a northwest passage and the economic implications thereof. And, of course, that means the debate is open again. Who exactly owns the North Pole and Arctic land that surrounds it? Canada? Russia? Denmark? The line-up of countries laying claim to the land and its resources is growing. Aboriginal people are caught in the crossfire, which affects where they live and the integrity of their traditional hunting, trapping, and fishing territories.

We remember vividly when a development project affected the fragile meeting of rivers and the ocean. The second the community made "noises" about this worry, the government suits arrived in a private jet, and we watched as they went door to door writing cheques to compensate Aboriginal residents. Talk about continuing a legacy of colonialism: exploit a people and then buy their silence – and, in the process, foster dependency and demotivation.

These policies have given rise to a vicious cycle of exploitation and guilt that continues to this day and, worse, that looks destined to keep going. As we noted earlier, there is a renewed Canadian economic focus on the North. Non-Aboriginal Canada sees dollar signs associated with the resources in Aboriginal regions, but blatant exploitation generates guilt. The result is that, instead of a genuine partnership, governments bend over backwards to compensate Aboriginal communities, thus fostering further dependency. Similarly, with the warming of Arctic waters and the prospect of a shipping lane across the North, issues over ownership of the Arctic lands have heated up. If Canadians are living on lands that are being disputed, that goes a long way to establishing ownership. Will we see a new round of forcing Aboriginal peoples to live on potentially disputed lands? The last time forced location was used to combat land claims from competing nations the result was disastrous. Ask the people of Inukjuaq. These colonial practices, coupled with feelings of guilt, virtually guarantee that communities will continue to be reinforced for adopting a passive, demotivated attitude towards constructive community change.

But, more broadly, we are concerned about the ongoing individualistic approach to what is a genuine collective problem. For example, non-Aboriginal school boards provide a host of specialized services for students, including "special needs" students, and counselling for career choices. Every Aboriginal school we have ever worked in offers these same services, with one noticeable difference. The phrase "but all our students are special needs students" is what you hear from educators in Aboriginal communities: And that's the issue. The same is true for social services workers who might seek to offer counselling to a fifteen–year-old youth who is in a volatile relationship and is already pregnant. But this is a challenge potentially confronting all young women in the community: the issue is collective, and a non-Aboriginal individualistic approach misses the point.

The police face the same dilemma. If you put every person engaged in a dangerous offence in jail, your jail will be the biggest building in the community. And it gets better. We have talked with a variety of young men from different communities in the Far North who have a unique strategy. They know the legal system so well that they manouevre to have jail time in the south during the winter but make sure they gain their freedom for the spring and summer. They say the southern jails are "great."

We could go on ad infinitum with examples of the collective challenges confronting Aboriginal communities. But, in the end, our point is simple. The challenges are collective, and they therefore require collective solutions.

## ENOUGH WITH THE CHALLENGES: TOWARDS CONSTRUCTIVE CHANGE

When it comes to real-life examples with respect to constructive solutions, our personal experiences are obviously limited. But we have seen enough to at least be encouraged by the potential for the three processes we outlined in chapters 7, 8 and 9, respectively: minority influence, zero tolerance, and engaging community members in survey research. Despite our optimism, we continue to be dismayed at not just the lack of imaginative government policy but the enthusiastic pursuit of thinly disguised self-interested projects that exacerbate the social and psychological outcomes of colonialism.

### Minority Influence

In a community the majority can influence the minority with relative ease. By contrast, for a minority to persuade the majority to change is no easy matter. We noted that, in Aboriginal communities, social change must begin with regrouping the functioning minority to collectively take on the challenge of changing attitudes and behaviour among the majority.

We cannot say that we have personally witnessed such a regrouping at the broad community level. We have, however, been involved in such regroupings for community change in specific domains. These include coping with the residential schooling experience and dealing with specific crises, such as community suicide and delinquent behaviour on the part of youth.

The regrouping of a small, functioning minority to spearhead constructive social change proved to be extremely difficult. The first challenge was trying to find the "right" people. These were precisely the people who were sought for every critical and non-critical community issue. They were spread so thin that they simply could not devote the concentrated collective effort needed to mobilize the majority into constructive change. They were willing planners with excellent ideas, but there was no one left over to execute or implement a detailed plan. The second problem we witnessed was more political. Often, mobilizing a group for constructive change required asking the head of each community organization to play a role. Protocol insisted that bypassing the head of even a single organization would be inappropriate. The problem, of course, was that the heads of organizations are not usually the members of the "functioning" minority and, in any case, are not typically inclined to engage in actual implementation.

Our experiences have taught us that regrouping a functioning minority for concerted, long-term action is not easy. But we must remember that this task has not been attempted with an accompanying clear rationale regarding its importance and its exact mission. So far our experience is limited to natural, informal groupings. With a well-defined game plan, minority influence may well be manageable.

## Zero Tolerance

Zero tolerance programs are easy to find. Bullying, drugs, risky sexual behaviour – you name it and it's zero tolerance. The problem is that none of these are "real" zero tolerance programs: they are publicity programs to raise awareness about a specific issue, and they simply don't work in an environment in which the vast majority of young people are vigorously engaged in the targeted behaviour.

We have been able to watch closely what amounts to an enlightened zero tolerance policy, and it had great promise. The program, unfortunately, is suffering the fate of most zero tolerance policies: it is not being strictly applied.

The program was built around the one thing that Aboriginal youth love to do, are willing to work at, and for which they have the support of the entire community: ice hockey. Communities have state–of-the-art arenas but often their use is compromised by poor maintenance and organization. In one community, inspired by enlightened leadership from a former professional player, a truly organized hockey program was introduced. The inspired feature was the linking of ice-hockey to education. For each age group, participation in the hockey program required that the boys and girls perform well at school. The punishment for not performing well at school was revocation of the privilege of playing on the hockey team. "Performing well" at school was defined modestly, in that all that was required was that students attended regularly and made an effort. There was no performance criterion: effort was the only focus. This required the cooperation of teachers who had to write weekly reports and school officials who had to monitor school attendance and attitude. Every student, every adult, every educator, and every member of the community was aware of the program and its contingencies.

So where did it all fall apart? An important regional hockey tournament was looming and one of the better players was not making the threshold in terms of his academic effort. He was warned, cajoled, encouraged, and monitored, with the constant threat that unless his effort improved, he would not be playing in the tournament. No improvement was forthcoming, but sure enough, when the hockey team boarded the plane to head off to the tournament, key community members made sure the delinquent "player" joined his teammates, hockey bag in hand. The message was clear to everyone in the community: the academic effort contract was mere rhetoric. The teachers who spent all their time preparing academic reports were disgusted and disillusioned. Students realized the heat was off. A few community members voiced their disapproval. At this moment zero tolerance for lack of academic effort seems doomed. The only hope is with the minority of community members who continue to voice their displeasure. They will have to be very insistent if the program is to survive intact.

Unfortunately, this is the only genuine example of the application of zero tolerance that we have witnessed personally. We have seen hundreds of so-called zero tolerance pronouncements, but they are mere pleas for students not to engage in certain targeted behaviours: there is never a serious commitment to follow through on the promised consequences for contravention of the policy.

## Survey Research to Engage Community Members

We have detailed our progress in using survey research as a vehicle for constructive social change. The essence of the process involves a mechanism for engaging in a one-to-one conversation with each and every community member. This level of engagement requires crossing the profound psychological divide that permeates every Aboriginal community. Survey research accomplishes this by involving everyone in the community in the process of generating data on constructive community norms. We have demonstrated in several communities across the country that it is realistic to survey the vast majority of community members and to obtain results to indicate that the vast majority at least "say" that they support education. The next step is to find the constructive minority who can be trained to make home visits. Their mission, armed with constructive norms substantiated by the survey results, will be to elicit a concrete commitment from each parent to engage in behaviours that would support their children's education. This process is now under way, but only time will tell if the last phase will be successful in the long term.

Meantime, we are expanding into other domains. For example, we are in the process of asking a group of Aboriginal young people to note on an hour-by-hour basis what they actually do throughout their entire day. We then ask questions about the purpose and importance of the hour-by-hour behaviour. The result is a profile of the group members that focuses on what they actually do and why they do it on a daily basis. The next step is to meet the group and share the results. We do not share any young person's profile but we do share the profile for the entire group: this is not a finger-pointing exercise. The group profile clearly indicates the extent to which the group as a whole is devoting time and energy to the things that really matter to its members. The group members, the students, stimulated by the group profile, discuss the implications for themselves. The profiles are for the most part positive, illustrating how much sleep they get and how much schoolwork and socializing they do as a group. Usually the group members are surprised at how much time they spend in random socializing and how much more private studying they should do. As an aside, we get approximately the same profile and reaction from non-Aboriginal students. The point is that the students are confronted with what they do as a group – their norms. And they are free to use that information in any way they see fit. Again, the point is to confront them with any disconnect between their stated goals and their actual behaviour, thus enabling them to learn from each other.

## IS CONSTRUCTIVE CHANGE POSSIBLE? WITH COLLECTIVE RESILIENCE, YES

We have come to that point at which we look ahead and ask: Is there any sign of hope on the horizon? We have catalogued a litany of challenges confronting Aboriginal communities. Indeed, we feel uncomfortable reiterating and providing examples that reinforce a negative stereotype of the communities we love and respect. We have argued for a new, collective approach to constructive community change, but these efforts are in their infancy.

Do we have any reason to be optimistic? We, of course, believe our proposals for a new collective direction will bear fruit. But, more important, every time we visit Aboriginal communities we cannot escape the realization that Aboriginal people have been, are, and will be a resilient people. And we focus here not on the usual preoccupation with personal resilience but, rather, on a _collective resilience_.

But what is resilience exactly? In physics, resilience means that a material can be bent but not broken, and this despite the extreme stress to which the material might be subjected. In the social sciences, resilience at the personal level represents the capacity of individuals to bounce back from extreme stress and adversity. If a mother can lose a child to suicide, and somehow continue to function effectively after a normal recovery period, we would conclude that she is highly resilient. At the collective level, resilience takes the form of an entire cultural group maintaining its capacity to function despite the dramatic social change that has challenged the core of its cultural identity. Dramatic social change is defined as "profound societal transformations that produce a complete rupture in the equilibrium of social structures because their adaptive capacities are surpassed" (de la Sablonnière et al. 2009, 325). The classic example of resilience at the collective level is the response of the Jewish people following events culminating in the Holocaust. Millions were killed, many more displaced, and their culture was challenged to its very core. Nevertheless, Jewish people somehow managed to rebuild an even stronger identity and to collectively pursue constructive paths to success.

Aboriginal people have collectively confronted dramatic social change brought about by the ravages of colonialsm. Social dysfunction is pervasive. If we take suicide as an example, the simple reality is that the rate of suicide is eleven times higher in Aboriginal communities than in non-Aboriginal communities. These apparently very "personal" events are in fact collective experiences because each member of the community is affected. Because everyone is related to everyone else, either by blood or close friendship, a dramatic event such as suicide is a truly collective trauma. The tangible evidence of this is the fact that for every suicide, indeed for every death in the community, the entire community, including offices and schools, shuts down.

Thus, these dramatic, seemingly personal events are really experienced at the collective level; thus, collective resilience will be required to cope with and recover from them. Given the ongoing collective challenges confronting the communities, nothing short of the highest level of collective resilience is needed in order for them to survive and thrive.

Visit any community and the signs of collective resilience are everywhere. In spite of ongoing collective trauma, communities are populated by individuals who are trying their best to adapt and institute positive changes. To begin with, it is surprising that so many Aboriginal communities around the world are still intact and thriving. They are actively struggling to maintain and grow their culture. For example, we have seen Inuit and First Nations colleagues devoting all their waking hours to developing a school curriculum so that the children in their community will have an education that is more culturally relevant than the one they received themselves. We have seen alcoholic Aboriginals become sober despite the fact that their family and friends continue to struggle with their own sobriety. We have seen victims of abuse bravely break the cycle of abuse by having the courage to move forward. For the most part, Aboriginal people do all this in spite of not having a supportive normative structure – a normative structure that, in non-Aboriginal communities, would help people to bounce back in the face of adversity.

We have always been amazed at the capacity of our Aboriginal friends and colleagues to find humour and touches of humanity against the backdrop of ongoing trauma. Recently, we were sitting in the staff room of the school with several of our Inuit friends and colleagues drinking coffee before they went off to teach their classes. Each of these teachers is struggling with personal and family challenges. They were teasing and laughing at us because one of us – don't ask why – kissed the toe of one of the teachers. In spite of their own challenges, and the prospect of going off to teach children who are not in a position to be able to mentally focus (let alone to be motivated to learn), these teachers display humour and optimism. Every day they get up in the morning and try to make a difference so that the children in the community might enjoy a brighter future than they themselves experienced. This is collective resilience at its best. They smile, laugh, and fight for their identity and for the survival of their language.

Is collective resilience enough? No. But it may provide the core collective energy to turn communities around. The challenges are collective, our proposed solutions are collective, and collective resilience can fuel constructive change.

# References

Aarts, H., and A. Dijksterhuis. 2003. "The Silence of the Library: Environment, Situational Norm, and Social Behavior." *Journal of Personality and Social Psychology* 84: 18–28. doi: 10.1037/0022-3514.84.1.18.

Adams, K. 2009. "John Beaucage Seeking National Leader's Role." *Bay Today*, 3 February. http://www.baytoday.ca/content/news/details.asp?c=29855.

Adlaf, E.M., P. Begin, and E. Sawka. 2005. *Canadian Addiction Survey (CAS): A National Survey of Canadian's Use of Alcohol and Other Drugs; Prevalence of Use and Related Harms – Detailed Report.* http://www.ccsa.ca/Eng/KnowledgeCentre/OurPublications/Pages/CCSAPublicationsA-F.aspx.

Advisory Group on Suicide Prevention. 2003. "Acting on What We Know: Preventing Youth Suicide in First Nations." Ottawa: Health Canada.

*American Heritage Dictionary of the English Language.* 2013. http://ahdictionary.com/word/search.html?q=zero%20tolerance#Z5013600.

American Psychological Association Zero Tolerance Task Force. 2008. "Are Zero Tolerance Policies Effective in the Schools? An Evidentiary Review and Recommendations." *American Psychologist* 63: 852–62. doi: 10.1037/0003-066X.63.9.852.

Amiot, C.E., R. de la Sablonnière, D.J. Terry, and J.R. Smith. 2007. "Integration of Social Identities in the Self: Toward a Cognitive-Developmental Model." *Personality and Social Psychology Review* 11 (4): 364–88. doi:10.1177/1088868307304091.

Anderson, J.F. 2007. "Screening and Brief Intervention for Hazardous Alcohol Use and Indigenous Populations: Potential Solution or Impossible dream?" *Addiction Research and Theory* 15 (5): 439–48. doi:10.1080/16066350701219210.

Anglican Church of Canada. 2009. "Residential Schools: The Living Apology." http://www.anglican.ca/rs/history/schools/index.htm.

Asch, S. 1955. "Opinions and Social Pressure." *Scientific American* 193: 31–5.

Ashmore, R.D., K. Deaux, and T. McLaughlin-Volpe. 2004. "An Organizing Framework for Collective Identity: Articulation and Significance of Multidimensionality." *Psychological Bulletin* 130 (1): 80–114. doi: 10.1037/0033-2909.130.1.80.

Assembly of First Nations. 2007. "Alcohol and Drug Abuse." In *First Nations Regional Longitudinal Health Survey: Results for Adults, Youth and Children Living in First Nations Communities*. http://www.rhs-ers.ca/english/pdf/rhs2002-03reports/rhs2002-03-technicalreport-afn.pdf.

– 2009. "AFN National Chief Calling for a First Nations Economic Stimulus Package at Meeting with First Ministers." http://64.26.129.156/article.asp?id=4400.

Atleo, S. 2009. "Four Pillar Strategy." http://www.shawnatleo.ca/modules /wfchannel/index.php?pagenum=7.

Baumgardner, A.H. 1990. "To Know Oneself Is to Like Oneself: Self-Certainty and Self-Affect." *Journal of Personality and Social Psychology* 58 (6): 1062–72. http://dx.doi.org/10.1037/0022-3514.58.6.1062.

Baumeister, R.F. ed. 1999. *The Self in Social Psychology*. Philadelphia, PA: Psychology Press.

Baumeister, R.F., E. Bratslavsky, M. Muraven, and D.M. Tice. 1998. "Ego Depletion: Is the Active Self a Limited Resource?" *Journal of Personality and Social Psychology* 74 (5): 1252–65.

Baumeister, R.F., T.F. Heatherton, and D.M. Tice. 1994. *Losing Control: How and Why People Fail at Self-Regulation*. San Dieago, CA: Academic Press.

Baumeister, R.F., and T.F. Heatherton. 1996. "Self-Regulation Failure: An Overview." *Psychological Inquiry* 7: 1–15. http://dx.doi.org/10.1207/s15327965pli0701_1.

Baumeister, R.F., B.J. Schmeichel, and K.D. Vohs. 2007. "Self-Regulation and the Executive Function: The Self as Controlling Agent." In *Social Psychology: Handbook of Basic Principles*, 2nd ed., ed. A. Kruglanski and E. T. Higgins, 516–39. New York: Guilford.

Baumeister, R.F., and J. Tierney. 2011. *Willpower: Rediscovering the Greatest Human Strength*. New York: Penguin.

Baumeister, R.F., K.D. Vohs, and D.M. Tice. 2007. "The Strength Model of Self-Control." *Current Directions in Psychological Science* 16 (6): 351–5. doi: 10.1111/j.1467-8721.2007.00534.x

Bellegarde, P. 2009. "Priorities." http://www.perrybellegarde.com/pdfs/Perry _Bellegarde_Priorities_E.pdf.

Benet-Martinez, V., and J. Haritatos. 2005. "Bicultural Identity Integration

(BII) Components and Psychosocial Antecedents." *Journal of Personality* 73: 1015–45. http://dx.doi.org/10.1111/j.1467-6494.2005.00337.x

Benet-Martinez, V., F. Lee, and J. Leu. 2006. "Biculturalism and Cognitive Complexity: Expertise in Cultural Representations." *Journal of Cross-Cultural Psychology* 37: 386–407. http://dx.doi.org/10.1177/0022022106288476.

Benet-Martinez, V., J. Leu, F. Lee, and M. W. Morris. 2002. "Negotiating Biculturalism : Cultural Frame Switching in Biculturals with Oppositional versus Compatible Cultural Identities." *Journal of Cross-Cultural Psychology* 33: 492–516. http://dx.doi.org/10.1177/0022022102033005005.

Bernard, V.W., P. Ottenberg, and F. Redl, 2003. "Dehumanization: A Composite Psychological Defense in Relation to Modern War." In *Behavioral Science and Human Survival* edited by A. Schwebel and M. Schwebel, 64–82. Lincoln, NE: iUniverse, Inc.

Berry J.W. 1990. "Psychology of Acculturation." In *Nebraska Symposium on Motivation, 1989: Cross-Cultural Perspectives*, ed. J.J. Berman. 201–34. Lincoln: University of Nebraska Press.

– 1997. "Immigration, Acculturation and Adaptation." *Applied Psychology* 46: 5–68. http://dx.doi.org/10.1080/026999497378467.

– 2005. "Acculturation: Living Successfully in Two Cultures." *International Journal of Intercultural Relations* 29 (6): 697–712. http://dx.doi.org/10.1016/j.ijintrel.2005.07.013.

– 2006a. "Contexts of Acculturation." In *The Cambridge Handbook of Acculturation Psychology*, ed. D.L. Sam and J.W. Berry, 27–42. New York: Cambridge University Press. http://dx.doi.org/10.1017/CBO9780511 489891.006.

– 2006b. "Stress Perspectives on Acculturation." In *The Cambridge Handbook of Acculturation Psychology*, ed. D.L. Sam and J.W. Berry, 43–57. New York: Cambridge University Press. http://dx.doi.org/10.1017/CBO9780511489891.007.

Berry, J.W., J.S. Phinney, D.L. Sam, and P. Vedder. 2006. "Immigrant Youth: Acculturation, Identity, and Adaptation." *Applied Psychology: An International Review* 55 (3): 303–32. http://dx.doi.org/10.1111/j.1464-0597.2006 .00256.x.

Berry, J.W., and D.L. Sam. 1997. "Acculturation and Adaptation." *Handbook of Cross-Cultural Psychology* 3: 291–326.

Bidell, T.R., and K.W. Fischer. 1996. "Between Nature and Nurture: The Role of Human Agency in the Epigenesis of Intelligence." In *Intelligence: Heredity and Environment*, ed. R.J. Sternberg and E. Grigorenko, 193–242. New York: Cambridge University Press. http://dx.doi.org/10.1017/CBO 9781139174282.008.

Bond, R., and P.B. Smith. 1996. "Culture and Conformity: A Meta-Analysis of Studies Using Asch's (1952b, 1956) Line Judgment Task." *Psychological Bulletin*, 119 (1): 111–37. doi: 10.1037/0033-2909.119.1.111.

Bonanno, G.A. 2004. "Loss, Trauma, and Human Resilience: Have We Underestimated the Human Capacity to Thrive after Extremely Aversive Events?" *American Psychologist* 59 (1): 20–8. doi: 10.1037/0003-066X.59.1.20.

Boothroyd, L.J., L.J. Kirmayer, S. Spreng, M. Malus, and S. Hodgins. 2001. "Completed Suicides among the Inuit of Northern Quebec, 1982–1996: A Case–Control Study." *Canadian Medical Association Journal* 165 (6): 749–55.

Borsuk, A.J., and M.B. Murphy. 1999. "Idle or Otherwise, Threats Bring Severe Discipline: Where Area Students Once Faced a Principal, Now They Face the Police." *Milwaukee Journal Sentinel*, 30 April.

Brady, M. 1995. "Culture in Treatment, Culture as Treatment: A Critical Appraisal of Developments in Addictions Programs for Indigenous North Americans and Australians." *Social Science and Medicine* 41 (11): 1487–98. Available at http://dx.doi.org/10.1016/0277-9536(95)00055-C.

– 2000. "Alcohol Policy Issues for Indigenous People in the United States, Canada, Australia and New Zealand." *Contemporary Drug Problems* 17 (3): 435–509.

Brady, P. 1996. "Native Dropouts and Non-Native Dropouts in Canada: Two Solitudes or a Solitude Shared." *Journal of American Indian Education* 35 (2): 10–20.

Brodeur, P. 1985. *Outrageous Misconduct: The Asbestos Industry on Trial*. New York: Pantheon Books.

Brug, J., M. Van Vugt, B. Van Den Borne, A. Brouwers, and H. Van Hooff. 2000. "Predictors of Willingness to Register as an Organ Donor among Dutch Adolescents." *Psychology and Health* 15: 357–68. http://dx.doi.org/10.1080/08870440008401998.

Brzozowski, J., A. Taylor-Butts, and S. Johnson. 2006. *Victimization and Offending among the Aboriginal Population in Canada*. Ottawa: Statistics Canada.

Burke, E., and D. Herbert. 1996. "Zero Tolerance Policy: Combating Violence in Schools." *NASSP Bulletin* 80: 49–54. doi: 10.1177/019263659608057909.

Campbell, J.D. 1990. "Self-Esteem and the Clarity of the Self-Concept." *Journal of Personality and Social Psychology* 59 (3): 538–49. http://dx.doi.org/10.1037/0022-3514.59.3.538.

Campbell, J.D., S. Assanand, and A.D. Paula. 2003. "The Structure of the

Self-Concept and Its Relation to Psychological Adjustment." *Journal of Personality* 71 (1): 115–40. http://dx.doi.org/10.1111/1467-6494.t01-1-00002.

Campbell, J.D., and L.F. Lavallee. 1993. "Who Am I? The Role of Self-Concept Confusion in Understanding the Behavior of People with Low Self-Esteem." In *Self-Esteem: The Puzzle of Low Self-Regard*, ed. R.F. Baumeister, 3–20. New York: Plenum Press. http://dx.doi.org/10.1007/978-1-4684-8956-9_1.

Canada. 2006. *The Human Face of Mental Health and Mental Illness in Canada 2006*. Ottawa: Minister of Public Works and Government Services.

Canadian Council on Social Development. 2009. *Social Challenges: The Well-Being of Aboriginal People*. http://www.ccsd.ca/cpsd/ccsd/c_ab.htm.

Canadian Labour Congress. 2005. *Aboriginal Rights Resource Tool Kit*. http://www.canadianlabour.ca/human-rights-equality/aboriginal-workers.

*Canadian Oxford Dictionary*. 2004. http://www.oxfordreference.com/view/10.1093/acref/9780195418163.001.0001/m-en_ca-msdict-00001-0079657.

Canadian Paediatric Society. First Nations and Inuit Health Committee. 2002. "Fetal Alcohol Syndrome." *Journal of Paediatric Child Health* 7: 161–74.

Carducci, B.J., and P.S. Deuser. 1984. "The Foot-in-the-Donor Technique: Initial Request and Organ Donation." *Basic and Applied Social Psychology* 5: 75–81. http://dx.doi.org/10.1073/pnas.1108561108.

Carducci, B.J., P.S. Deuser, A. Bauer, M. Large, and M. Rameakers. 1989. "An Application of the Foot in the Door Technique to Organ Donation." *Journal of Business and Psychology* 4: 245–49. http://dx.doi.org/10.1007/BF01016444.

Casella, R. 2003. "Zero Tolerance Policy in Schools: Rationale, Consequences, and Alternatives." *Teachers College Record* 105 (5): 872–92. http://dx.doi.org/10.1111/1467-9620.00271.

Casey, B.J., L.H. Somerville, I.H. Gotlib, O. Ayduk, N.T. Franklin, M.K. Askren, and Y. Shoda. 2011. "Behavioral and Neural Correlates of Delay of Gratification 40 years Later." *Proceedings of the National Academy of Sciences* 108 (36): 14998–15003.

Chandler, M.J., and C. Lalonde. 1998. "Cultural Continuity as a Hedge against Suicide in Canada's First Nations." *Transcultural Psychiatry* 35 (2): 191–219. http://dx.doi.org/10.1177/136346159803500202.

Chandler, M.J., C.E. Lalonde, B.W. Sokol, D. Hallett, and J.E. Marcia. 2003. "Personal Persistence, Identity Development, and Suicide: A Study of Native and Non-Native North American Adolescents." *Monographs of the Society for Research in Child Development*, i–138. Boston: Wiley Blackesll.

Chansonneuve, D. 2007. *Addictive Behaviours among Aboriginal People in Canada*. Ottawa: Aboriginal Healing Foundation.

Chénier, N.M. 1995. "Suicide Among Aboriginal People: Royal Commission Report." 23 February. http://www.parl.gc.ca/Content/LOP/research publications/mr131-e.pdf.

Christian, W.M., and P.M. Spittal. 2008. "The Cedar Project: Acknowledging the Pain of Our Children." *Lancet* 372 (9644): 1132–33. http://dx.doi.org /10.1016/S0140-6736(08)61460-9.

Cialdini, R.B. 2003. "Crafting Normative Messages to Protect the Environment." *Current Directions in Psychological Science* 12: 105–9. http://dx .doi.org/10.1111/1467-8721.01242.

Cialdini, R.B., and N.J. Goldstein. 2004. "Social Influence: Compliance and Conformity." *Annual Review of Psychology* 55(1): 591–621. http://dx.doi.org /10.1146/annurev.psych.55.090902.142015.

Cialdini, R.B., C.A. Kallgren, and R.R. Reno. 1991. "A Focus Theory of Normative Conduct: A Theoretical Refinement and Reevaluation of the Role of Norms in Human Behavior." *Advances in Experimental Social Psychology* 21: 201–34. http://dx.doi.org/10.1016/S0065-2601(08)60330-5.

Cialdini, R.B., R.R. Reno, and C.A. Kallgren. 1990. "A Focus Theory of Normative Conduct: Recycling the Concept of Norms to Reduce Littering in Public Places." *Journal of Personality and Social Psychology* 58: 1015–26. http://dx.doi.org/10.1037/0022-3514.58.6.1015.

Cocker, Mark. 1998. *Rivers of Blood, Rivers of Gold: Europe's Conflict with Tribal Peoples*. London: J. Cape.

Cohen, S. 2004. "Social Relationships and Health." *American Psychologist* 59 (8): 676–86. http://dx.doi.org/10.1037/0003-066X.59.8.676.

Congress of Aboriginal Peoples. 2009. "Employment, Empowerment and Enrichment: Human Resources Development and Canada's Off-Reserve Aboriginal Community." http://www.abopeoples.org/programs /Employment%20empowerment%20final.pdf.

de la Sablonnière, R., R. Debrosse, and S. Benoit. 2010. "Comparaison de Trois Conceptualisations de L'intégration Identitaire: Une étude auprès d'immigrants Québécois [Comparison of three identity integration conceptualizations: A Study among Quebec immigrants]." *Cahiers Internationaux de Psychologie Sociale* 88: 663–82.

de la Sablonnière, R., D.M. Taylor, C. Perozzo, and N. Sadykova. 2009. "Reconceptualizing Relative Deprivation in the Context of Dramatic Social Change: The Challenge Confronting the People of Kyrgyzstan." *European Journal of Social Psychology* 39 (3): 325–45.

Del Litke, C. 1996 "When Violence Came to Our Rural School." *Educational Leadership* 54: 77–80.

Dingle, S. 2009. "NT Educators Responsible for Indigenous 'Underclass.'" *ABC News*. 13 April. http://www.abc.net.au/news/2009-04-13/nt-educators-responsible-for-indigenous-underclass/1649030.

Dorais, L.-J. 1996. "The Aboriginal Languages of Quebec, Past and Present." In *Quebec's Aboriginal Languages: History, Planning, Development.* ed. J. Aurais, 43–100. Clevedon, UK: Multilingual Matters Ltd.

Drug-Free Schools and Campuses Act. 1989. Public Law 101–226. *US Statutes at Large* 103 (1989) 1928.

*Economist*. 2009. "Joining the Stimulating Party: A Pragmatic Budget has Given Stephen Harper's Government a New Lease of Life – But Not Necessarily a Long one." 29 January. http://www.economist.com/research/articlesBySubject/displaystory.cfm?subjectid=548577&story_id=13022147

Feda, D.M.G. 2008. "Written Violence Policies and Assault Deterrents in Minnesota Schools: Impact on Educators' Risk of Physical Assault." Pro-Quest digital dissertations.

Festinger, L. 1954. "A Theory of Social Comparison Processes." *Human Relations* 7: 117–40. http://dx.doi.org/10.1177/001872675400700202.

First Nations Centre. 2005. *First Nations Regional Longitudinal Health Survey (RHS), 2002/03: Results for Adults, Youth and Children Living in First Nations Communities.* Ottawa: First Nations Centre.

First Nations Child and Family Caring Society of Canada. 2002. *Affirming and Promoting Indigenous Knowledge and Research.* http://www.fncfcs.com/projects/FNRS.html.

Fischer, K.W. 1980. "A Theory of Cognitive Development: The Control and Construction of Hierarchies of Skills." *Psychological Review* 87: 477–531. http://dx.doi.org/10.1037/0033-295X.87.6.477

Freedman, J.L., and S.C. Fraser. 1966. "Compliance without Pressure: The Foot-in-the-Door Technique." *Journal of Personality and Social Psychology* 4 (2): 195–202.

Frideres, J.S. 1987. "Native People and Canadian Education." In *The Political Economy of Canadian Schooling*, ed. T. Wotherspoon, 275–89. Toronto: Methuen.

Gaertner, L., C. Sedikides, J.L. Vevea, and J. Iuzzini. 2002. "The" I," the" We," and the "When": A Meta-Analysis of Motivational Primacy in Self-Definition. *Journal of Personality and Social Psychology* 83 (3): 574–91. http://dx.doi.org/10.1037/0022-3514.83.3.574

Garrick, R. 2008. "Research Must Respect Aboriginal Communities."
*Wawatay News*, 13 November.

Gionet, L. 2008. *Inuit in Canada: Selected Findings of the 2006 Census.*
Ottawa: Minister of Industry

– 2009a. *First Nations People: Selected Findings of the 2006 Census.* Ottawa:
Minister of Industry.

– 2009b. *Métis in Canada: Selected Findings of the 2006 Census.* Ottawa: Minister of Industry.

Goldstein, A.P. 2001. "Low-Level Aggression: New Targets for Zero-Toler-
ance." In *Handbook of Psychological Services for Children and Adolescents*, ed.
J.N. Hughes, A.M. La Greca, and J.C. Conoley, 161–81. New York: Oxford
University Press.

Goldstein, N.J., R.B. Cialdini, and V. Griskevicius. 2008. "A Room with a
Viewpoint: Using Social Norms to Motivate Environmental Conservation
in Hotels." *Journal of Consumer Research* 35 (3): 472–82.
http://dx.doi.org/10.1086/586910

Graham, J. 2008. "Native Leader Urges Governments to Help First Nations
Tackle Substance Abuse." *Brantford Expositor*, 5 February.
http://www.brantfordexpositor.ca/2008/02/05/native-leader-urges-help-
tackling-substance-abuse

Granberg, D., and S. Holmberg. 1992. "The Hawthorne Effect in Election
Studies: The Impact of Survey Participation on Voting." *British Journal of
Political Science* 22: 240–7. http://dx.doi.org/10.1017/S0007123400
006359.

Greeley, H. 1860. *An Overland Journey, from New York to San Francisco, in the
Summer of 1859.* New York: C.M. Saxton, Barker and Co. https://play
.google.com/store/books/details?id=v3EFAAAAQAAJ&rdid=book-
v3EFAAAAQAAJ&rdot=1.

Greenberg, J., X. Pyszczynski, and S. Solomon. 1986. "The Causes and Con-
sequences of the Need for Self-Esteem: A Terror Management Theory." In
*Public Self and Private Self,* ed. Roy. F. Baumeister, 189–212. New York:
Springer-Verlag.

Greenwald, A.F., C.G. Carnot, R. Beach, and B. Young. 1987. "Increasing Voting Behavior by Asking People if They Expect to Vote." *Journal of Applied
Psychology* 72: 315–18. http://dx.doi.org/10.1037/0021-9010.72.2.315.

Greenwald, A.G., and M. R. Banaji. 1995. "Implicit Social Cognition: Attitudes, Self-Esteem, and Stereotypes." *Psychological Review* 102 (1): 4–27.
http://dx.doi.org/10.1037/0033-295X.102.1.4.

Haritatos, J., and V. Benet-Martinez. 2002. "Bicultural Identities: The Inter-
face of Cultural, Personality, and Socio-Cognitive Processes." *Journal of*

*Research in Personality* 36: 598–606. http://dx.doi.org/10.1016/S0092-6566(02)00510-X.

Harrell-Bond, B.E. 1986. *Imposing Aid: Emergency Assistance to Refugees.* Oxford: Oxford University Press.

Harter, S. 1999. *The Construction of the Self: A Developmental Perspective.* New York: Guilford.

– 2003. "The Development of Self-Representations during Childhood and Adolescence." In *Handbook of Self and Identity*, ed. R.R. Leary and J.P. Tangney, 610–42. New York: Guilford.

Health Canada. 1996. *Joint Statement: Prevention of Fetal Alcohol Syndrome (FAS) Fetal Alcohol Effects (FAE) in Canada.* Ottawa. http://www.phac-aspc.gc.ca/hp-ps/dca-dea/prog-ini/fasd-etcaf/index-eng.php.

– 1998. *National Native Alcohol and Drug Abuse Program: General Review.* Ottawa. http://www.hc-sc.gc.ca/fniah-spnia/pubs/substan/_ads/1998_rpt-nnadap-pnlaada/index-eng.php.

– 2003a. *Acting on What We Lnow: Preventing Youth Suicide in First Nations.* Advisory Group on Suicide Prevention. Ottawa. http://www.hc-sc.gc.ca/fniah-spnia/pubs/promotion/_suicide/prev_youth-jeunes/index-eng.php.

– 2004. *Health Sectoral Session.* http://www.aboriginalroundtable.ca/sect/hlth/bckpr/HC_BgPaper_e.pdf.

– 2006. *First Nations and Inuit Health: Suicide Prevention.* http://www.hc-sc.gc.ca/fniah-spnia/promotion/suicide/index-eng.php.

– 2009. *A Statistical Profile on the Health of First Nations in Canada: Determinants of Health, 1999 to 2003* http://www.hc-sc.gc.ca/fniah-spnia/alt_formats/fnihb-dgspni/pdf/pubs/aborig-autoch/2009-stats-profil-eng.pdf.

Heckewelder, J.E.G. 1876. *History, Manners and Customs of the Indian Nations who once Inhabited Pennsylvania and the Neighbouring States.* Vol. 12. Philadelphia: Historical Society of Pennsylvania. https://play.google.com/store/books/details?id=F8wLAAAAYAAJ&rdid=book-F8wLAAAAYAAJ&rdot=1.

Henault, C. 2001. "Zero Tolerance in Schools." *Journal of Law and Education* 30 (3): 547–53.

Henderson, A. 1999. "Political Constructions of National Identity in Scotland and Quebec." *Scottish Affairs* 29: 121–38.

Heymann, J. 2013. *Children's Chances: How Countries Can Move from Surviving to Thriving.* Cambridge, MA: Harvard University Press.

Hogg, M.A., and B.A. Mullin. 1999. "Joining Groups to Reduce Uncertainty: Subjective Uncertainty Reduction and Group Identification." In *Social*

*Identity and Social Cognition*, ed. D. Abrams and M.A. Hogg, 249–79.
Malden, IL: Blackwell.

Hogg, M.A., D.K. Sherman, J. Dierselhuis, A.T. Maitner, and G. Moffitt.
2007. "Uncertainty, Entitativity, and Group Identification." *Journal of
Experimental Social Psychology* 43 (1): 135–42. http://dx.doi.org/10.1016
/j.jesp.2005.12.008.

Holmes, T.R., and J. Murrell. 1995. "Schools, Discipline, and the Uniformed
Police Officer." *NASSP Bulletin* 79 (569): 60–4.

Huberdeau, M.-E., D. Cárdenas, and R. de la Sablonnière. 2014. "Writing
about Conflicting Identities: A Concrete Strategy Facilitating Well-
Being." Paper to be presented at 22nd Congress of the International Association for Cross-Cultural Psychology, summer, Reims, France.

Human Resources and Skills Development Canada. 2009. *Aboriginal Labour
Market Programs: Employment Programs.* http://www.hrsdc.gc.ca/eng
/jobs/aboriginal/index.shtml.

Inuit Tapiriit Kanatami. 2005. "State of Inuit Learning in Canada." In *The
Canadian Council on Learning*, ed. ITK Socio-Economic Department. 1–12.
Ottawa: Government of Canada. http://www.ccl-cca.ca/NR/rdonlyres
/03AC4F69-D0B8-4EA3-85B1 56C0AC2B158C/0/StateOfInuitLearning
.pdf.

Jetten, J., M.A. Hogg, and B.A. Mullin. 2000. "In-Group Variability and
Motivation to Reduce Subjective Uncertainty." *Group Dynamics: Theory,
Research, and Practice* 4 (2): 184–98. http://dx.doi.org/10.1037/1089-
2699.4.2.184.

Ji, L.J., R.E. Nisbett, and Y. Su. 2001. "Culture, Change, and Prediction." *Psychological Science* 12 (6): 450–6. http://dx.doi.org/10.1111/1467-9280
.00384.

Juran, J.M. 1954. "Universals in Management Planning and Controlling."
*Management Review* 43 (11): 748–61.

Kachanoff, F., D.M. Taylor, S. Neufeld, and M. Rossignac-Milon. 2013. "The
Daily Diary Project: A Collective Approach for Achieving Success."
Report, Kativik School board, Nunavik, 21 June.

Kendall, J. 2001. "Circles of Disadvantage: Aboriginal Poverty and Underde-
velopment in Canada." *American Review of Canadian Studies* 31 (1–2):
43–59. http://dx.doi.org/10.1080/02722010109481581.

Khan, S. 2008. "Aboriginal Mental Health: The Statistical Reality." *Visions:
BC's Mental Health and Addictions Journal* 5 (1): 6–7.

King, M.L. 1963. "I Have a Dream." Speech, Washington, DC, 28 August. US
National Archives and Records Administration. http://www.archives.gov
/press/exhibits/dream-speech.pdf.

King, T. 2012. *The Inconvenient Indian*. Toronto: Doubleday Canada.

Kircher, R. 2009. "Language Attitudes in Quebec: A Contemporary Perspective." PhD diss., University of London.

Kirmayer, L.J. 1994. "Suicide among Canadian Aboriginal peoples." *Transcultural Psychiatric Research Review* 31 (1): 3–58. http://dx.doi.org/10.1177/136346159403100101.

Kirmayer, L.J., B. Hayton, M. Malus, V. Jimenez, R. Dufour, C. Quesney, and N. Ferrara. 1993. "Suicide in Canadian Aboriginal populations: Emerging Trends in Research and Intervention. Prepared for the Royal Commission on Aboriginal peoples." *Culture and Mental Health Research Unit, Institute of Community and Family Psychiatry* MBD-JGH McGill University. Report No.1. Montreal. http://www.mcgill.ca/files/tcpsych /Report1.pdf.

Kirmayer, L.J., G.M. Brass, T. Holton, K. Paul, C. Simpson, C. Tait. 2007. "Suicide among Aboriginal People in Canada." *Aboriginal Healing Foundation.* Available at http://www.ahf.ca/downloads/suicide.pdf.

Kirmayer, L.J., S. Dandeneau, E. Marshall, M.K. Phillips, and K.J. Williamson. 2011. "{Kirmayer, 2011 #78}Rethinking Resilience from Indigenous Perspectives." *Canadian Journal of Psychiatry* 56 (2): 84–91.

Kirmayer, L.J., M. Sehdev, R. Whitley, S.F. Dandeneau, and C. Isaac. 2009. "Community Resilience: Models, Metaphors and Measures." *International Journal of Indigenous Health* 5 (1): 62–117.

Kitayama, S, H.R. Markus, H. Matsumoto, and V. Norasakkunkit. 1997. "Individual and Collective Processes in the Construction of the Self: Self-Enhancement in the United States and Self-Criticism in Japan." *Journal of Personality and Social Psychology* 72: 1245–67 http://dx.doi.org/10.1037 /0022-3514.72.6.1245.

Knowles, E, ed. 2009. *Oxford Dictionary of Quotations*. 7th ed. Oxford: Oxford University Press. http://www.oxfordreference.com/

Koestler, A. 1944. "On Disbelieving Atrocities." *New York Times Magazine,* January. (Reprint, Arthur Koestler, *The Yogi and the Commissar*. New York: Macmillan).

Kumar, A. 1999. "Suit Fights School Alcohol Policy." *St. Petersburg Times*, 28 December.

LaFromboise, T., H.L. Coleman, and J. Gerton. 1993. "Psychological Impact of Biculturalism: Evidence and Theory." *Psychological Bulletin* 114 (3): 395–412. http://dx.doi.org/10.1037/0033-2909.114.3.395.

Lambert, W.E., R.C Hodgson, R.C. Gardner, and S. Fillenbaum. 1960. "Evaluational Reactions to Spoken Language." *Journal of Abnormal and Social Psychology* 60(1): 44–51. http://dx.doi.org/10.1037/h0044430.

Lambert, W.E., and G.R. Tucker. 1972. *Bilingual Education of Children: The St. Lambert Experiment*. Rowley, MA: Newbury House.

*Lau v. Nichols*. 1974. 414 US 563.

Leary, M.R., and J. P. Tangney, eds. 2003. *Handbook of Self and Identity*. New York: Guilford Press.

Leclerc, F. 1972. "Les 100,000 façons de tuer un homme [100,000 ways to kill a man]." *L'alouette en colère* (CD). Paris: Philips.

Ledlow, Susan. 1992. "Is Cultural Discontinuity an Adequate Explanation for Dropping out?" *Journal of American Indian Education* 31 (3): 21–36.

Lipsett, H. 1999. "Zero Tolerance: No Excuses Approach." *Orbit* 29 (4): 40–1.

Maass, A., and R.D. III Clark. 1984. "Hidden Impact of Minorities: Fifteen Years of Minority Influence Research." *Psychological Bulletin* 95: 428–50. http://dx.doi.org/10.1037/0033-2909.95.3.428.

MacMillan, H.L., A.B. MacMillan, D.R. Offord, and J.L. Dingle. 1996. "Aboriginal Health." *Canadian Medical Association Journal* 155 (11): 1569–78.

Malchy, B., M.W. Enns, T.K. Young, and B.J. Cox. 1997. "Suicide among Manitoba's Aboriginal People, 1988 to 1994." *Canadian Medical Association Journal* 156 (8): 1133–38.

Markus, H.R., and S. Kitayama. 1991. "Culture and the Self: Implications for Cognition, Emotion, and Motivation." *Psychological Review* 98 (2): 224–53. http://dx.doi.org/10.1037/0033-295X.98.2.224.

Marshall, J. 1999. *Zero Tolerance Policing*. www.ocsar.sa.gov.au/docs /information_bulletins/IB9.pdf

Mascolo, M.F., and K.W. Fischer. 1998. "The Development of Self through the Coordination of Component Systems." In *Self-Awareness: Its Nature and Development*, ed. M.D. Ferrari and R.J. Sternberg, 332–94. New York: Guilford.

McAdams, D.P. 2006. "The Problem of Narrative Coherence." *Journal of Constructivist Psychology* 19 (2): 109–25.

Mendelson, M. 2006. *Aboriginal People and Postsecondary Education in Canada*. Ottawa: The Caledon Institute of Social Policy.

Metcalfe, J., and W. Mischel. 1999. "A Hot/Cool-System Analysis of Delay of Gratification: Dynamics of Willpower." *Psychological Review* 106: 3–19. http://dx.doi.org/10.1037/0033-295X.106.1.3

Milgram, S. 1963. "Behavioural Study of Obedience." *Journal of Abnormal and Social Psychology* 67: 371–8. http://dx.doi.org/10.1037/h0040525

Miller, D.T., and D.A Prentice. 1996. "The Construction of Social Norms and Standards." In *Social Psychology: Handbook of Basic Principles*, ed. E.T. Higgins and A.W. Kruglanski, 799–829. New York: Guilford.

Mischel, W., and E.B. Ebbesen. 1970. "Attention in Delay of Gratification."

*Journal of Personality and Social Psychology* 16: 329–37. http://dx.doi.org
/10.1037/h0029815.

Mischel, W., E.B. Ebbesen, and A.R. Zeiss. 1972. "Cognitive and Attentional
Mechanisms in Delay of Gratification." *Journal of Personality and Social
Psychology* 21: 204–18. http://dx.doi.org/10.1037/h0032198.

Mischel, W., Y. Shoda, and P.K. Peake. 1988. "The Nature of Adolescent
Competencies Predicted by Preschool Delay of Gratification." *Journal of
Personality and Social Psychology* 54: 687–96. http://dx.doi.org/10.1037
/0022-3514.54.4.687.

Moffitt, T.E., L. Arseneault, D. Belsky, N. Dickson, R.J. Hancox, H. Harring-
ton, and A. Caspi. 2011. "A Gradient of Childhood Self-Control Predicts
Health, Wealth, and Public Safety." *Proceedings of the National Academy of
Sciences* 108 (7): 2693-98. http://dx.doi.org/10.1073/pnas.1010076108.

Monchalin, L. 2009. "Aboriginal People's Safety." In *Making Cities Safer:
Action Briefs for Municipal Stakeholders*, ed. I. Waller, 31–4. Ottawa: Institute for the Prevention of Crime. http://www.sciencessociales.uottawa
.ca/ipc/eng/documents/full_text_eng.pdf.

Moscovici, S. 1994. "Three Concepts: Minority, Conflict and Behavioral
Style." In *Minority Influence*, ed. S. Moscovici, A. Mucchi-Faina, and A.
Maass, 233–51. Chicago: Nelson-Hall Publishers. http://dx.doi.org
/10.2307/2786541.

Moscovici, S., E. Lage, and M. Naffrechoux. 1969. "Influence of a Consistent
Minority on the Responses of a Majority in a Color Perception Task."
*Sociometry* 32: 365–80. http://dx.doi.org/10.2307/2786541.

Movement for Canadian Literacy. 2004. "Literacy in Canada: It's Time for
Action." http://www.nald.ca/library/research/mcl/present/submiss
/brief.pdf.

Mucchi-Faina, A., A. Maass, and C. Volpato. 1991. "Social Influence: The
Role of Originality." *European Journal of Social Psychology* 21 (3): 183–97.
http://dx.doi.org/10.1002/ejsp.2420210302.

Muraven, M., and R.F. Baumeister. 2000. "Self-Regulation and Depletion
of Limited Resources: Does Self-control Resemble a Muscle?" *Psychological Bulletin* 126: 247–59. http://dx.doi.org/10.1037/0033-2909.126
.2.247.

Nancrede, S.F. 1998. "School to Take Foul Mouths to Task: Southport High
Will Institute Zero-Tolerance Policy on Profanity." *Indianapolis Star*, 20
August.

Nemeth, C., and J. Wachtler. 1974. "Creating the Perceptions of Consistency
and Confidence: A Necessary Condition for Minority Influence." *Sociometry* 37 (4): 529–40. http://dx.doi.org/10.2307/2786425.

Norenzayan, A., and R.E. Nisbett. 2000. "Culture and Causal Cognition." *Current Directions in Psychological Science* 9 (4): 132–5. http://dx.doi.org/10.1111/1467-8721.00077.

Norris, F.H., S.P. Stevens, B. Pfefferbaum, K.F. Wyche, and R.L. Pfefferbaum. 2008. "Community Resilience as a Metaphor, Theory, Set of Capacities, and Strategy for Disaster Readiness." *American Journal of Community Psychology* 41 (1–2): 127–50. http://dx.doi.org/10.1007/s10464-007-9156-6.

Norris, M.J. 2007. "Aboriginal Languages in Canada: Emerging Trends and Perspectives on Second Language Acquisition." *Canadian Social Trends* 83: 20–8.

Ogbu, J.U. 1992. "Understanding Cultural Diversity and Learning." *Educational Researcher* 218: 5–14.

Paluck, E.L. 2009. "Reducing Intergroup Prejudice and Conflict Using the Media: A Field Experiment in Rwanda." *Journal of Personality and Social Psychology* 96 (3): 574–87.

Pauktuutit Inuit Women of Canada. 2005. "National Strategy to Prevent abuse in Inuit Communities." http://www.pauktuutit.ca/nuluaq/abuse preventionstrategy.pdf.

– 2006. *National Strategy to Prevent Abuse in Inuit Communities and Sharing Knowledge, Sharing Wisdom: A Guide to the National Strategy.* http://pauktuutit.ca/wpcontent/blogs.dir/1/assets/InuitStrategy_e.pdf.

Pelham, B.W., and W. B Swann. 1989. "From Self-Conceptions to Self-Worth: On the Sources and Structure of Global Self-esteem." *Journal of Personality and Social Psychology* 57 (4): 672–80. http://dx.doi.org/10.1037/0022-3514.57.4.672.

Peterson, R.S., and C.J. Nemeth. 1996. "Focus versus Flexibility: Majority and Minority Influence Can Both Improve Performance." *Personality and Social Psychology Bulletin* 22 (1): 14–23. http://dx.doi.org/10.1177/01 46167296221002

Petrillo, L. 1987. "8-Year-Old May be Expelled under 'Zero-Tolerance' Code." *San Diego Union-Tribune*, 29 October.

Ponting, J.R. 1986. *Arduous Journey: Canadian Indians and Decolonization.* Toronto: McClelland and Stewart.

Preston, Jane. P. 2008. "The Urgency of Postsecondary Education for Aboriginal Peoples. *Canadian Journal of Educational Administration and Policy* 86: 1–22.

Prime Minister of Canada. 2008. "PM Offers Full Apology on Behalf of Canadians for the Indian Residential Schools System." 11 June. http://www.pm.gc.ca/eng/media.asp?id=2146.

– 2009. "Priorities." http://www.pm.gc.ca/eng/feature.asp?pageId=133.

Prochaska, J.O., C.C. DiClemente, and J.C. Norcross. 1992. "In Search of How People Change: Applications to Addictive Behaviors." *American Psychologist* 47 (9): 1102–14. doi: 10.1037/0003-066X.47.9.1102.

Quebec. 2009. *L'école, j'y tiens – tous ensemble pour la réussite scolaire.* http://www.mels.gouv.qc.ca/sections/publications/publications/EPEPS/Formation_jeunes/LEcoleJyTiens_TousEnsemblePourLaReussiteScolaire.pdf.

Rhee, E., J.S. Uleman, H.K. Lee, and R. J Roman. 1995. "Spontaneous Self-Descriptions and Ethnic Identities in Individualistic and Collectivistic Cultures." *Journal of Personality and Social Psychology* 69 (1): 142–52. http://dx.doi.org/10.1037/0022-3514.69.1.142.

Richards, J. 2006. "Aboriginal Education in Quebec: A Benchmarking Exercise." C.D. Howe Institute Commentary 328. http://www.cdhowe.org/pdf/Commentary_328.pdf.

Richards, J., and A. Vining. 2004. "Aboriginal Off-Reserve Education: Time for Action." *Education Papers* 198: 1–31.

Robin, R.W., J.C. Long, J.K. Rasmussen, B. Albaugh, and D. Goldman. 1998. "Relationship of Binge Drinking to Alcohol Dependence, Other Psychiatric Disorders, and Behavioral Problems in an American Indian Tribe." *Alcoholism, Clinical and Experimental Research* 22 (2): 518–23. http://dx.doi.org/10.1111/j.1530-0277.1998.tb03682.x.

Rojas, E.Y., and H.M. Gretton. 2007. "Background, Offence Characteristics, and Criminal Outcomes of Aboriginal Youth who Sexually Offend: A Closer Look at Aboriginal Youth Intervention Needs." *Sex Abuse: A Journal of Research and Treatment* 19 (3): 257–83. http://dx.doi.org/10.1177/107906320701900306.

Royal Commission on Aboriginal Peoples. 1996. *Report of the Royal Commission on Aboriginal Peoples.* 5 vols. Ottawa: Supply and Services.

Ryder, A.G., L.E. Alden, and D.L. Paulhus. 2000. "Is Acculturation Unidimensional or Bidimensional? A Head-to-Head Comparison in the Prediction of Personality, Self-Identity, and Adjustment." *Journal of Personality and Social Psychology* 79 (1): 49–65. http://dx.doi.org/10.1037/0022-3514.79.1.49.

Saggers, S. 1998. *Dealing with Alcohol: Indigenous Usage in Australia, New Zealand and Canada.* Cambridge: Cambridge University Press.

Schreiner, M.E. 1996 "Bold Steps Build Safe Havens." *School Business Affairs* 62 (11): 44–6.

Shannon, M.M., and D.S. McCall. 2000. "Zero Tolerance Policies in Context: A Preliminary Investigation to Identify Actions to Improve School Discipline and School Safety." http://www.safehealthyschools.org/whatsnew/capzerotolerance.htm.

Shkilnyk, A. 1985. *A Poison Stronger Than Love*. New Haven: Yale University Press.

Shoda, Y., W. Mischel, and P.K. Peake. 1990. "Predicting Adolescent Cognitive and Self-Regulatory Competencies from Preschool Delay of Gratification: Identifying Diagnostic Conditions." *Developmental Psychology* 26: 978–86. http://dx.doi.org/10.1037/0012-1649.26.6.978.

Skiba, R.J. 2000. "*Zero Tolerance, Zero Evidence: An Analysis of School Disciplinary Practice*." Bloomington: Indiana Education Policy Center, Indiana University.

Skiba, R.J., and R.L. Peterson. 1999. "The Dark Side of Zero Tolerance: Can Punishment Lead to Safe Schools?" *Phi Delta Kappan* 80 (5): 372–82.

Stader, D.L. 2006. "Zero Tolerance: Safe Schools or Zero Sense?" *Journal of Forensic Psychology Practice* 6 (2): 65–75. doi: 10.1300/J158v06n02_05.

Statistics Canada. 2003. "Aboriginal Peoples Survey 2001: Initial Release – Supporting Tables 2." http://www.statcan.gc.ca/pub/89-595-x/index-eng.htm.

– 2006a. "Aboriginal People as Victims and Offenders." http://www.statcan.gc.ca/daily-quotidien/060606/dq060606b-eng.htm.

– 2006b. "Measuring Violence Against Women." http://www.statcan.gc.ca/pub/85-570-x/85-570-x2006001-eng.pdf.

– 2006c. "Aboriginal Peoples in Canada in 2006: Inuit, Métis and First Nations, 2006 Census." Ottawa: Ministry of Industry. http://www12.statcan.ca/census-recensement/2006/as-sa/97-558/pdf/97-558-XIE2006001.pdf#page=14.

– 2007. "Nunavut Crime Statistics Profile, 2007." http://www.gov.nu.ca/eia/stats/StatsData/Crime/Nunavut%20Crime%20Statistics%20Profile,%202007%20(by%20Statistics%20Canada).pdf.

– 2008. "Labour Force Historical Review 2007." http://www4.hrsdc.gc.ca/.3ndic.1t.4r@-eng.jsp?iid=16.

Tajfel, H., and J.C. Turner. 1979. "An Integrative Theory of Intergroup Conflict." In *The Social Psychology of Intergroup Relations*, ed. W.G. Austin and S. Worchel, 33–48. Pacific Grove, CA: Brooks/Cole.

– 1986. "The Social Identity Theory of Intergroup Behavior." In *Psychology of Intergroup Relations*, 2nd ed., ed. S. Worchel and W. G. Austin, 7–24. Chicago: Nelson-Hall.

Taylor, D.M. 1991. "The Social Psychology of Racial and Cultural Diversity: Issues of Assimilation and Multiculturalism." In *Bilingualism, Multiculturalism and Second-language Learning*, ed. A.G. Reynolds, 1–19. Hillsdale, NJ: Lawrence Erlbaum Associates.

– 1997. "The Quest for Collective Identity: The Plight of Disadvantaged

Ethnic Minorities." *Canadian Psychology* 38 (3): 174–90. http://dx.doi.org
/10.1037/0708-5591.38.3.174

– 2002. *The Quest for Identity: From Minority Groups to Generation Xers.*
Westport, CT: Praeger.

Taylor, D.M., and R. de la Sablonnière. 2013. "Why Interventions in Dysfunctional Communities Fail: The Need for a truly Collective Approach."
*Canadian Psychology* 54 (1): 22–9.

Terry, D.J., and M.A. Hogg. 1996. "Group Norms and the Attitude-Behavior
Relationship: A Role for Group Identification." *Personality and Social Psychology Bulletin* 22 (8): 776–93.
http://dx.doi.org/10.1177/0146167296228002.

Thorndike, R.L. 1938. "The Effect of Discussion upon the Correctness of
Group Decisions, When the Factor of Majority Influence Is Allowed For."
*Journal of Social Psychology* 9: 343–62.
http://dx.doi.org/10.1080/00224545.1938.9920036.

Tjepkema, M. 2002. "The Health of the Off-Reserve Aboriginal Population."
In *Health Reports: How Healthy Are Canadians?* Ottawa: Statistics Canada.
http://www.statcan.gc.ca/pub/82-003-s/2002001/pdf/4195132-eng.pdf.

Tookenay, V.F. 1996. "Improving the Health Status of Aboriginal People in
Canada: New Directions, New Responsibilities." *Canadian Medical Association Journal* 155 (11): 1581–3.

Twemlow, S.W., P. Fonagy, F.C. Sacco, M.L. Gies, R. Evans, and R. Ewbank.
2001. "Creating a Peaceful School Learning Environment: A Controlled
Study of an Elementary School Intervention to Reduce Violence." *American Journal of Psychiatry* 158: 808–10.  http://dx.doi.org/10.1176/appi
.ajp.158.5.808.

Usborne, E., J. Caouette, Q. Qumaaluk, and D.M. Taylor. 2009. "Bilingual
Education in an Aboriginal Context: Examining the Transfer of Language Skills from Inuktitut to English or French." *International Journal of
Bilingual Education and Bilingualism* 12 (6): 667–84. http://dx.doi.org
/10.1080/13670050802684388.

Usborne, E., and D.M. Taylor. 2010. "The Role of Cultural Identity Clarity
for Self-Concept Clarity, Self-Esteem, and Subjective Well-
Being. *Personality and Social Psychology Bulletin* 36 (7): 883–97.

US Department of Education. Institute of Education Sciences. 2001. *Indica-
tors of School Crime and Safety: 2001* (NCES 2002113), ed. P. Kaufman, X.
Chen, S.P. Choy, K. Peter, S. A. Ruddy, A.K. Miller, amd M.R. Rand.
Washington, DC. http://nces.ed.gov/pubsearch/pubsinfo.asp?pubid
=2002113.

Vohs, K.D., and T.F. Heatherton. 2000. "Self-Regulatory Failure: A Resource-

Depletion Approach. *Psychological Science* 11 (3): 249–54. http://dx.doi.org/10.1111/1467-9280.00250.

Wacquant, L. 1999. "*L'idéologie de l'insécurité: Ce vent punitif qui vient d'Amérique. Le Monde Diplomatique* [The ideology of insecurity: This punitive wind coming from America]." April. http://www.monde-diplomatique.fr/1999/04/WACQUANT/11910.

Waldram, J.B. 2004. *Revenge of the Windigo: The Construction of the Mind and Mental Health of North American Aboriginal Peoples.* Vol. 26. Toronto: University of Toronto Press.

Waldram, J.B., D.A. Herring, and T. Kue Young. 1995. *Aboriginal Health in Canada: Historical, Cultural and Epidemiological Perspectives.* Toronto: University of Toronto Press.

Ward, C., C.-H. Leong, and M. Low. 2004. "Personality and Sojourner Adjustment: An Exploration of the Big Five and the Cultural Fit Proposition." *Journal of Cross-Cultural Psychology* 35 (2): 137–51. http://dx.doi.org/10.1177/0022022103260719.

Washburn, W.E. 1975. *The Indian in America.* Vol. 436. New York: Harper and Row.

Webb, P., and W.A. Kritsonis. 2006. "Zero-Tolerance Policies and Youth: Protection or Profiling?" *Doctoral Forum* 3 (1): 1–8. http://citeseerx.ist.psu.edu/viewdoc/download?doi=10.1.1.120.8375&rep=repi&type=pdf.

*West's Encyclopedia of American Law.* 2005. http://www.encyclopedia.com/doc/1G2-3437704780.html.

White, P. 2010. "Inuit Mothers Fight Lonely Battle for Their Children's Health." *Globe and Mail,* 5 June.

White, J., and N. Jodoin. 2003. "Aboriginal Youth: A Manual of Promising Suicide Prevention Strategies." http://suicideinfo.ca/LinkClick.aspx?fileticket=xYw_rxl1F7w%3d&tabid=475.

Wilson, J.Q., and G.L. Kelling. 1982. "Broken Windows." *Atlantic Monthly* 249 (3): 29–38.

Willson, S.A., and J.B. Sanborn. 1887. *Magazine of Western History* 7: 666–75. (Cleveland: Magazine of Western History Publishing Co.) https://play.google.com/store/books/details?id=rPQOAAAAYAAJ&rdid=book-rPQOAAAAYAAJ&rdot=1.

World Health Organization. 2009. "Mental Health: Suicide Prevention." http://www.who.int/mental_health/prevention/suicide/suicideprevent/en/index.html.

Yan, Z., and K. Fischer. 2002. "Always under Construction: Dynamic Variations in Adult Cognitive Microdevelopment." *Human Development* 45: 141–60. http://dx.doi.org/10.1159/000057070.

Zimbardo, P.G. 1982. "Understanding Psychological Man: A State of the Science Report." *Psychology Today* 16: 17–18.

– 2008. *The Lucifer Effect: Understanding How Good People Turn Evil.* New York: Random House.

Zimbardo, P.G., and J.N. Boyd. 1999. "Putting Time in Perspective: A Valid, Reliable, Individual-Differences Metric." *Journal of Personality and Social Psychology* 77: 1271–88. http://dx.doi.org/10.1037/0022-3514.77.6.1271.

– 2008. *The Time Paradox: The New Psychology of Time That Will Change Your Life.* New York: Free Press.

# Index